28254612

BALLOU ...
BUENA V...
610 WES...
STORM L...

D0206258

FROM THE CHILD'S POINT OF VIEW

BALLOU LIBRARY
BUENA VISTA UNIVERSITY
610 WEST FOURTH STREET
STORM LAKE, IA 50588-1798

From the
Child's
Point
of
View

Denny Taylor

 Heinemann
Portsmouth, NH

HEINEMANN
A division of Reed Publishing (USA) Inc.
361 Hanover Street   Portsmouth, NH 03801-3912
Offices and agents throughout the world

Copyright © 1993 by Denny Taylor. All rights reserved. No part of this book may be reproduced in any form or by electronic or mechanical means, including information storage and retrieval systems, without permission in writing from the publisher, except by a reviewer, who may quote brief passages in a review.

Every effort has been made to contact the copyright holders for permission to reprint borrowed material where necessary. We regret any oversights that may have occurred and would be happy to rectify them in future printings of this work.

Editor: *Philippa Stratton*   Production: *J. B. Tranchemontagne*
Design: *Mary C. Cronin*   *Drawing by Andrew*

The author and publisher are grateful to the following for permission to reprint previously published material:

Chapter 1, "Ethnographic Education Evaluation for Children, Families, and Schools" first appeared in *Theory Into Practice*, 27(1):67–76. (Theme issue on "Becoming A Student.") Copyright 1988 College of Education, The Ohio State University.

Chapter 2, "Toward a Unified Theory of Literacy Learning and Instructional Practices" first appeared in *Phi Delta Kappan*, November 1989.

Chapter 3, "Teaching Without Testing: Assessing the Complexity of Children's Literacy Learning" first appeared in *English Education*, February 1990.

Page 157, HUBBA BUBBA and the HUBBA BUBBA Wrapper design are registered trademarks of Wm. Wrigley Jr. Company.

Library of Congress Cataloging-in-Publication Data
Taylor, Denny, 1947–
    From the child's point of view / Denny Taylor.
        p.   cm.
    Includes bibliographical references (p.   ) and index.
    ISBN 0-435-08793-2
    1. Students—United States—Self-rating of.   2. Educational tests and measurements—United States—Evaluation.   3. Learning, Psychology of.   I. Title.
LB1131.T267   1993
371.2′6—dc20   93-25140
                                                                      CIP

Printed in the United States of America on acid-free paper
97 96 95 94 93   EB   7 6 5 4 3 2 1

Testing children is a political activity and a commercial enterprise.

This book is dedicated to all teachers who resist unnecessary testing and who work as advocates for children.

CONTENTS

Foreword   ix

Introduction   **1**

References   9

1   **Ethnographic Educational Evaluation for Children, Families, and Schools**   **10**

The Ethnographic Perspective   12
The Contextual Worlds of Childhood   13
Families as Educators   14
Schools as Academic and Social Institutions   16
Reading and Writing Behaviors of Young Children   20
Ethnographic Evaluations   22
Commentary   26
Postscript: Autumn 1987   27
Notes   27
References   28

2   **Toward a Unified Theory of Literacy Learning and Instructional Practices**   **31**

Debunking Reductionist Research   31
Giving Up Simplistic Notions About Complex
    Behaviors   33
Descriptions of Observable Literacy Behaviors   34
Literacy Profiles of Third Graders   38
Blurring the Boundaries   42
Toward a Unified Theory   46
References   50

3   **Teaching Without Testing: Assessing the Complexity of Children's Literacy Learning**   **52**

Teaching, Learning, and Schooling from the
    Perspective of the Learner   57
Seeing the Project Through Its Objectives   60
Teaching, Learning, and Schooling: What Happens
    When You Make a Paradigm Shift?   115

Postscript: Teaching as a Subversive Activity 129
Participants in the *Biographic Literacy Profiles Project* 137
Works Cited and Project Bibliography 138

4 Early Literacy Development and the Mental Health of Young Children **143**

Nicola: A Biographical Literacy Profile of a
Kindergarten Child 145
What Nicola Can Teach Us About Early Literacy
Development 167
Postscript: December 2, 1992 172
Notes 173
References 174

5 Assessing the Complexity of Students' Learning: A Student Advocacy Model of Instructional Assessment **176**

Phase One: Classrooms as Critical Sites of Inquiry 179
Phase Two: Assessing the Learning of Students for
Whom Teachers Are Concerned 192
Phase Three: Analyzing Information and Making
Decisions About the Types of Support That Will
Best Fit the Student's Needs 203
Phase Four: Adjusting the Student Support Plan Based
on the Ongoing Collection of Information 217
Commentary 219
Implementation of the Student Advocacy Model of
Instructional Assessment 225
Appendix: The Presupposition of Human Pathology 228
Notes 228
References 230

Index 233

FOREWORD

In this textured and often evocative book, Denny Taylor makes a compelling case for the primacy of children's worlds as sources of knowledge for key educational decision-making. The rich ethnographic portraits of learners that have become a hallmark of her work—stories of Nicola and Andrew, Evan and Margaret, Bobby and many others—here inform her central argument: that designing appropriate curriculum, instruction and assessment requires that we understand the complex ways children construct their own literacies and learning environments in everyday life. In short, we need to observe children—in school and out—and to learn from them, focusing not on what's missing or what's wrong but on what's present and palpable and ultimately what's patterned or thematic in their efforts to make sense of experiences in their daily lives.

Denny Taylor's focus on the child's point of view is familiar and yet radical, carrying with it significant implications for rethinking practice and policy at all levels of the educational system. To educate from the child's point of view means more than making the children the referents or subjects. She is positing here a vision of education in which children's perspectives do not just enhance but in a fundamental way drive the system. In this effort, we are all in different ways both implicated and responsible. Researchers, teachers, administrators, specialists, families, state level educators and policy makers— all have vital roles to play in effecting the systemic change such a vision entails. In reading together texts originally addressed to differently positioned players in the educational scene, we are invited into the same conversation and offered both a heuristic framework and inventive tools for working these ideas out together. Arguing elegantly and often passionately for a "between-heads" view of learning and for the complexity of learners' observable literacy behaviors, Taylor attacks reductionist research paradigms and simplistic assessment practices, contending that many children are in fact "disabled" by the ways they are currently taught to read and write.

Denny Taylor's own close observations of children and her deep professional relationships with families and other educators infuse both her critique and her recommendations for action. In the essays and documents collected here, she particularly emphasizes the critical role of teachers who are uniquely positioned to access and make visible the child's point of view and thus to be the most knowledgeable observers, constructing curriculum based on real data. Teaching here is portrayed as ongoing and systematic inquiry, a 'way of knowing' embedded in the everyday events of classroom life. As adults and children in classrooms make learning environments for one another, teachers can make informed judgments or assessments as well as interpret information collected from other sources. Importantly, teachers function as knowledge generators and policy-makers, not simply (or even primarily) as implementers of the insights of those outside the classroom. As Denny Taylor's work in a number of settings richly illustrates, when teachers pose questions based on such a conceptual framework, they build synergistic communities for collegial learning and their classrooms change, creating more responsive environments for children whose lives, she reminds us, always need to be understood within the larger social, cultural and political contexts that determine what and how they learn.

In a poem entitled *To Be of Use,* Marge Piercy writes of her own admiration for "people who harness themselves . . . who strain in the mud and the muck to move things forward, who do what has to be done, again and again." I too love "people who submerge in the task, who go into the field to harvest and work in a row and pass the bags along, who are not parlor generals . . . but move in a common rhythm." Denny Taylor is such a person, working alongside others, living as she writes, revealing her intense respect for children, teachers, parents, and communities and her unwavering commitment to social justice. This is writing for action—strong, and as it should be, sometimes unsettling. As Piercy writes,

> But the thing worth doing well done
> has a shape that satisfies, clean and evident.

From a Child's Point of View is such a "thing," an immensely important book coming at a critical moment of possibility for educational equity and reform.

Susan L. Lytle
University of Pennsylvania

INTRODUCTION

A ndrew drew two pyramids. At the top of one he drew a stick person, and in a bubble from the person's mouth he wrote, "Guess I'll never know the enternal answer." At the bottom of the second pyramid Andrew drew an entrance to a "buriel chamber." He then drew a speech bubble coming out of the chamber, and in it he wrote, "A'nt that the enternal question?" Then he drew another stick figure and another speech bubble in which he wrote, "Mummies can be so capreshet." (See Figure I–1.) He then gave the paper to his third-grade teacher.

I think about Andrew's message whenever I think about him. When I first met Andrew he was in the first grade and had a thick special education folder. The specialists, who had evaluated him when he was in kindergarten, wrote that he had "below average understanding of semantics" and "morphological markers," which is difficult to understand given the later observations of Andrew's teachers in first, second, and third grade. The specialists focused on the errors that he made on the tests that they administered to him. The reports in Andrew's file tell us that he "demonstrated errors" in "articles, pronouns and contractions," and that these "errors" corresponded to certain percentiles and stanines that were used to rank him with other children of his age. But the reports don't tell us how Andrew *used* language when he was not being tested.

Many of the children with whom I have worked in the last six years have been evaluated in similar ways to Andrew as educators have searched for the eternal answer to the eternal question "What's wrong with this child?" In each chapter of this book, I will show that this question is capricious, that the answers that are given to the question are eccentric and erratic, and that neither the question nor the answer makes any sense at all when we stop looking for errors and try to understand learning *from the point of view of the child.*

The first chapter, "Ethnographic Educational Evaluation for Children, Families, and Schools," was published in *Theory into Practice (TIP)* in 1988. Judith Green was an associate editor for the journal, and she encouraged me to submit the piece. I had presented the research at the National Council of Teachers of English and the Na-

FIGURE I-1   **Andrew's two pyramids**

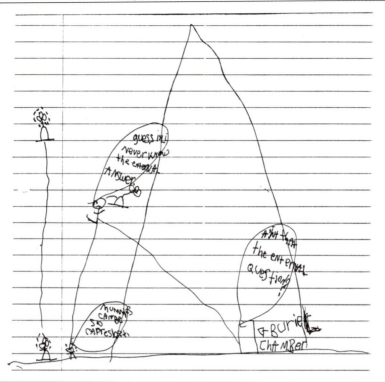

tional Reading Council at the invitation of Donald Graves, who at the time was president of the National Council of Research in English. Don had asked me to write a theoretical paper about "ethnographic assessment" for NCRE. Since theoretical explanations need a practical foundation, I found two children who had been identified as possible special needs students and who were being evaluated by their respective schools. One of the children was Patrick, whom many of you have read about in my book *Learning Denied* (1991).

Central to the theoretical position presented in the *TIP* paper is the belief that *"in-the-head" analysis of human behavior is beyond our present capability.* Instead I suggested a *"between heads"* view of human learning. This is the foundation on which all the chapters in this volume rest. It is the central tenet of all my research, so it is not surprising that it is the thread that runs through each piece of writing presented here.

"Toward a Unified Theory of Literacy Learning and Instructional Practices," first published in *Phi Delta Kappan* in 1989, picks up on the *TIP* argument that "in our in-the-head tests in the educational system, we consistently *underestimate* the enormous potential of children to participate in the construction of their own learning environments." I was working with teachers and children in New Hampshire schools when I read Marie Carbo's critique of Jeanne Chall's research in *Phi Delta Kappan*, and Chall's response to Carbo's critique. As I wrote at that time I was disturbed that the complex subject of children's learning had been reduced by both of these researchers to a trivial debate over methods. I was deeply concerned that the reading and writing of the children with whom I was working was not reflected in the dialogue that was taking place. Classroom observations of children actively engaged in reinventing both the functions and forms of written language made it clear to me that neither Carbo nor Chall had made any attempt to consider learning to read and write from the child's point of view. "Toward a Unified Theory of Literacy Learning and Instructional Practices" was my attempt to rectify this situation. By juxtaposing my observations of the complexities of children's literacy behaviors with the simplistic reductionist arguments of Chall and Carbo, I hoped to shift the focus of attention away from reductionist research and synthetic methods of instruction and towards the consideration of the literacy learning that takes place when children are given the opportunity to participate actively in the reinvention of both the forms and functions of written language.

In the *TIP* article, I wrote:

> We can begin by observing children, learning with them and from them as they learn with us and from us. . . . In this way we can create philosophical and theoretical frames for our observations of the learning environments we make for one another.

This statement is at the very heart of the Biographic Literacy Profiles Project, which is described in Chapter 3, "Teaching Without Testing."

In the summer of 1989 I participated in an institute at Lehman College. There I met Gordon Pradl, who was then the editor of *English Education*. Gordon invited me to write an article for the journal, and I discussed with him the possibility of writing a paper about the Biographic Literacy Profiles Project. Much to my surprise, Gordon said that he was willing to devote an entire issue to the project. The only snag was the deadline: Gordon wanted the paper to be published in the first volume of *English Education* in 1990, to mark the beginning of the new decade which was only three months away. "Teaching Without Testing" was the first volume to be published in 1990. In an editorial Gordon wrote:

> As we begin the last decade of this century much remains to be accomplished in our educational systems. Nowhere is this more evident than in how we assess student growth and achievement in the language arts and then in turn use such assessments to modify and encourage instruction. At the heart of this assessment struggle are divisive educational questions: Who gets to define and describe student's competence and accomplishments? Can one statistically measure the complexities of literacy development? Should a testing bureaucracy be allowed to hold such power over the professional decision making of teachers? (p. 3)

He goes on to state that "one cannot approach assessment in a new way without also altering what passes for teaching and learning in a school setting" (p. 3). For one brief moment, that is exactly what we did. Over a hundred teachers took part in the Biographic Literacy Profiles Project, working together to redefine teaching and learning in school settings in ways that enabled them to focus on teaching and learning from the child's point of view. We concentrated on what children can do and not on what they can't do, and we said in loud voices, "There is nothing wrong with the child." There are only children who are trying to make sense of the complexities of their everyday lives, whose behavior might not always appear to be appropriate, and whose learning might puzzle us. This does not mean that there is something *wrong* with them. As teachers, our task is to stand side by side with the children we teach and to imagine the world from their individual and shared perspectives. It is only then that we can come to understand the complex ways in which children construct and use both the functions and forms of written language.

Much of "Teaching Without Testing" was written on the telephone. I would write all day and talk with teachers at night. Our conversations focused on what they were doing, what they saw happening, what it was like for them as they worked to base instruction on their observations of children's literacy behaviors. At that time, in addition to my classroom visits, I was meeting with project teachers in the boardroom of a bank that had donated the space for us to come together to discuss children's literacy learning. When our "board meetings" took place, I would work late into the night writing "Teaching Without Testing" and then drive for an hour and a quarter the next morning to meet with project teachers at the bank. I never arrived on time, but I always arrived with drafts of the paper for teachers to read. At each meeting, copies of the draft were passed around the table and teachers were given the opportunity to edit the piece. At the end of the day I would drive home to write some more about the conversations that had taken place that day and to incorporate into the text the new ways of analyzing children's work that we were developing at the "board meetings."

I then sent sections of the manuscript on disk to Gordon. On the telephone I expressed my concern that time was running out. "I can't make the deadline," I said. Gordon said, "Just keep writing." Then he added that the manuscript was "refreshingly devoid of commas." "And semicolons," I said, regaining my sense of humor enough to keep writing. We cut several sections, including one on families: even using the entire issue there was too much to print. It was the end of November when the manuscript was finally completed. The first issue of *English Education* in the 1990s was published two months later.

The "Teaching Without Testing" that appears in this book carries a postscript. The work we did goes on, but not as before. We are less optimistic about both the empowerment of teachers and the empowerment of children in the Granite State. As you will read, in my opinion and in the opinion of many project teachers, the New Hampshire State Board of Education is working openly to deconstruct the state's public school system. Teachers have become pariahs. The chair of the State Board has referred to them as a "special interest group," and she has made it clear that the expertise of teachers is not recognized in New Hampshire. Under these conditions, it is difficult for teachers to continue their pioneering work of redefining teaching and learning from the child's point of view. But quietly, in classrooms, the work continues as teachers create literacy environments for children that celebrate children's lives and support their learning in ways that will prepare them for the changing world in which they live.

I ended the *TIP* article with a reference to Dewey and by stating, "It is 'the intimate and necessary relation between the processes of actual experience and education' . . . that we must come to understand." In the year that followed the writing of "Teaching Without Testing" the teachers in the Biographic Literacy Profiles Project spent more and more time considering the learning of children about whom they were seriously concerned. It became increasingly evident to us that the number of children who had been hurt by life's experiences was growing. New Hampshire's economy was in a state of collapse. Banks were failing, the job market was shrinking, and people were losing their homes. Many families were unable to cope, and children were (and are still) suffering as a consequence. Child abuse was on the rise. One project teacher had seven children at one time in her classroom whose parents were under investigation for child abuse. Project teachers were anxious to provide safe places for children in their classrooms, and they worked to understand and support the learning of the children for whom they were seriously concerned.

At our meetings and institutes we focused on literacy and the mental health of young children. We used our observations of children's explorations of the functions and forms of written language as one way in which we could support them, both academically and socially, as they tried to cope with the events that had taken place in their everyday lives. It was at one of our project institutes that Sharron, a kindergarten teacher, shared with us the portfolio that she had created to reflect Nicola's early literacy development. When you read the fourth chapter of this book, "Early Literacy Development and the Mental Health of Young Children," you will meet Nicola and learn about the events that had taken place that changed her young life. As Sharron shared Nicola's portfolio it became clear to us that our ways of working with children provided us with an opportunity to build on the necessary relationships between processes of actual experience and education. For Sharron this meant that understanding the ways in which Nicola used print enabled her to support the coping strategies that Nicola was constructing as she tried to overcome the difficulties that she faced in her everyday life.

It was at this time, in the fall of 1990, that I read *Beginning to Read: Thinking and Learning about Print* by Marilyn Jager Adams (1990). I found it difficult to think about Nicola and read the text at the same time. Her learning did not fit with the pronouncements that Adams was making about the ways in which young children learn to read and write. There was nothing in the text that reflected the complexities of Nicola's learning as she was actively engaged in reconstructing both the functions and the forms of written language. It occurred to me then that I had learned more from Nicola about the early literacy development of young children than from all the research studies in Adams' book combined. By juxtaposing my analysis of Adams' text with Sharron's observations of Nicola's literacy learning I hoped that it would be possible to raise questions not only about the acceptance by so many in the reading field of such studies of early literacy development but also, and more important, to raise the question of the consequences of such acceptance for children whose lives and learning do not fit into the reductionist research paradigm that dominates what happens to children when they learn to read and write in school. There is no doubt in my mind that many children are disabled by the ways in which they are taught to read and write. When we break the intimate connection between experience and learning, children are cut off from their own problem-solving abilities. We sever the link between their lives and their learning, and they suffer as a consequence.

The final chapter in this volume focuses on what happens to children when this link is broken. In the summer of 1991 I received a call from Richard Figueroa, who is director of the California Research Institute on Special Education and Cultural Diversity, inviting me to join an advisory committee that was being formed to consider alternative ways of assessing children's learning for special education in the state of California. Richard said he had read *Learning Denied,* and I gathered from our conversation it was Patrick's story that had prompted him to invite me to become a member of the advisory committee. I agreed to participate and sent Richard a copy of "Teaching Without Testing." In October 1991, the advisory committee met in Sacramento at the California State Department of Education. It was an exciting meeting. Much of the discussion focused on the development of alternative assessment procedures that would not lead to an overrepresentation of African American and Latino American students in special education classes, an increasing problem in all our nation's schools. As members of the advisory team talked with members of the State Department of Education it became clear that there was general concern for all children who step into the special education arena. There was general agreement that our knowledge of the ways in which children learn render current assessment procedures obsolete.

In January 1992, Richard telephoned and asked me if I would develop an alternative assessment model, to be considered with several other models, that could be used to assess the special needs of students in California schools. At that time I was working with Project teachers to develop alternative assessment procedures for students in Project schools. We were working intensively to understand how we could use our ways of assessing students' learning to inform the special education process, which seemed so mired in rules and regulations and in the dogma of human pathology. The model that Richard was asking me to develop was already under way. We focused on using disciplined and systematic ways of observing children to inform and ultimately change the special education process that handicaps so many children in our schools.

The student advocacy model of instructional assessment builds on the theoretical position that I presented in my *TIP* article. At the time the model was developed, I wrote:

> To evaluate, we need to build descriptions of children as they participate in the social construction of their own environments. The ways in which we develop our explanations should be imaginative and intuitive, as well as analytic and well trained.

This is how we tried to understand Nicola's learning, and how we tried to understand the learning of Andrew, whose search for the eternal answer begins this introduction to *From A Child's Point of View*.

The student advocacy model builds on the ideas in "Toward a Unified Theory of Literacy Learning and Instructional Practices," though the ways in which we have learned to base instruction on children's observable literacy behaviors are more clearly defined. In addition, the model incorporates expanded versions of the analytic grids described in "Teaching Without Testing." Finally, children such as Nicola are represented in the student advocacy model. Writing in support of Nicola in "Early Literacy Development and the Mental Health of Young Children" helped me to understand how important it is that we reject any assessment model that makes the assumption that there is something wrong with the child.

The student advocacy model of instructional assessment places teachers at the center of the problem-solving process to discover how learning takes place from the perspective of the child. In my work with teachers in schools I have learned that it is teachers' expertise that creates significant ways of knowing the local complexities of children's everyday lives, the ways in which children construct and use language, the ways in which children participate in problem-solving situations, and how children's learning can be supported in classroom settings. It is teachers' collaborating with other teachers and with individual children that can make a difference in the life of a young child.

The student advocacy model of instructional assessment is now under consideration for use in California's public schools. As I write, three models are being considered; each model is being rated by an Advisory Committee to the California State Department of Education. Richard Figueroa has developed the rating scale, based upon criteria for assessment reform consistent with those established by the National Academy of Sciences.

Finally, know when you read this book that it is not a fait accompli. It is, rather, a working document meant to help us think about learning from the child's point of view. Take it and use it. Make it work for you. Move back and forth between the chapters. Look for the connections between the pieces. Ask yourself if there is theoretical cohesion. Question the practicality of the statements that are made. Challenge the assumptions on which it is based. Bring your own experience to the text. Spend time observing children. Take notes. Ask the eternal questions of those in the field of reading instruction. Look for the eternal answers. But at all costs try not to be too capricious as you work to understand learning from the child's point of view.

REFERENCES

Adams, Marilyn Jager. 1990. *Beginning to Read: Thinking and Learning about Print*. Cambridge, MA: The MIT Press.
Pradl, Gordon. 1990. Editorial. *English Education*. 22(1):3.
Taylor, Denny. 1991. *Learning Denied*. Portsmouth, NH: Heinemann.

1

ETHNOGRAPHIC EDUCATIONAL EVALUATION FOR CHILDREN, FAMILIES, AND SCHOOLS

Central to an ethnographic perspective of human behavior is the belief that "in-the-head" analysis of human behavior is beyond our present capability.

E *van:*[1] Evan was referred by his school for testing and psychological evaluation when he was in the second grade and again in the third grade. The reason for the repeated referral is stated in his fourth-grade psychological evaluation as "a lack of production in academic subjects, despite the perception that he is a bright, capable youngster. . . . Then, as now, his work was completed correctly but often late and of minimal quality. Also, then and now he was perceived disorganized and a daydreamer and sometimes socially isolated."

In the third grade the WISC-R was administered (other tests unknown). The following year tests were given that the subsequent report states included the Thematic Apperception Test, Draw Your Family, Oral Sentence Completion Test, 3 Wishes, and the Piers-Harris Children's Self-Concept Test.

Evan was also observed in his classroom and participated in a clinical interview. The psychologist wrote: "I see Evan as manifesting a classic underachievement syndrome. The primary underpinnings are insecurity and denial of feelings with a secondary component of passive aggression." Evan received psychological counseling in his fourth- and fifth-grade years, and in the classroom his desk was separated from the desks of the other children. At the end of the fall semester of his sixth-grade year the school once again recommended psychological counseling.

Patrick: At the age of 6 years and 10 months, Patrick was tested by a clinical psychologist. His parents speak of the evaluation procedures lasting an entire day. Patrick's mother remembers her concern about the amount of time and not knowing what to do about the situation. Painfully she recalls that as the psychologist came out of his office with Patrick he told her that her son had severe neurological problems but he would not tell her what they were.

The parents received the report from the day of testing four months later. The psychologist wrote that his "impression" was that Patrick's disabilities included "developmental dyslexia," "attention deficit disorder," and "developmental language disorder."

Preceding the independent evaluation by the clinical psychologist Patrick had been evaluated in school. The disparities in the tests that Patrick had taken in his kindergarten year prompted his parents to seek another evaluation. However, instead of clarifying the problem the evaluation just added to the confusion. In less than a year Patrick had been given the following tests: WISC-R, CELF Screen, Beery VMI, Wide Range Achievement Test, Personality Inventory for Children, Peabody Picture Vocabulary, Expressive One Word Picture Vocabulary Test, Stanford Early School Achievement Test, Murphy Durrell Reading Readiness Test, Southern California Sensory Integration Tests, Goodenough Draw-a-Person Test, Lateral Dominance Examination, Aphasia Screen, Sensory and Perceptual Exam, Trail Test, Gesell, and a second administration of the Gesell. In February of Patrick's first-grade year, a re-evaluation of Patrick's abilities was recommended by the school.

Despite this exhaustive testing, little progress was made toward understanding the school problems of Evan and Patrick.

In a critical editorial on evaluation, Dillon (1987) writes that "evaluation remains one of the most characteristic traits of our educational system." He goes on to state that until "we develop alternatives, any progress we make in language arts curriculum and instruction will remain severely hampered. The system—or at least this one very powerful aspect of it—will continue determining what we can and can't do."

As the educational system insists on formally teaching and evaluating the reading abilities of children in kindergarten and first-grade classrooms, we are faced with the fact that children are failing before they have been given the opportunity to even begin their elementary school education. The consequences of this situation are serious indeed. In my own experience of working with parents and teachers, I am overwhelmed by the impact upon families and schools when children are evaluated and found wanting. But most of all I am overwhelmed by the impact on the children themselves, who find they are not meeting the expectations of an educational system that judges their abilities by external measures that have very little to do with their everyday lives.

Dillon ends his editorial by stating, "We can accept and live with these limits or we can develop practical alternatives in actual practice in real schools and school districts." This article is a response to his challenge. It begins by identifying some of the theoretical constructs that underpin an ethnographic approach to evaluation. It then describes some of the practical ways this theoretical framework has been used to develop ethnographic educational evaluations of the two children, Evan and Patrick, who are mentioned above. Thus, theory is balanced with practice to offer the beginnings of an alternative paradigm that can be used as a stepping stone to the development of more humane evaluation procedures for use in schools. The position is interpretive and the descriptions fluid and open for reconstruction by other researchers and educators who are ready to bring their own academic training and practical experience to this forum.

THE ETHNOGRAPHIC PERSPECTIVE

Central to an ethnographic perspective of human behavior is the belief that "in-the-head" analysis of human behavior is beyond our present capability. McDermott and Roth (1978) speak to this issue when they state, "Mental events are never directly available for analysis; they can only be modeled by inference from people's behavior in extremely well-defined environments."

The perspective they propose views human behavior as socially ordered (Durkheim, 1895/1938), and as involving the "reactions of individuals to the reactions of other individuals" (Bateson, 1958, 1972). If we accept this view of the social organization of human behavior, "what happens between heads," we can no longer accept the mentalistic metaphors that refer to "what happens in the head" that have emerged from research conducted in artificial environments and laboratory settings. In terms of evaluation, this perspective suggests that we must focus on "situated practical accomplishments" that are "internal to the situation at hand." But more than this, we must "look across situations" as we move "from rhetorics of the head to descriptions of the environments that people build for each other" (McDermott and Roth, 1978).

In adopting this ethnographic perspective of the social construction of behavior, the oversimplified pronouncements based on traditional evaluative procedures have to be rejected or redefined. Instead of analyzing the "in-the-head" knowledge of children we have to examine the environments in which that knowledge is applied. Such a reassessment of our position has far reaching consequences for Evan and Patrick. Essentially it means taking the ascribed "problems" out of their heads and relocating them within the socially constructed frameworks of their day-to-day lives. We have to try to get as close as we can to the ways in which Evan and Patrick see what's happening to them. They become our informants. We have to get to know them so that we can eventually build adequate descriptions of the environments of which their knowledge is constitutive and in which it is displayed.

THE CONTEXTUAL WORLDS OF CHILDHOOD

Children's knowledge is not available for the asking. We do not know how they think about the world. We can only make tentative ("modeled by inference") interpretations based on our observations of children as they go about their daily lives. In another article I have tried to accomplish this by drawing a visual representation (Taylor, 1987) of what I imagine childhood to be. It is consistent with the ethnographic perspective of the social organization of behavior discussed briefly above. In this representation children are participating in and helping to construct their own environments:

> Whether it is an apartment building on a busy city street or a farmhouse on a country dirt road, the (con)textual worlds of childhood begin wherever the young child lives. A *very small place* is home. It is a place filled with an abundance of objects, images, and impressions, where nothing is trivial and details are not so much irrationally irrelevant as irrationally significant. In this place the child experiences a sense of wonder at the freakiness of "ordinary" events and an intense interest in the magic of plain and simple things. From these experiences of the intimate detail in a very small place, each child (that is afforded the opportunity) creates an authentic foundation for his or her own existence. (see Coe, 1984)

Central to this interpretation of the contextual worlds of childhood are the people with whom the child shares his or her young life. The emphasis is upon the child's everyday experiences, made visible through social interactions with family and friends. Thus language is placed at the heart of the model. This child-oriented view of the world is based to a large extent on the ethnographic narratives that I have written of my observations of children with their families. The perspective comes of talking with children, listening to them, and trying to understand what is important to them in their everyday lives. Let's consider what we learn from Evan and Patrick from observations of their everyday lives:

> *Evan:* In adopting this position with Evan, we learn what is important to him. We learn that he is interested in computers, and when we provide him with an opportunity to use a computer, he tells us he is not allowed to be in the computer club at school because he does not complete his

homework assignments. However, he does manage to use the computer through one of his friends. Evan has signs for his door and posters for his walls that were designed by him and made by his friend who is a "legitimate" member of the school's computer club.

Patrick: Focusing upon Patrick, we learn that he loves to play the card game Concentration. When we play the game with him, we learn that he is practically unbeatable. Patrick has played the game with members of his family since he was "a baby." As he works to match the cards, he talks about the games he has played with his dad, and the games he has won when he has played with friends of the family who did not believe he could beat them.

Programming computers and playing card games are among trivial details that become important to us if we wish to gain some insights into the ways Evan and Patrick participate in the construction of their own environments. By watching and listening to them, we learn of questions that need to be asked when we look across situations at the "situated practical accomplishments" that are occurring in other settings. Such information is not accessible through traditional testing and traditional observation of children.

FAMILIES AS EDUCATORS

From the ethnographic perspective, Patrick and Evan are not seen as isolated individuals, but rather as members of families in which the education of children is very different from the education of children in schools (Taylor, 1981, 1982, 1983a, 1983b, 1987, in press). Leichter (1974), influenced by the work of Bateson (1972), Chapple (1970), Dewey (1916), and Mead (1970), among others, presents what she refers to as "models" of the family as an educational system. She writes of "encouraging sensitivity to the multiplicity of meanings that any event may have for different individuals within a particular family and to the shift of meanings that can occur from one moment to another." Leichter stresses the need to scrutinize educational encounters in families from a perspective that "takes multiple levels of experience into account," and she reminds us that not all educational influences are intentional.

To adopt Leichter's theoretical framework necessitates relinquishing our roles as experts, as we place ourselves in the extremely uncomfortable position of *not* knowing. This means assuming the role of neophyte each time we work with a child and his or her family. But it also means that the system remains *open*, affording us the opportunity to gain some appreciation of the education of the particular child without the intrusion of school models of learning.

Our biggest assets, if we are willing to take this approach, are families themselves. Parents and children become our informants as we try to interpret the "situated practical accomplishments" of children that are "internal to the situation at hand." A mother (or a father) knows her child in ways beyond the capabilities of the researcher, evaluator, or educators. The parent is able to achieve what Erickson (1982) describes as an "overall contextual perspective" that can "only come through intimate and continuous acquaintance." Mothers, fathers, and children are our *interpreters* (Frake, 1962/ 1981) of the lives they share as they work together in *becoming* (Wolcott, 1982) a family.

In trying to understand the educational influences in the lives of young children, then, our task is to listen and to observe and not to restrict ourselves to the information on a preset questionnaire. If we are willing, we can become privy to the multiple levels of experience that are characteristic of family life, and we can gain some understanding of the "trivial" details that are so important to the education of the child.

We can begin by asking ourselves, "How do these parents and these children construct the contexts of their everyday lives?" and "What can we learn of the social organization of behavior from the ways in which they live together?" These questions can only be answered through careful, systematic, ethnographic observations of the families and through conversations with family members. Consider the following information about Evan and Patrick obtained by such observations and discussions.

Evan: Evan's mother is very concerned about Evan, and during our early conversations she talked about the problems he was having in school. She spoke of when he was a baby, and of the time they spent alone because her husband worked away from home every other week.

She talked about the birth of her daughter when Evan was two, her divorce, moving to another town, and her recent remarriage. Evan was always central to her interpretation of the family's life history. She spoke of the changes in his young life, including changing schools. She appeared to be searching through the events of the past as she tried to explain "his problem." For years she had been told that *she* was the problem, that Evan's difficulties were somewhere rooted in her past. She spoke of the sessions with the psychologist, which she had hoped would help her child.

She talked about everyday life—mealtimes, bedtimes, things that made them laugh, and bad behavior that was punished with chores. She talked about the split week, and of the different parenting styles in the two homes in which her children live. Later, conversations with Evan's father added to the detailed descriptions that were being constructed of Evan's family life.

Patrick: The first conversations with Patrick's parents focused both on the tests and the results of the tests Patrick had been given during his kindergarten year. His mother talked of the school's initial concern because he did not "alternate" as he climbed up and down the stairs. She spoke of the first time the Gesell test was administered, and of his complaining on the way to the testing center that he had a sore throat. Patrick's mother explained that she had suggested, to no avail, that they postpone the testing. On the way home she had stopped at the doctor's office where Patrick, who had developed a fever, was tested for strep. It was positive; he did have a strep infection. However, the Gesell report remains a part of his school record.

Much of this early talk focused on the parents' concern that *if* Patrick had so many problems, why hadn't they seen them at home? His mother spoke of his curiosity about the world around him and of his interest in plants and animals. His father talked about the time he spent with Patrick. He commented that Patrick sometimes helped him and he never seemed to have any difficulty in following directions.

Both parents spoke of how they came to doubt themselves and of the ways they began to doubt Patrick. But they also shared other images of family life. Meals, bedtimes, going for walks, picnics in summer, visiting relatives, and children playing with friends were all talked about as they talked about Patrick.

When we listen to parents and view families as educational institutions, we add yet another level of "local knowledge" (Geertz, 1983) to our interpretations of the social and academic lives of young children.

SCHOOLS AS ACADEMIC AND SOCIAL INSTITUTIONS

To this point I have focused on developing a picture of the child *outside* the school setting. However, the child's "problems" are school defined. Thus, it is necessary to examine our interpretation of school just as we examined those of the worlds of childhood and the family.

In trying to gain some understanding of the social and academic accomplishments of teachers and children in classrooms, we need to make explicit the complexity of classroom life. We must examine the everyday life of classrooms in which the failure of the child is evidenced. The work of Green (1983) and other ethnographers of communication (Cook-Gumperz, 1986; Erickson, 1982; Gumperz, 1981, 1982; Hymes, 1982; McDermott, 1974; Mehan, 1979) makes apparent the complexity of classroom life and provides an approach and a language to talk about daily life. Green and her colleagues (Green, Weade, and Graham, 1988) make visible "the invisible or ordinary social processes of classroom life in which academic information is embedded." They show how children's opportunities to learn are influenced by the social and instructional demands of the lesson.

This work demonstrates how the ways in which teachers and children work together to accomplish the *academic* task that they must fulfill influences what gets learned and what counts as knowledge. From this perspective lessons (or tests) are a product of the interactions among participants. More importantly, in adopting this definition we become concerned with *what counts as a lesson to the participants,* as appropriate performance, and as evidence of competence.

Green, Weade, and Graham (1988) capture the complexity facing the child who must participate appropriately and accurately in the lesson when they write:

> Lesson construction . . . can be likened to the construction of a group composition that is simultaneously being written, read, and revised. In order to contribute to the developing lesson, participants must interpret both the information to be presented (academic text) and the appropriate form for presentation or addition of information (social text). . . . Thus for teachers and students, lesson construction involves a range of strategies including but not limited to monitoring, interpreting, re-establishing, modifying, and suspending expectations, actions, meanings, and themes of the developing social and academic texts (13-14).

Clearly from this perspective, lessons can no longer be thought of as just a matter of the teacher giving the children a set of instructions for the completion of tasks. Rather, lessons must be viewed as jointly constructed events. Thus we must ask ourselves about: (a) what individuals bring to the task (personal frames of reference); (b) what academic information is constructed during "teacher-student(s)-material(s) interactions" (academic frames); (c) what expectations evolve through the "unfolding actions of the participants" (social frames); (d) what instructional strategies are used in the accomplishment of the task (instructional frames); and (e) what producers (publishers and test makers) provide in terms of form and content of materials (material frames) (Green, Harker, and Golden, 1986).

If we stop now and reconsider the world of childhood and the family as educator, we see that these overall interpretations of classroom life are consistent with the perspective of the social organization of behavior presented earlier. Thus, it is not difficult to imagine the contextual worlds that are embedded in the personal frames of reference that a child brings to the task. Nor is it difficult to imagine the ways in which the education of children in family settings influences every level of the social and academic construction of lessons by teachers and children in school. If we *really* want to know about the children in our classrooms, ethnographic observations in classrooms can tell us more than any test. The richness of information that can be obtained in these observations is reflected in the following narrative:

> *Evan:* Evan spends his school day in two classrooms. Before visiting his school, we talked about his teachers and the children in his classes. Evan talked as he played a computer word game and then stopped for a moment to draw a diagram of one of his classrooms. We used the diagram as we talked about his school day. He indicated where he sat and talked about his friends as he marked the position of their seats on his drawing. He drew the teacher's desk but said he (the teacher) rarely used it. Then he drew a circle to the left of the chalkboard and said it was the teacher's stool.
>
> Evan said the arrangement of the other classroom was similar to the one he had drawn, except that there the working tables were used as computer tables. He said he was not allowed to use the computers, explaining that he did not keep up with his work and so he was not in the computer club.
>
> Evan continued playing the computer game as he talked about school. We looked through his textbooks and at the pieces of paper folded in his books, on which he had written his assignments. He was not interested in some of the work and so he didn't do it. He spoke of there being too many assignments, and when asked what he would prefer to do, he said he would like to be able to do one or two assignments in detail. The conversation shifted to his teachers and the children in his classes. He said he would like to stay in the one teacher's room because the other teacher shouted at him and made fun of him in front of the other kids. Evan added that sometimes when that happened the children also made fun of him.
>
> This synthesis of a conversation that lasted several hours provides us with an opportunity to think about the classroom from the child's perspective. We cannot see what he sees, but we can begin to imagine what it looks like from his point of view. From these interviews, I knew something of Evan's personal frames of reference when I entered the classroom to observe his behavior and therefore I was able to ask myself questions that focused on the academic, social, instructional, and mate-

rial frames. In this perspective, I as the observer became the instrument in the reconstruction of the classroom environments that the teachers and children were building for one another. Strips of behavior became visible.

For instance, in both classrooms it became evident that there were times when Evan tuned out. He read the book he'd brought from home, organized the papers in his notebook, sorted out his pencil box, and interacted with the children sitting near him. Consistently throughout the observations, these activities occurred during the time when his teachers were talking to the class, explaining assignments, or giving directions.

Patrick: Patrick told us as much by what he didn't say as by what he actually said. He avoided the few questions that he was asked about school. Our conversations were about his family and friends. On the few occasions when school was mentioned, his face would visibly cloud over and he would talk about something else. Much of our initial information came from his teacher. The ambiguities in the test results made classroom decisions extremely difficult. Patrick's teacher did not want to add to his distress, and so she tried to "take the pressure off him." He was removed from his reading group, and she worked with him on an individual basis using Distar. She told him he did not have to alphabetize his spelling words (a weekly class assignment) or do the dictation exercise, a daily assignment in the handwriting program.

Thus, Patrick attended school, but he was not expected to participate in many of the activities in his classroom. Observations were made when Patrick was playing with cuisenaire rods and working on Distar with his teacher. Patrick was asked to pronounce the words and then "say them fast." He then did a workbook page from the Distar program. Much of the time Patrick appeared to be watching the other children. When his teacher spoke to him, he hesitated before answering and sometimes he did not speak. Again the task is to try and understand something of the ways in which Patrick sees his classroom and to combine this imaginative interpretation with the more analytic resources on which we can draw. Listening to Patrick, observing him in his classroom, listening to his teacher and examining the materials used in instruction all come together in the reconstruction of the environment of which he is a part.

In constructing descriptions of the children, as they build unique personal configurations of participation in the lives of their families and their classrooms, we can begin to appreciate the possibilities of ethnographic educational evaluations. A between-heads perspective limits the possibilities of blaming Evan and Patrick for the difficulties they face in school. The reified in-the-head descriptors ascribed to them no longer apply.

READING AND WRITING BEHAVIORS OF YOUNG CHILDREN

Given the centrality of literacy in the lives of children in schools, this section will focus on interpretations of the reading and writing behavior of young children. Becoming literate is a dynamic process that cannot be measured by traditional tests or controlled by texts. This view is captured and reflected in a joint statement (*Literacy Development*, 1985) in which six national associations[2] emphasize that "many pre-first grade children are subjected to rigid, formal pre-reading programs with inappropriate expectations and experiences for their levels of development" and that "pressure to achieve high on standardized tests" results in program content that denies "curiosity, critical thinking and creative expression." Among the recommendations are the following:

1. Build instruction on what the child already knows about oral language, reading, and writing. Focus on meaningful experiences and meaningful language rather than isolated skill development.
2. Respect the language the child brings to school, and use it as a base for language and literacy activities.
3. Ensure feelings of success for all children, helping them see themselves as people who can enjoy exploring oral and written language.
4. Encourage children's first attempts at writing without concern for the proper formation of letters or correct conventional spelling.
5. Encourage children to be active participants in the learning process rather than passive recipients of knowledge by using activities that allow for experimentation with talking, listening, writing, and reading.

Fifteen recommendations are made in the joint statement. Every statement is consistent with current research findings on young children's literacy behaviors that have emerged in recent years (see Hall, 1987) as we have watched and listened to children actively reconstruct oral and written language within the social contexts of their everyday lives (see, among others, Clay, 1979; Goodman, 1986; Graves, 1978; Harste, Woodward, and Burke, 1984; Schickedanz, 1986; Sulzby, 1986; Taylor, 1983a; Taylor and Dorsey-Gaines, 1988; Taylor and Strickland, 1986a, 1986b). We know that children are socially constructing reading and writing behaviors long before they enter elementary school. Oral and written language are a part of the contextual worlds of childhood, and if we are to facilitate their development in school, we must understand how children, given the opportunity, construct language for themselves. This is true whether the child is a pre-first grader or already into the early elementary years. Thus to really understand Evan's and Patrick's classroom failure, it becomes necessary to examine in depth their reading and writing behavior both in and out of school.

Evan: Insights about Evan's reading and writing behaviors can be found in the ways he talks about the books he has read and the stories he has written. In the ways his parents talk about his literacy activities, and in the ways his teachers talk about his reading and writing activities at school. Other insights can be gained from observations of Evan as he reads and writes and from an analysis of the materials he reads. During one of our earliest conversations Evan talked about the books he liked to read. One book, *The Sword of Shannara* (Brooks, 1977) had captured his imagination, and he talked enthusiastically of reading it whenever he got the chance. *Lord of the Rings* (Tolkien, 1984) was another book he had read and enjoyed. When we talked of the books he was reading at school, Evan said, "I'm reading books six levels above my reading book in school." He showed with his thumb and first finger the size of the print in the basal he was reading at school. When asked why he was in that particular reading group, Evan said it was because he did not complete his assignments. Why didn't he complete them? Evan said, "I'm not interested in some of the work, so I don't do it."

At that time Evan was staying after school to "catch up" with his assignments. He had been away with his family to meet the parents of his new stepfather. As he was already behind with his work he was given a package of assignments to do during his six-week winter vacation in New Zealand. He took the work with him but spent little time on it. However, when he returned he did spend a great deal of his free time working on the story he was submitting to the Young Authors competition. He talked about the story and on several occasions gave it to me to read. He wrote the story by hand, and then used his mother's computer (to which he had not previously had access) to edit the story.

Patrick: The first impressions we have of Patrick's reading and writing behaviors are of the tasks he could not do. During the classroom observation children were writing out their spelling lists in "ABC order." Patrick copied the list but did not alphabetize the words. He was not reading in the basal series with the rest of the children, and he spent very little time writing in his classroom. However, out of school he talked about the books in his bedroom and the books about dinosaurs. His parents talked about reading stories to him since he was a baby, and of how he loved to sit and listen. During our first meeting, Patrick drew a picture of the mountains he could see out the window, and he drew a picture of himself skiing. I wrote the word *skiing* and we talked about the word, and Patrick wrote a sentence. I then wrote the word *mountain* and

FIGURE 1–1 Patrick's mountain story

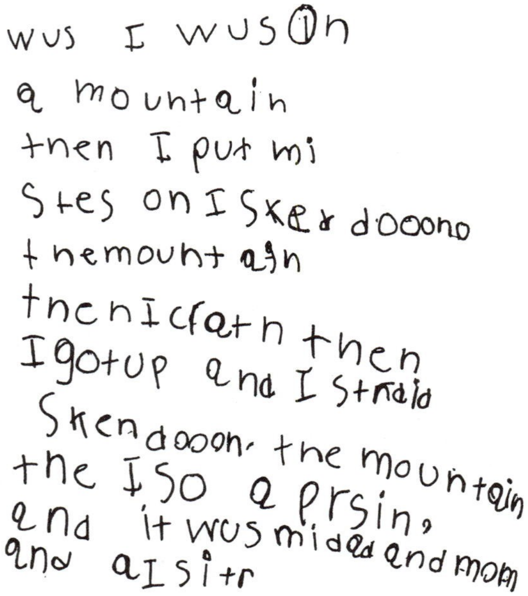
wus I wus On
a mountain
then I put mi
Stes on I Sker dooono
themountagn
thenIcratn then
Igotup and I Strdid
Skendooon. the mountain
the I So a prsin,
and it wus midead and mom
and aIsitr

again we talked. Patrick took another piece of paper and wrote a story that was cohesive and in an appropriate register (see Figure 1–1).

When we consider the information within the multiple contexts of their everyday lives, these interpretations of the reading and writing behaviors of Evan and Patrick provide important insights into the difficulties both children experience at school.

ETHNOGRAPHIC EVALUATIONS

The alternative approach to evaluation has made a difference in the lives of Evan and Patrick. The information gathered through observations and working with these children, together with the data collected during discussions with their parents and their teachers, was reconstructed into social histories of their lives. These interpretations were then shared with their families and schools, and parents and teachers were asked to verify them: "Does this make sense?" "Is this a reasonable interpretation of what is happening with Patrick at home and at school?" "Do you think that is what's happening to Evan?"

Evan: The evaluation of Evan began with the child. We talked about trying to see the world from his point of view. The description began with comments Evan had made and observations about things he liked to do. It included his comments about being shouted at in school and being made fun of by some of the children. Attention was given to the changes that had taken place in his young life, and of the ways in which he moved between his mother and father, living in two homes and sharing two very different ways of life. Evan's comments about the computer club and his reading group were included in the descriptions of his school life. Emphasis was placed on the ways the children received information about their assignments, on the levels of abstract thinking required to process the information, and on the "decontextualized" tasks that were prescribed.

Both of Evan's teachers became involved in the evaluation. Both responded to the observation that Evan did not listen when they talked, acknowledging that this was a difficulty they faced in trying to work with him on a daily basis. We looked at the kinds of information Evan was given and his teachers talked of how they could change the ways in which assignments were arranged. Without actually mentioning frames, their discussion was about their personal frames of reference and their interpretations of the personal frames of reference that Evan brings to his classes.

We reconstructed not only the social and academic frames, but also the instructional frames of pedagogical strategies, and examined some of the materials that were used in their classes. This particular discussion lasted for several hours as we considered explanations, modified and qualified our interpretations, and constructed acceptable meanings for what was happening in Evan's life that had resulted in his yearly reevaluation.

The principal talked of the system failing Evan, and of the opportunity the teachers had to institute some changes that would make a difference. All those involved were ready to look at the situation a little differently, and to at least consider the possibility that Evan's problem was *not* in his head, but somewhere between heads, historically located, in the social organization of his elementary school classrooms.

The principal talked of starting over, of giving Evan the opportunity to be in the computer club, of moving him into the reading group where he would read "great books," and of giving him the support he needed to keep up with his assignments. Evan was brought into the meeting and told of the changes that were going to be taking place. He was asked to play his part, to work with his teachers as the changes were made. Evan's parents also agreed to help Evan by trying to provide consistent support for him, especially with his homework.

In the weeks that followed Evan worked hard. His mother talked of him getting up early so that he could read the "great books" and of his enthusiasm for the computer club. Evan talked some weeks later about the changes that were taking place. The computer club and his new reading group are important to him but so are the changes that he sees in his teachers and the other children. Evan said his teachers do not shout at him as much now and that the children are more accepting. Today most of Evan's assignments are completed. When they are not finished he stays in school to catch up and he takes the late bus home. He still has difficulties sometimes with the other children, and occasionally his teachers become frustrated. But the principal talks to them and says, "Just think where we've been and how far we've come."

Evan is making progress. While five years of questioning do not simply go away, the teachers were ready to see a little differently, to imagine what it is like for the child, and everyone has benefited. Everyone has to work at it, and they are. The meetings continue and reinterpretations are being made. The administration, the teachers, and the parents are all working together, taking risks with and for the child.

Patrick: The situation with Patrick has taken a little more time. The ethnographic assessment began when the school wanted to begin retesting Patrick so that he could be given learning disabled status (a prerequisite for him to receive special services). Thus, there was some uncertainty about the potential outcomes of an alternative evaluation. Again we began with the child. The card game Concentration became important. We looked at the skills needed to play and we tried to imagine the complex social and academic strategies that Patrick uses when he plays the game. We examined Patrick's stories, and talked about the information embedded in these texts that told us that Patrick is actively constructing language, generating hypotheses, and solving problems. We established a between-heads perspective and focused on the social organization of the academic life in his classroom.

We then talked about the extraordinary number of tests Patrick has taken and of the ambiguity of his nonparticipatory position in the classroom—not being expected to alphabetize his words or complete the dictation exercises—and of how this had affected his position as a member of his class. Several meetings took place and as time went by Patrick's teacher, the language arts coordinator, and the director of special services cautiously considered the possibilities of the alternative evaluation. "What can we do?" "How can we change the ways in which we work with Patrick?" "How can we make him feel comfortable in the classroom so that he can participate in the reading and writing activities?" Distar was abandoned. Patrick read the books with his teacher that his reading group had read since his absence from the group. We talked of creating a supportive, noncorrective environment.

We discussed letting Patrick know when he had accomplished a task. If Patrick was asked to alphabetize his spelling words and he successfully placed three words in ABC order these words would be talked about and not those incorrectly ordered. In addition to the changes made in school, Patrick's parents agreed to read with him at home in a slightly different way. Now when they share stories with Patrick they invite him to participate when he feels comfortable with the story.

In addition, Patrick visits me. Sometimes if he has had a busy day I will read to him, but he usually takes over after a few pages and reads to me. He asks questions such as, "How come there's a *k* at the beginning of some words, like at the beginning of *knee?*" On other occasions he comments, "Marvin K. Mooney. I must remember Mooney." Then for a while he writes stories. "Do you know what I'm going to write next?" "Does this make sense?" "Can you read that?" "Read it to me." "Read it again." One story leads into another. They are all connected, variations on the themes that Patrick has invented, and each one is a little more complex than the one before.

For a few minutes we work on school tasks. (These tasks may not be ones that we would have chosen, but they are important if Patrick is to survive in school.) Alphabetizing his spelling words was one task we worked on. Patrick and I spent time looking through my old leather-bound Oxford Dictionary with its 2,536 pages of words. We felt the paper and the writing that is raised on the page. We talked about why words are alphabetized. We played at finding words beginning with various letters of the alphabet. We talked about his spelling words, and we problem-solved our way through the task of placing them in alphabetical order. Patrick tried on his own and succeeded. "How can you alphabetize your words at school?" We imagined the task. The chalk board. Patrick's desk. Transferring the words. Getting them in the right order.

Another meeting of parents, teachers, and administrators took place some weeks later, in March, at which information was gathered as well as shared. At that time, Patrick's teacher said she was pleased with his progress. He was reading with her and completing most of his assignments. He was writing in his own way in his diary, his dictation was completed, and he was alphabetizing his spelling words. Patrick's parents said that for the first time, Patrick had volunteered to read in Sunday school in front of the other children.

Patrick's father talked about the children's dictionary that they had bought for him. He talked of Patrick taking the dictionary to bed with him and he spoke of the ways in which his son prolonged saying good-night by looking up words. One night Patrick said he had to look up the word *baseball* before he went to sleep, and found the word without any assistance from his dad. Patrick is beginning to see himself as a reader and he likes writing stories. He is building on what he knows, socially constructed personal knowledge that was *never discovered* during the extensive testing procedures. It will take time. He is shy of new tasks and it is not easy for him to go to school. But he is learning. His ideas are accepted. On some level, I think he knows that his understandings of written language are respected.

COMMENTARY

As suggested in this chapter, we can build alternative paradigms and broad-based theories that give children a chance to participate in the educational system that shapes their lives. Parents and children, teachers, and administrators *can* work together to change their fail-ure-producing ways. At the present time children are grouped, sorted, retained, and labeled as "learning disabled" based on evaluations that are made through the use of large-scale manufactured measures. Thus children are diagnosed as suffering from "a chronic fear-of-failure syndrome," "developmental dyslexia," or "attentional deficit dis-order," as if these were tangible diseases such as the measles or chicken pox that must be treated with extra doses of isolated skills, separate instruction away from friends, or, in the case of attentional deficit disorder, treated on occasion with drugs such as ritalin.

When we evaluate children we get lost in our own abstractions and children fail. When children fail, families are placed in jeopardy. Sometimes families fail. When children fail, teachers are held ac-countable. In essence, they too are found wanting. The ultimate irony of this situation is that when children are given the opportunity to create an authentic foundation for their own existence, they do not fail. In our adult-made, in-the-head-tested educational system, we consistently *underestimate* the enormous potential of children to par-ticipate in the construction of their own learning environments. We ignore their abilities, preferring instead the artificial glitz of publish-ers' programs (see Peetoom, 1987). Then when children "get it wrong" we blame them and try to rescue them through further syn-thetic measures.

To evaluate, we need to build descriptions of children as they participate in the social construction of their own environments. The ways in which we develop our explanations should be imaginative and intuitive, as well as analytic and well-trained. In my own experi-ence, teachers are ready for this change. We can begin by observing children, learning with them and from them as they learn with us and from us (see Teale, 1986). In this way we can create philosophical and theoretical frames for our observations of the learning environments we make for one another. We are lucky in this endeavor, for a precedent has already been established. Dewey (1938/1963) makes as much sense today as he did fifty years ago. It is "the intimate and necessary relation between the processes of actual experience and education" (p. 20) that we must come to understand.

POSTSCRIPT: AUTUMN 1987

Evan is in seventh grade. His school and family have worked together to help him keep up with his school assignments and to help him make the transition from the elementary school to the junior high. At the present time the school, which is recognized for academic excellence, is considering the broad-range uses of ethnographic educational evaluations. Meetings are taking place with the superintendent of schools, principal, and faculty members to determine how the approach can be adapted for use within the system.

Patrick is in second grade. Although the school staff showed an initial interest in the possibilities of the ethnographic educational evaluation, they subsequently urged his parents to agree to more traditional evaluation procedures. At the end of Patrick's first-grade year the school advocated retention and retesting. His parents refused. They have maintained their storybook reading, and he reads books and writes stories on a regular basis with me. In August I wrote a profile of Patrick's literacy behaviors, and his parents submitted it to the school. To the best of my knowledge the report has not been considered. At the present time, retesting and coding appear to be the only option the school is willing to consider.

NOTES

I would like to thank Don Graves for asking me to address the question of assessment and evaluation from the perspective of my own research for the National Conference on Research in English. I would also like to thank Ray McDermott, who listened to sections of the paper over the telephone, and Angela Jaggar, for her support at the NCRE presentation of the research at the NCTE Spring Conference in Louisville, Kentucky. Most of all, I want to thank the parents and children, and the teachers and administrators who were willing to participate in the evaluations.
1. "Evan" and "Patrick" are not their real names.
2. The associations are the Association for Childhood Education International, Association for Supervision and Curriculum Development, Interna-

tional Reading Association, National Association for the Education of Young Children, National Association of Elementary School Principals, National Council of Teachers of English.

REFERENCES

Bateson, G. 1958. *Naven.* Stanford, CA: Stanford University Press.
──────. 1972. *Steps to an Ecology of Mind.* New York: Ballantine.
Brooks, T. 1977. *The Sword of Shannara.* New York: Random House.
Chapple, E. D. 1970. *Culture and Biological Man: Explorations in Behavioral Anthropology.* New York: Holt, Rinehart & Winston.
Clay, M. 1979. *Reading: The Patterning of Complex Behavior.* Portsmouth, NH: Heinemann.
Coe, R. N. 1984. *When the Grass Was Taller: Autobiography and the Experience of Childhood.* New Haven, CT: Yale University Press.
Cook-Gumperz, J. 1986. *The Social Construction of Literacy.* New York: Cambridge University Press.
Dewey, J. 1916. *Democracy and Education.* New York: Macmillan.
──────. 1963. *Experience and Education* (Kappa Delta Pi. The Collier Books Edition). London: Collier-Macmillan. (Original work published 1938.)
Dillon, D. 1987. Editorial on Evaluation. *Language Arts* 64: 271.
Durkheim, E. 1938. *The Rules of Sociological Method.* 8th ed. S. Solovay & J. Mueller, trans.; G. Catlin, ed. New York: The Free Press (Macmillan). (Original work published 1895.)
Erickson, F. 1982. "Taught Cognitive Learning in Its Immediate Environments: A Neglected Topic in the Anthropology of Education." *Anthropology of Education* 13(2): 149–180.
Frake, C. O. 1981. "Cultural Ecology and Ethnography." In A. S. Dil, ed., *Language and Cultural Description: Essays of Charles O. Frake* (pp. 18–25). Stanford, CA: Stanford University Press. (Original work published 1962.)
Geertz, C. 1983. *Local Knowledge: Further Essays in Interpretive Anthropology.* New York: Basic Books.
Goodman, Y. 1986. "Children Coming to Know Literacy." In W. H. Teale & E. Sulzby, eds., *Emergent Literacy: Writing and Reading* (pp. 1–14). Norwood, NJ: Ablex.
Graves, D. H. 1978. *Balance the Basics: Let Them Write* (Report to the Ford Foundation). New York: Ford Foundation.
Green, J. L. 1983. "Research on Teaching as a Linguistic Process: A State of the Art. In E. Gordon, ed., *Review of Research in Education* (pp. 151–252). Washington, DC: American Educational Research Association.
Green, J., J. O. Harker, and J. M. Golden. 1986. "Lesson Construction: Differing Views." In D. W. Noblit & W. T. Pink, eds., *Schooling in Social Context: Qualitative Studies* (pp. 46–77). Norwood, NJ: Ablex.

Green, J., R. Weade, and K. Graham. 1988. "Lesson Construction and Student Participation: A Sociolinguistic Analysis." In J. L. Green & J. O. Harker, eds., *Multiple Perspective Analysis of Classroom Discourse*. Norwood, NJ: Ablex. 11–48.

Gumperz, J. J. 1981. "Conversational Inference and Classroom Learning." In J. Green & C. Wallat, eds., *Ethnography and Language in Educational Settings* (pp. 3–23). Norwood, NJ: Ablex.

————. 1982. *Discourse Strategies*. London: Cambridge University Press.

Hall, N. 1987. *The Emergence of Literacy*. Portsmouth, NH: Heinemann.

Harste, J. C., V. A. Woodward, and C. L. Burke. 1984. *Language Stories and Literacy Lessons*. Portsmouth, NH: Heinemann.

Hymes, D. 1982. "What Is Ethnography?" In P. Gilmore & A. Glatthorn, eds., *Children in and out of School* (pp. 21–32). Washington, DC: Center for Applied Linguistics.

Leichter, H. J. 1974. "The Family as Educator." *Teachers College Record* 76: 175–217.

Literacy Development in Pre-First Grade: A Joint Statement of Concern About Present Practices in Pre-First Grade Instruction and Recommendations for Improvement. 1985. Available from the International Reading Association, 800 Barksdale Road, Newark, DE 19714-8139.

McDermott, R. P. 1974. "Achieving School Failure: An Anthropological Approach to Illiteracy and Social Stratification." In G. Spindler, ed., *Education and Cultural Process* (pp. 82–118). New York: Holt, Rinehart & Winston.

McDermott, R. P., and D. R. Roth. 1978. "The Social Organization of Behavior: Interactional Approaches." *Annual Review of Anthropology* 7: 321–45.

Mead, M. 1970. *Culture and Commitment: A Study of the Generation Gap*. New York: Natural History Press.

Mehan, H. 1979. *Learning Lessons*. Cambridge, MA: Harvard University Press.

Peetoom, A. 1987. "Educational Publishing: A Personal Perspective." *Language Arts* 64: 402–406.

Schickedanz, J. A. 1986. *More than the ABC's: The Early Stages of Reading and Writing*. Washington, DC: National Association for the Education of Young Children.

Sulzby, E. 1986. "Writing and Reading: Signs of Oral and Written Language Organization in the Young Child." In W. H. Teale & E. Sulzby, eds. *Emergent Literacy: Writing and Reading* (pp. 50–89). Norwood, NJ: Ablex.

Taylor, D. 1981. "The Family and the Development of Reading Skills and Values." *Journal of Research in Reading* 4: 92–103.

————. 1982. "Translating Children's Everyday Uses of Print into Classroom Practices." *Language Arts* 59: 546–549.

————. 1983a. *Family Literacy: Young Children Learning to Read and Write*. Portsmouth, NH: Heinemann.

———. 1983b. "Reflections on Parenting." *Family Process* 22: 341–346.

———. 1987. "The (Con)textual Worlds of Childhood: An Interpretive Approach to Alternative Dimensions of Experience." In B. Fillion, C. Hedley, & E. DiMartino, eds., *Home and School: Early Language and Reading* (pp. 93–107). Norwood, NJ: Ablex.

Taylor, D., and C. Dorsey-Gaines. 1988. *Growing up Literate: Learning from Inner-City Families*. Portsmouth, NH: Heinemann.

Taylor, D., and D. S. Strickland. 1986a. *Family Storybook Reading*. Portsmouth, NH: Heinemann.

———. 1986b. "Family Literacy: Myths and Magic." In M. R. Sampson, ed., *The Pursuit of Literacy: Early Reading and Writing* (pp. 30–48). Dubuque, IA: Kendall/Hunt Publishing.

Teale, W. H. 1986. "The Beginnings of Reading and Writing: Written Language Development During the Preschool and Kindergarten Years." In M. R. Sampson, ed., *The Pursuit of Literacy: Early Reading and Writing* (pp. 1–29). Dubuque, IA: Kendall/Hunt Publishing.

Tolkien, J. R. R. 1984. *The Lord of the Rings* (trilogy). New York: Ballantine Books. (Original work published 1945.)

Wolcott, H. F. 1982. "The Anthropology of Becoming." *Anthropology and Education Quarterly* 13: 83–108.

2

TOWARD A UNIFIED THEORY OF LITERACY LEARNING AND INSTRUCTIONAL PRACTICES

In our in-the-head-tested educational system, we
consistently *underestimate* the enormous potential
of children to participate in the construction of
their own learning environments.

M y writing of this article was provoked by Marie Carbo's critique of Jeanne Chall's research and by Chall's rebuttal, for I find myself disagreeing with both of them and disturbed that the complex subject of children's early literacy development has been reduced in their debate to a battle over methods (Carbo, 1988; Chall, 1989). When viewed against the broader context of the past twenty years of research into the ways in which young children learn to read and write, the "Great Debate" can be seen as little more than a trivial argument over an issue that has no scientific relevance. Thus I would urge both researchers and educators to look beyond this petty squabble. I am firmly convinced that if we can ignore such reductionist disagreements about currently dominant methodologies, we will be able to concentrate on building theoretically grounded explanations of reading and writing that will eventually enable us to develop a unified theory of literacy learning and instructional practices.

DEBUNKING REDUCTIONIST RESEARCH

In his discussion of economics, James Gleick cites the Nobel laureate Wassily Leontief, who is reported to have said that "in no field of empirical inquiry has so massive and sophisticated a statistical machinery been used with such indifferent results" (quoted in Gleick, 1988, p. 84). Leontief's comment could very well have been made about the use of statistics in the plethora of reading studies cited by Chall and Carbo. However, Carbo, herself a reductionist, never quite gets a handle on the problem, even though she raises some serious concerns about the surface-level accuracy of Chall's "garden-variety studies." To understand the underlying problem we must dig much deeper. In her rebuttal Chall writes, "The essence of scholarship, then, is in creating a theory, an explanation, that best fits the research. Synthesizing research, to a great extent, is creating order out of *chaos*" (Chall, 1989, p. 528, emphasis added).

This totally artificial, reductionist approach to science leads to synthetic explanations that do not reflect the complexity of the phenomena being studied. It seems appropriate to quote Gleick again, for in the introduction to *Chaos: Making a New Science* he writes:

> [C]haos is a science of process rather than state, of becoming not being.
> . . . [It] breaks across the lines that separate scientific disciplines . . .
> [and] poses problems that defy accepted ways of working in science, . . .
> turning back a trend in science toward reductionism. (p. 5)

The argument that Gleick pursues throughout his text is that *patterns* of behavior are nonlinear—globally stable but locally unpredictable. If we accept this interpretation of science, then the idea that the essence of scholarship is the creation of theories that best fit the research breaks down, especially in research studies that are based on the underlying assumption that human behavior (reading, writing, literacy, or whatever) can best be described by linear, hierarchical models (Chall, 1983b).

Clearly, Chall and the researchers she cites would argue that it *is* possible to reduce language to an orderly, sequential set of graphophonemic features that can be presented to children in a series of training episodes. They would also argue that it is possible to determine the effects of such experimentation using tests of statistical significance, analysis of variance, and linear regression. However, stripping away the noise and color of children's literacy learning—removing the complexity of real phenomena—may well produce statistically predictable global patterns, but I would argue that these patterns are locally unpredictable, inherently unstable, and completely inapplicable to the learning behaviors of *individual* children (see Brown, 1989; Jervis, 1989; Johnston, 1989; Meisels, 1989; Shepard, 1989). Only when we use statistical procedures to artificially simplify human activity to fit our research models do such explanations work. While it might be possible to fit simplistic notions of decoding to the "normal" distribution described by the bell-shaped curve and then to produce training programs for children based on the results of such studies, the underlying assumptions totally ignore what we have come to understand of the complexity of the literacy behaviors of young children.

The essence of scholarship does *not* lie in creating theories that fit our research, in synthesizing the chaos of our findings. Instead, scholarship should be an attempt to create theories or explanations that tell us something about the phenomena we are studying.

With regard to literacy, our task as researchers is not to control isolated bits of reading or writing, nor to modify learning in artifically defined training situations (classrooms or laboratories) so that we can test our methods. Instead, our task as social scientists is to try to understand the complexity of the literacy behaviors of young children. And our task as educators is to use these understandings to support and enhance children's learning opportunities, guiding them in both direct and indirect ways as they develop *personal* understandings of literacy that are both socially constructed and individually situated in the practical accomplishments of their everyday lives. Ironically, when such a theoretical and pedagogical framework is established, children become immersed in the reconstruction of genuine functions, uses, and forms of written language. They become immersed in the dialectics of their own chaotic discoveries, and much of their time is spent in solving problems that have to do with the relationships between sounds and systems of symbols.

GIVING UP SIMPLISTIC NOTIONS ABOUT COMPLEX BEHAVIORS

The methods of instruction that are now dominant dictate that, when a young child comes to school, learning to read is presented as an orderly, linear, hierarchical sequence of tasks (Chall, 1983b). How a child measures up to this theory of instruction becomes the benchmark of his or her early reading development (Gerald Coles, personal communication, April 1989; Chall acknowledges this fact when she discusses the influence that *Learning to Read: The Great Debate* has had on standardized tests: see Chall, 1983a, p. 3). When an individual child's learning does not fit the instructional training program, "problems" are diagnosed and "remediated," using more intensive doses of linearly sequenced decoding skills. Children are labeled and pigeonholed, and their own learning is denied (Taylor, in press). What researchers and educators who support such methods fail to appreciate is that the "errors" that they mark on workbook pages are not aberrations in the learning abilities of young children but are merely reflections of their own aberrant theories and pedagogical practices.

They have learned not to see that children's early literacy behaviors are disorderly, seemingly erratic, and incomprehensibly chaotic.

Giving up simplistic notions about complex behaviors is not a "charismatic solution" to a "very serious problem," nor is this view of literacy "couched in the rhetoric of warmth, openness, and great promise, (Chall, 1989, p. 532). There are no cuddly solutions to the problems posed by children's literacy learning, and I offer none. The task is as serious as any we face. We must give up the security of prepackaged programs built upon stage theories and stop trying to fit children's early reading and writing experiences into some model or other. This is the only way that we will ever be able to see how language is both constructed and used by children when adults are not blatantly distorting the process.

Acknowledging the complexity of early reading and writing development means that we must try to understand literacy from the child's perspective, and that involves disciplined, systematic observation of children as they work at reading and writing in and out of classroom settings. Above all, it demands an awareness that the literacy behaviors of young children are sensitively dependent on *initial conditions* (Gleick, 1988).

DESCRIPTIONS OF OBSERVABLE LITERACY BEHAVIORS

The following descriptions of children's observable literacy behaviors illustrate the importance of providing children with opportunities to reconstruct the functions and uses of written language without the intrusion of prepackaged training programs. The first two descriptions were written by Leigh Walls, a kindergarten teacher. In her classroom, literacy is used in many playful situations, in the "hospital" and in the "post office," as well as in the reading corner and the writing center (Schickedanz, 1988). Leigh wrote of one of her students:

> *September:* For Mark, writing is a social process which must be shared at many points as he works on his drawings. He works quickly and his art work is representational, frequently including backgrounds (sky, water, sun, etc.) which are so enthusiastically added that they may obscure the major features of the drawing. Mark draws upon many kinds of experiences and interests in determining topics for his pictures: a fair he attended, castles, boats, rainbows, spiders (and their webs!), a crane wrecking a building. Mark feels a real sense of ownership towards his

work, as evidenced by this inventory, which he shared after a neighboring child added a sun to "complete" his picture: "I made a house on the land. And this is the water. And this is the sky. And I didn't want the sun [with a significant glance at the other child], so *don't* give me the sun!" Mark knows many alphabet letters and corresponding sounds and is beginning to use this knowledge to label his pictures with critical features of the needed word: "SR" for *spider*web. He writes his name in all capitals or a mixture of capital and lower-case letters. He remembers many of his key words and is quick to use the context of the print he encounters in the classroom to predict—and frequently read correctly—what it says.

January/February: Mark continues to describe his pictures in great detail orally. Sometimes he notes every single thing he has drawn: "This is a Mickey Mouse watching Pluto in the shade beside the doghouse under the tree on the nice grass. And Mickey's standing on his front porch. And that's his house with his windows, his basement, his stairway, and his front porch." Other times he tells a story: "This is a Tiger Shark shooting. The Cobra shot at him and missed. And the Tiger Shark shot at him but he missed the buddy and hit the sand. That's why I did yellow. So the Tiger Shark shot at the Cobra plane and the Cobra hit himself and shot off one wing. I'm glad he shot himself. He's bad. He wants to destroy the world. And the Tiger Shark shot at the Cobra and blew it to smithereens!" His own writing varies from none to the initials "USA" on a truck, to a single word ("VOOKANOO"—"volcano"), to several words ("SKAEHS KAD"—"sky house cloud") or a complete sentence ("DSAPNGOTORC"—"This is a person going to work"). Mark prefers to write words he knows from memory, such as "Mickey Mouse." He also integrates print into his art work; in addition to USA on a truck, he made a sign which said, "Mark," and he told me, "It says, 'Mark's town, next stop!' " When he reads his own writing, he pays attention to the letters he has used. One day, I asked him to read "TKK" at the top of his paper. He started to read, "Tiger Sh . . . ," but then he grabbed a pencil to add "AK" at the end to complete it: "TKK AK"—"Tiger Shark." He has accumulated 20 key [personal] words, which he generally reads "on sight."

The literacy biographies that Leigh writes provide a narrative description of the literacy behaviors of each child in her kindergarten class. No two profiles are the same. Each biographical account provides a social/historical context for understanding the many complex ways in which individual children are coping with the task of learning to read and write.

Another profile from Leigh's literacy biographies helps us see the difference in the ways that individual children reinvent the functions,

Toward a Unified Theory of Literacy Learning and Instructional Practices

uses, and forms of written language. This biographical profile includes the entries Leigh made for May and June so that we can see what happens over time when a young child is given the opportunity to play with print in a kindergarten classroom:

September: Christopher's drawings are frequently of himself and his family, and his people are generally happy and brightly colored, with distinctive facial features, including ears and hair. At first, Christopher drew small figures, taking up just a corner of the page. After several weeks, he started using the whole page, covering it with shapes and numerals (he appears to love numbers and counting!) or squiggles which he calls mazes (after our field trip to the farm, where we walked in a maze of shapes). Christopher labels pictures of himself and his brother (Jack) with their names, written in all capital letters, "CHRIƧTOPHER" and "ԼACK." He is beginning to label other pictures with beginning sounds: "F" for "flower," "Y" for the "m" sound at the start of "maze." His oral descriptions of his work are frequently listings of what he drew: "I wrote my name and two balls," "I wrote a devil and my name," and so on. Christopher also copies his key words onto his paper occasionally, progressing from left to right until he runs out of space and then putting the remaining letters at the beginning of the word that he is writing so that all the letters are together on one line.

October: In early October Christopher's pictures were generally experiments with dots, lines, and colors. By midmonth they became more representational again, with recognizable mountains, monsters, etc. His oral descriptions continue to be listings of what he's drawn: "A castle. A werewolf. A skeleton and a bat and a vampire and a spider and spider webs." Christopher is labeling more often with beginning sounds: "M" for "mountain," "Ƨ2" for "snakes" and for "skeleton," and "BB" for "bumblebee." His interest in copying words from other sources continues.

January/February: Christopher has begun to use some lower-case letters when writing his name: "CHRiƧtoPHER." The class was introduced to initials as the abbreviation for their names, and he began writing "CR" on his journal pages to identify them as his own. He still writes beginning sounds of words as labels, as well as occasionally using other critical features, such as "M" for "grand*m*a." The day Christopher drew E.T. and labeled the picture "E," I asked if he could finish the name, and he quickly added "T." Another time, he wrote "KNT" for "*king*," with encouragement to listen for sounds beyond the first one. On January 23, Christopher made a book with a different animal on each page. He told me all the animals he had drawn and then said, "It's *Brown Bear, Brown Bear, What Do You See?*" He wrote "B" for "Brown Bear"

and "C" for "see." On each page he wrote "iCA" for "I see a . . . " and
then the picture of a bird, a duck, a horse, and a frog, making his own
version of a story which he enjoys hearing and reading. He seems to like
using the pens that a classmate brought in and is inspired to make detailed drawings with them. These he may describe by giving a detailed
inventory: "This is the bow and arrow, and this is the alligator. And this
[an arrow] is going all the way there. This is the 'frigerator. It has a
sword inside. That's the sun, and that's the cloud. And that's the castle,
and that's the window. And that's the bridge, and that's the water. And
that's the guard. And that's the king."

May/June: Christopher's avid interest in monsters continues. At the library, he chooses "monƨter" books. At writing time, he draws monsters
and copies his key word, "monƨter," repeatedly. He even uses his library books to help him in his drawing, copying, for example, a picture
from the story *Harry and the Terrible Whatzit* (May 9). When he
checked out a book about famous monsters from the movies, Christopher worked on a single page of his journal every day for a week as he
tried to draw every kind of monster shown in the book. He used pencil
only so that he was able to draw and erase and redraw until he was
happy with his product, and the content of the page changed daily. This
page is an excellent indication of his skills to this point as he labeled his
art in a variety of ways (May 31–June 6): using beginning and ending
sounds ("SR" for "star" and "BT" for "bat"); using words which are
part of his (memorized) independent spelling vocabulary ("Matt"); copying from his book ("DRACULA"); using the combination of a known beginning sound and his key words (he wrote "M" and then looked in his
key words for the remainder of "MAИ"), using invented spelling to create a phrase ("ƐGƧ + MWN" for "three ghost women"); and using invented spelling to write an entire sentence ("i MPUB" for "I made a
bird"). Christopher's independent writing tends to be copied words and
words he has memorized, but he will use invented spelling with little or
no assistance when an adult [who supports such behavior] is present
or when he can think of no other source of the words he needs
("iMrnDoblr" for "I am riding on Big George"). At the present time, he
rereads some, but not all, of his invented spelling; for example, looking
at "I ROPIƧtPLOL" (May 4), he said, "It says, 'I wrote . . . '—I can't
remember the rest."

Christopher is very aware of print in the environment and is beginning to pick up sight words in addition to his key words. One day, as he
worked on his journal, he glanced at a neighbor's paper, on which she
had written another child's name: "EMBER." Commented Christopher,
"I like her name." That he is thinking about sound/symbol relationships
is obvious: one day (June 8) he came to me, clearly distressed, pointing
to our daily schedule and saying, "Mrs. Walls! 'Gym' should start with a

'J' and it doesn't!" I explained that some letters have more than one sound and that the "G" has a "hard" sound (as in "goat") and a soft sound (as in "gym"). Christopher is still musing over this confusing bit of information!

Leigh's descriptions of the ways in which Christopher is learning to read and write as he and other children *use* literacy in the everyday activities of their classroom provide evidence of the individual interpretations that children construct of the functions, uses, and forms of written language when their learning is not restricted by artificial workbook activities.

Let me reemphasize that these children are working in a kindergarten classroom in which reading and writing are purposeful activities. In such classrooms, patterns of literacy are constantly evolving to accommodate the everyday experiences of both teachers and children, and new understandings of reading and writing can lead to the systematic restructuring of classroom routines. Many of the children's deliberate uses of literacy occur when their purposeful engagement in print activities is used to call attention to the functions and uses of reading, together with *context-specific analysis of language structure and skills*. Over time, literacy becomes more complex and is transformed through the dialectical relationship established between the activity and the setting.

LITERACY PROFILES OF THIRD GRADERS

These transformations are clearly visible in the literacy profiles written by Kathy Matthews, a third-grade teacher. Once again, I have included two biographical accounts to emphasize the ways in which children reconstruct the functions, uses, and forms of written language in very personal ways. The biographies record the evolution of each child's literacy development, and Kathy's descriptions serve to emphasize that there is no generic pattern that can be encapsulated in a basal reader or on a workbook page:

September: "I don't know what's different," Rob told me one day. "Last year I thought reading was, you know, just okay. But this year I *love* reading! It's my best thing!" Rob's enthusiasm for reading also appears in his reading journal: "I feel like I read a million pages. It is a wonderful book." Rob generally chooses reading as an independent activity, sometimes bemoaning the fact that he has to stop reading to participate in other activities. Rob often talks about books and how he feels about the stories he reads. He is attentive to his peers' opinions about books and their reading choices and frequently becomes involved in lively, spontaneous discussions: "That was a great book!"; "I heard that one was good"; "I'm gonna read that one next!" As he reads, Rob gives me casual reports on his progress: "It was kinda hard at first but now I really think I'm doin' good"; "This book is gettin' boring"; "This one's easy! Look at how much I read today!"; "This one is hard! I don't think I'm ready for this one yet!"

The few entries that Rob has written in his reading journal are either brief descriptions of the story he is reading or simple, evaluative comments: "I really like *Little House in the Big Woods*. I think it is comfortable." Similarly, his daybook entries are surface descriptions of the activities and events that are important to him. His morning entries generally pertain to home issues, while the afternoon entries center on the most significant activity of the day or on his relationships with peers. ("The nicest thing [was] N. let me play football all the time and J. couldn't get me, and the other team said, 'You're fast!' ")

Rob has worked for some time on his story, "Hidden Crown," an adventure tale which bears some resemblance to the "Choose-Your-Own-Adventure" books that he often seeks in the school library. Rob spends an extensive amount of time creating detailed illustrations to carry the action of his narrative. He frequently confers with others and often appears to shift the focus of his story to accommodate the new ideas generated by such discourse.

Rob's concepts of the phonetic and structural aspects of written language place him in the mid-transitional stage of spelling achievement. When constructing words, he uses all consonants, long, open-syllable vowels, simple short vowels, blends, digraphs, and final consonant clusters -NT and -CK, as well as silent E and -ING. He writes chapter headings, uses a caret to insert information, paginates, shows a mixed use of periods, and uses question marks appropriately.

October: Rob's enthusiasm for our focus on prehistoric life has prompted him to create a new story titled "The Cave," a chapter book about the adventures and escapades which he and his peer-characters heroically survive. Much of the story occurs in the dialogue, which moves the characters and the action across time and space. ("When?" said Rob. "How about tomorrow?" said Adam. "Okay," said Rob. "Where?" "How about Hawaii?") Rob spends most of each writing period drawing and redrawing the illustrations or consulting with friends. He often reads his story to classmates, describes what he might do next, and then actively role-plays the parts with his peers. Rob tends to subvocalize as he composes, particularly when sketching action scenes. He uses enlarged print for sound effects and for emphasis.

Rob wrote brief, often unfinished entries in both his reading journal and his daybook this month. His first entry in his new learning log reflected some of the new information he had acquired ("I never knew the knee was one of the fragilest spots") and included an illustration of a human skull with its parts appropriately labeled. Another time he speculated about being an archaeologist and still another time wistfully wrote, "I wish I knew more about rocks." Rob used written language to compose riddles, jokes, and letters which he sent to friends; to write notes to me requesting assistance or asking for specific information; to collect, organize, and describe data from a field experience (an archaeological dig); and to share his personal feelings with a classmate.

For most of this month, Rob has been reading *Chester Cricket's Pigeon Ride*, which in his reading journal he describes as being "good in one way and good in another way." The reading journal entries that he wrote were one- or two-sentence descriptions of the main idea behind what he read.

September: Jill's ambivalent feelings about reading are revealed in the first entry in her reading journal: "I don't like reading that much but it's nice. I love writing but you need to read to write. I do like it if I really think about it. . . . " Her ambivalence seems confined to independent reading, because she is an enthusiastic participant in class experiences with reading, including shared-book and read-aloud times. Jill often seeks out favorite books and poems that have been shared, particularly the poetry of Robert Frost, whom she even quotes in her daybook. When asked to choose a story for independent reading, Jill's first tendency is to select simple chapter books or stories that she has already successfully read. Suggested books are sometimes dismissed as being "probably too hard." When asked how she went about the process of choosing a book that would appeal to her, she replied, "I don't know, I guess I just look at the covers to see if I'll like it or if it's gonna be too hard. Sometimes I ask people, too." In her journal she wrote, "CHARLOTTE'S WEB is great. Each time [I hear it] I want to read it but I don't so I'm reading it now. I just love it."

Jill is able to adjust her writing to her audience and to the purpose that her writing serves. Her reading journal letters to me are chatty accounts of her feelings about reading, questions to me as a reader ("What book are you reading?"), or reviews of the stories she reads. In her daybook, Jill often summarizes the day's events, tells her feelings about those events, and inquires about the readers' feelings even though she knows there will be no response. She also uses the daybook as a forum for experimenting with language and thought, as when she tries out something new like poetic description ("I love the music playing and the trees swaying in the light breeze").

Writing is, in Jill's words, "the best thing of all." She often speaks of "wishing we could write all day." Jill prefers to work in the company of others and, in fact, once stated that she didn't think she wrote as well when she had to work by herself. As she works, she continually seeks others' feedback—less, it seems, for assistance with the problems of content than for confirmation of her own process of planning and designing the story. Her conferences often become opportunities to role-play the story, which she then adjusts accordingly.

Most of Jill's effort has been focused on composing a multiple-part story whose tone and content are imitative of teenage novels like the Sweet Valley High series. Each part bears a separate title and has illustrations that are detailed and carefully drawn (especially the characters' clothing). The story's point of view is first person, it occurs primarily in dialogue, and it centers on themes of boy/girl relationships, jealousy, fashion, and friendship. Each of the separate parts ends with a suspenseful turn of events that is conveniently resolved in the beginning of the next part. Jill told me she had written the story this way so that it would be "like a TV show where they leave you hanging," because she felt it made the story "more exciting."

October: Jill added two new parts to the story she has been working on since early September and then completed two more similar pieces of writing. All her stories are written in first person and center on the fictitious exploits of her best friends, whom she consults frequently, and herself. She sometimes includes the specific friends with whom she has occasional conferences as characters. Her stories are told through her characters' conversations. The dialogue includes slang and popular expressions which serve to maintain the tone of the story. Jill often uses onomatopoeia and enlarged print to create sound effects or to emphasize meaning. Her illustrations have changed to simple, yet active, stick figures that are often accompanied by dialogue balloons. Because her stories are told in ordinary conversation, the written vocabulary of these narratives is more confined than in her daybook and reading journal, where she experiments with different forms of description and expression.

Jill's awareness of the many functions language can serve shows itself in numerous ways. She used written language to interact with others through her stories, notes, and letters. She used her learning log to speculate about experiences, to create hypotheses based on her own experiences and information ("The person who lived here was a doctor and they liked pottery"), and to ask questions and seek new information. She used her daybook as a means of expressing her moods, feelings, and creativity; to report to me about the activities of others; and to summarize the events that were of significance to her. Jill also used her reading journal to discuss her feelings about books and to connect with me, reader to reader.

The phonetic and structural concepts of written language that Jill has developed place her in the early to mid-transitional stage of spelling.

She uses the standard form of many high-frequency words and uses most consonants, blends, long vowels, short vowels, and digraphs. Jill uses question marks, exclamation points, mixed capitals, and occasional periods. Her revisions consist of crossing out or erasing specific words or using carets to insert words.

These literacy biographies illustrate Kathy Matthews' attempt to catalog systematically the configurations of the functions and uses of reading and writing. Kathy observes each child's literacy behavior, takes notes, and develops individual portfolios. As she attempts to understand literacy learning from each child's point of view, patterns emerge from the seemingly disorderly collections of data. Recently, in preparation for parent conferences, Kathy encouraged her students to help evaluate their own literacy development. The children were asked to reflect on their own learning. Kathy asked the children, "How have you changed? What do you do well? How do you want to improve?" At the conferences, the children shared with their parents and Kathy their observations of themselves as learners. Then Kathy shared the biographical accounts that she had written. What Kathy and her students found was that there were many similarities in the observations that they had made.

BLURRING THE BOUNDARIES

Across the United States, teachers are working in ways similar to those used by the teachers whose work I've excerpted above. They are blurring the boundaries between language as a topic of study and language as a means of communication (Taylor 1988; Taylor 1991a; Taylor, 1991b). In their classrooms, print is incorporated into knowledge-generating activities, including science, math, and social studies, so that children can use their creativity and ingenuity to theorize about learning and about using written language in problem-solving situations. Children are not disenfranchised, nor are their experiences marginalized. In such classrooms, teachers and children work together, becoming co-informants, as the reading and writing strategies of the one inform those of the other. This approach enables teachers to rethink the ways in which they can provide realistic instruction in situations that make sense to the children and to themselves. It also enables children to become involved in personal evaluations of the ways in which they are becoming literate.

In these classrooms, literacy becomes a dynamic, complex, multidimensional phenomenon that is transformed through the interdependence of activity and setting (see Taylor, 1989; Carraher, 1986; Carraher, Carraher, and Schliemann, 1985; de la Rocha, 1985; Lave, 1985; Lave, Murtaugh, and de la Rocha, 1984; Scribner, 1984). When reading and writing become problem-solving activities, print is used to:

*   recast (reconstitute) the relationships between problems and solutions;
*   examine variations in procedural possibilities;
*   discuss contradictions in interpretations of relationships between problems and solutions;
*   depart from literal formats through the reorganization of tasks;
*   develop least-effort strategies;
*   arrive at "instrumental" (purposeful) solutions;
*   theorize about "doing";
*   lead others in problem solving;
*   invent new procedures; and
*   generate problems as well as solutions.

In Betty Jacks' first-grade classroom the children were making books about dinosaurs. Betty had talked with them about some of the ways in which they could find important information about dinosaurs in books. Betty modeled the process and then gave each child an empty book cut in the shape of a brontosaurus. On the cover of hers, Margaret had written:

A Book
abut
Brontosaurus
by Margaret

Inside the front cover she had written:

This
Book
is
Dadcad
to
Kim
Roberts

On the next page Margaret had written:

I LOVe
Brontosa
it is
Nete

itwad abot
20 pons
+ abot
6 alfis

Margaret read, "It weighed about twenty tons—that equals plus about six elephants." She then told me she had found the information in the book that was on her desk: *The Monsters Who Died: A Mystery About Dinosaurs,* by Vicky Cobb, a tough text for a first grader. Margaret said that her mom, who had been helping in the classroom, had helped her. Then she added that she could read some of it. Margaret read, "It was named brontosaurus—" She paused and looked at me. I read, "meaning 'thunder reptile' because—" Margaret continued, "it must have made—" Margaret waited. "Thunderous—" I filled in. "Noise," Margaret read quickly, and then she finished the sentence, "as it tramped over the ground."

Margaret skipped chunks of text, looked down the page, and said, "And now here's the story about the head." Again we worked together to read, "For more than fifty years the head of the brontosaurus was thought to be very small compared to the rest of its body. The entire skull was smaller than one of its neck bones." Margaret stopped. After a moment she said, "Really?" And then she began to read again, "There was room only [reading *only* with some help] for a tiny brain." With support she continued, "If this skull truly belonged to the dinosaur, the beast must have been very slow and stupid." Margaret laughed, and then she wrote:

Thae Had
Small
brains [quickly found in the text]

Thae Had
Loing
Tals

On the next page she wrote:

Thae
Had
Loing
Nags
Thae
Had
big
bodese

Margaret made a bookmark and put it in the reference book. She put the book away and put the book she was writing in her writing folder. She put the folder with the rest of the children's folders.

When Margaret wanted information from *The Monsters Who Died: A Mystery About Dinosaurs*, she had collaborated with her mother, who had been in the classroom on the day that Betty had talked about finding information in books. Together, Margaret and her mother *recast* the problem so that Margaret could gain access to the text. Thus she participated in the *generation* of a new problem and in the *invention* of a new procedure for getting information from books, *departing from the literal format* through the reorganization of the task.

When I arrived in the classroom, Margaret's mother had left to pick up her son from a day-care center, so Margaret led me in the problem-solving activities. She applied the strategy that she had used with her mother to read the text with me. When Margaret skipped down the page, leaving out large chunks of the text, she demonstrated the use of a *least-effort* procedure. We can also surmise that at some time Margaret and her mother had collaborated in *generating* the problem of how Margaret could use complex texts as a basis for her own writing and that they might, perhaps, have *examined variations* in procedures. All of these social interpretations of the task would engage Margaret in *theorizing about doing.*

If we consider the concept of *theorizing* (an unobservable complex mental activity) from another perspective, we can use the same categories of behavior listed above to analyze how Margaret wrote her straightforward descriptions of brontosaurus based on her reading of such a complicated text. We could state that it appears to us that Margaret *recast* the problem/solution relationships, *departing from the literal format*, *inventing* new procedures and *using least-effort strategies* to arrive at an instrumental solution.

From Margaret's observable literacy behaviors, we can talk about her book knowledge, which she displayed in the way she read the reference book and in the ways she constructed her own written text. We can talk about the development of her graphophonemic representations; her knowledge of initial, medial, and final consonants; the complexity of her long vowels; her use of critical features; and her awareness of short vowels and of silent *e*. We could list the sight words that she used and note the way she returned to the reference text when she wanted to know how to spell *brain*. We could talk about her ability to draw inferences, for the book never actually said that dinosaurs had big bodies—only that they had small heads. We could describe Margaret's ability to organize, her use of word bound-aries, her use of capital and lower-case letters, her use of mathematical symbols, her curiosity and interest in learning, her willingness to take risks, and the confidence she displayed when she invented writ-ten words such as *Dadcad, alfis,* and *nete.*

If we try to synthesize all of this information, we can state that Margaret was able to use the social, symbolic, and material resources at her disposal to participate in the generation of nonroutine problem-solving procedures. There is no linear progression in such situated ac-tivities, and none is ascribed. The complexity of the process involved cannot be teased apart by statistical analysis, nor can such complex sociocognitive activity be simulated in a basal reading series. In trying to figure out how such processes function, I have found it help-ful to try to imagine possible global patterns of the locally chaotic problem-solving procedures that are inherent in learning to use writ-ten language in everyday classroom life. Thus the image is one of a kaleidoscope of patterns and shifting formations, of infinite variation that cannot be depicted in a hierarchy of skills or represented on a workbook page.

TOWARD A UNIFIED THEORY

The interpretations presented above provide us with one perspective on children's early literacy development. But it is just one perspec-tive, and there are many others. In the last twenty years, educational researchers, anthropologists, sociolinguists, psycholinguists, and so-ciologists have been involved in research studies that focus on read-ing and writing. Their research has taught us much about the ways in which young children learn to read and write and about the ways in which we teach them. The interpretations that they have created move us from the reductionist thinking of laboratory studies. Even though there are many differences among these researchers, they and we are bound together by the belief that we must understand literacy development from the point of view of the child. In other words, we do science *with* the participants in our research. Our subjects are not under the microscope; we do not practice on them. None of these re-searchers are represented or even considered in the arguments put forth by Jeanne Chall in favor of synthetic phonics.

When I first read Chall's response to Carbo in the March 1989 *Kappan,* I wondered if I had imagined these last twenty years of research. Implicit in her article is the assumption "If it doesn't have a number, it doesn't count."

But sometimes the numbers don't count. As I stated in the first section of this article, the scientific use of parametric statistics has a narrow application and is generally ill-suited to measuring the types of things that reading researchers are trying to measure. Even if, for one second, we adopt Chall's point of view and agree to waive the limitations of the tests (Shepard, 1989), how can we be sure that the underlying assumptions about literacy that are implicitly embedded in such a perspective are valid enough to allow the use of such measures? What if Chall's point of entry distorts the phenomena to be studied? What if the researchers Chall cites simply got it wrong? What if children's learning has been turned into a mirror image of the researchers' own convoluted theories? In "The Hollow Men" T. S. Eliot writes, "Between the conception / And the creation / . . . Falls the Shadow." What if they have failed "Between the idea / And the reality" because the basic conceptions of these research studies are flawed? Then we have failed through the creation of the debate and through our perpetuation of a dead issue.

Perhaps our failure would not matter if we were content to practice this "science" without practicing on children. But when educational theories leave the universities in which they were conceived, they change. *Theories become fact.* Publishers use them to produce textbooks, and programs are adopted. The artificial concepts expounded by the proponents of these theories are taught, tests are developed to determine knowledge and understanding of these concepts, and children's success or failure is measured by their performance on such tests. When this happens, children's learning is lost in the clean copy of a phonics workbook page (or in a test of learning styles or in some other reductionist trick).

Reading does not develop in predefined "stages." This myth has grown out of the reductionist research in which there is an artificial separation between reading and writing. Reading is dissected into predefined, linear, component parts that are divorced from the naturally occurring dialectical structures that constitute purposeful literacy activities. To my knowledge, none of the research that has focused on the sociocognitive organization of the functions and uses of literacy supports the stage theory advocated by Chall. To the contrary, many well-documented research studies, when combined, provide compelling evidence to support the proposition that there is infinite variety in the patterns of young children's early literacy development.

At the conclusion of her March 1989 *Kappan* article, Chall writes:

> In education as in national and world affairs, history teaches us that in times of desperation we have a tendency to look for global, charismatic, single solutions to very serious problems. Only after these fail—often at great cost—are we prepared to look for solutions that are more firmly based in reality. (p. 532)

I would argue that the proponents of reductionist, hierarchical models of early reading development have looked for a "global, charismatic, single solution" to a very serious problem and that in doing so they have created global patterns that exist only in artificial simulations of teaching and learning. But worse, when these aberrant theories left the universities in which they were created, they became commercialized in packaged programs and politicized in standardized tests. Some children are thought to need more practice, some less. But it would appear from this research perspective that the stages remain the same. The impact of this approach is made evident in the lack of problem-solving skills reported by the National Assessment of Educational Progress. Lauren Resnick (1987) writes:

> [E]vidence is beginning to accumulate that traditional schooling's focus on individual, isolated activity, on symbols correctly manipulated but divorced from experience, and on decontextualized skills, may be partly responsible for the school's difficulty in promoting its in-school learning goals. (p. 18)

If we try to change the ways in which children learn, if we impede the ways in which they solve problems in an effort to learn language, then why should we expect them to use language to perform well on "more complex and challenging tasks" (Applebee, Langer, and Mullis, 1987, p. 4) or to use their problem-solving capabilities when they leave school?

It is imperative that we make the connection between the ways in which children learn language and the ways in which they use language. When researchers move away from a reductionist approach to early reading instruction and spend time observing children in families and in classrooms, different patterns of reading and writing emerge. These patterns, which are theoretically grounded in the studies cited above, provide us with insights not only into the complex and seemingly chaotic ways in which individual children's reconstructions are encoded and processed into coherent patterns of symbolic relationships, but also into the equally complex and chaotic ways in which their symbolic inventions are transformed into functional forms that they use in both classroom and everyday settings. We cannot predict the ways in which individual children will encode and use language, but we can be informed of the many aspects of the global patterns that appear to come into play. Thomas Newkirk (1989) writes:

> We must be capable of believing two contradictory ideas: We must understand that individuals are distinctive, with particular abilities and interests, living out their lives in environments that are also unique, yet we must also act upon general understandings of human behavior and growth—we need to identify patterns, categories, and principles that transcend individual instances. (p. 32)

Newkirk refers to this stance as "walking a tightrope," and so it is. We do need to understand graphophonemic relationships so that we can support children in their reconstructions. But we also need to discern children's personal understandings of the forms and functions of written language. Our task is to insure that the voices of children become embodied in the ways in which we teach. The poet James Fenton (1989) writes:

> What you need for poetry is a body and a voice. It doesn't have to be a great body or a great voice. But it ought ideally to be your body, and it ought to be your voice. (p. 22)

It is the voices of the children that we want to hear—but not in an echo of our own dried-up abstractions. If we want to insure that all children's voices are constitutive of American society, then we must examine the underlying assumptions on which reductionist educational arguments are based. We must consider what we mean by *science* and by *scholarship*, and we must acknowledge, as David Bloome so cogently does, that there is "an inseparable link between the way we do research and what we research" (Bloome, 1989). I would extend that link to the ways in which we eventually teach.

I would like to conclude by reiterating what I stated earlier. Our task as social scientists is to try to understand the complexity of the literacy behaviors of young children, and our task as educators is to use these understandings to support and enhance children's learning opportunities. We can provide guidance in both direct and indirect ways as they develop their own personal understandings of literacy— understandings that are both socially constructed and individually situated in the practical accomplishments of their everyday lives. Ironically, when such a theoretical and pedagogical framework is established, children become immersed in the reconstruction of genuine functions, uses, and forms of written language. They become immersed in their own chaotic discoveries, and much of their time is spent in solving problems associated with the relationships between the ways in which they learn and the ways in which they use written language. When we tamper with their discoveries in artificial ways and impose our hierarchies upon them, we impede their thinking and limit their chances of becoming active members of what should be, in its ideal state, a democratic society.

REFERENCES

Applebee, Arthur N., Judith A. Langer, and Ina V. S. Mullis. 1987. *Learning to Be Literate in America*. Princeton, NJ: National Assessment of Educational Progress.

Bloome, David. 1989. "Concluding Commentary." Paper presented at the Conference on Ethnographic and Qualitative Research in Education, University of Massachusetts, Amherst. June.

Brown, Rexford. 1989. "Testing and Thoughtfulness." *Educational Leadership* 46(7): 31–33.

Carbo, Marie. 1988. "Debunking the Great Phonics Myth." *Phi Delta Kappan* (November): 226–40.

Carraher, Terezinha Nunes. 1986. "From Drawings to Buildings: Working with Mathematical Scales." *International Journal of Behavioral Development* 9: 527–44.

Carraher, Terezinha Nunes, David William Carraher, and Analucia Dias Schliemann. 1985. "Mathematics in the Streets and in the Schools." *British Journal of Developmental Psychology* 3: 21–29.

Chall, Jeanne S. 1983a. *Learning to Read: The Great Debate*. Updated ed. New York: McGraw-Hill.

———. 1983b. *Stages of Reading Development*. New York: McGraw-Hill.

———. 1989. "*Learning to Read: The Great Debate* Twenty Years Later—A Response to 'Debunking the Great Phonics Myth.' " *Phi Delta Kappan* (March): 521–38.

de la Rocha, Olivia. 1985. "The Reorganization of Arithmetic Practice in the Kitchen." *Anthropology and Education Quarterly* 16: 193–98.

Fenton, James. 1989. "Manila Manifesto." *London Review of Books*. May 18.

Gleick, James. 1988. *Chaos: Making a New Science*. New York: Penguin Books.

Jervis, Kathe. 1989. "Daryl Takes a Test." *Educational Leadership* 46(7): 10–15.

Johnston, Peter. 1989. "Constructive Evaluation and the Improvement of Teaching and Learning." *Teachers College Record* (Summer): 509–28.

Lave, Jean. 1985. "The Social Organization of Knowledge and Practice: A Symposium." *Anthropology and Education Quarterly* 16: 171–176.

Lave, Jean, Michael Murtaugh, and Olivia de la Rocha. 1984. "The Dialectic of Arithmetic in Grocery Shopping." In Barbara Rogoff and Jean Lave, eds., *Everyday Cognition: Its Development in Social Context*, pp. 67–95. Cambridge, MA: Harvard University Press.

Meisels, Samuel J. 1989. "High-Stakes Testing in Kindergarten." *Educational Leadership* (April): 16–22.

Newkirk, Thomas. 1989. *More Than Stories: The Range of Children's Writing*. Portsmouth, NH: Heinemann.

Resnick, Lauren. 1987. "Learning in School and Out." *Educational Researcher* 16(9): 13–20.

Schickedanz, Judith. 1988. "Play Contexts for Literacy Activities." Paper presented at the annual meeting of the International Reading Association, Toronto.

Scribner, Sylvia. 1984. "Studying Working Intelligence." In Barbara Rogoff and Jean Lave, eds., *Everyday Cognition: Its Development in Social Context*, pp. 9–40. Cambridge, MA: Harvard University Press.

Shepard, Lorrie A. 1989. "Why We Need Better Assessments." *Educational Leadership* 46(7): 4–9.

Taylor, Denny. 1988. "Ethnographic Educational Evaluation for Children, Families, and Schools." *Theory into Practice* 27(1): 67–76.

———. 1989. "Learning in the Workplace: A Theoretical Perspective." Unpublished report prepared for the Institute on Education and the Economy, Teachers College, Columbia University, New York.

———. 1991a. "Family Literacy: Text as Context." In James Flood et al., eds., *Handbook of Research on Teaching the English Language Arts*. New York: Macmillan.

———. 1991b. "Learning Denied: Inappropriate Educational Decision Making." *Harvard Educational Review*

3

TEACHING WITHOUT TESTING: ASSESSING THE COMPLEXITY OF CHILDREN'S LITERACY LEARNING

> We can begin by observing children, learning with
> them and from them as they learn with us and
> from us. In this way we can create philosophical
> and theoretical frames for our observations of the
> learning environments we make for one another.

O n the last day of the 1989 Summer Institute for new teachers
and administrators in the Biographic Literacy Profiles Project
everyone participated in a literacy "dig." Mary Yates, a teacher participating in the project, had brought into the institute a voluminous
collection of her daughter's early explorations of written language.
Mary spread Katie's work across several large tables and explained
that the books and papers had been done between November and
May of Katie's kindergarten year. Mary told us that while she was
teaching Katie went home from school at lunchtime and spent the
afternoon with her grandmother, who lived with them. Mary said that
it was in November, during the time that Katie spent with her grandmother, that she started making books out of everything from brown
paper grocery bags to brightly colored wrapping paper. Some of these
books were displayed on the table; the other pieces of writing represented the various books and papers that Katie had brought home
from school during that year.

Together the teachers and administrators began their "dig." At
first it seemed like an overwhelming task. We had been talking about
the ways in which young children figure out problems and reinvent
the forms of written language as they learn to problem-solve and reconstruct the functions and uses of print. We had explored our own
"literacy configurations," emptying briefcases and pocketbooks, and
sharing with each other the ways in which we ourselves use literacy
in our everyday lives. "Literacy configurations are like thumbprints,"
I had said, somewhat flippantly. "No two are quite the same." So
what of Katie's literacy configuration? Did she already have one in
kindergarten? Was it possible to describe how the ways in which she
was using print produced a unique patterning of early literacy behav-

iors? On the surface, her discoveries appeared lost in the chaos of her crumpled papers, but a pattern slowly emerged as Mary took the pieces one by one and talked to us about her daughter's writings. Gradually, as we discussed the writing that Katie had done in November and then December, the teachers started to respond and make notes about the personally distinctive features of Katie's writing that were beginning to be identified. For as they wrote about the ways in which Katie reconstructed the functions, uses, and forms of written language, forming in their own minds was a changing order that they could now describe.

Over lunch and into the early afternoon, the participants began to develop their own biographic profiles of Katie's early literacy behaviors. For several hours the teachers and administrators examined Katie's writing and tried to create a systematic account of what appeared on the surface to be a disorderly confusion of erratic discoveries.

Marcy Mager, a principal, wrote:

In November Katie spontaneously began writing books. She had an understanding of the construction of a book which included the binding, cover, ordered progression of pages and the combination of pictures and texts. Katie had a sense of authorship and ended her books with "by Katie Yates." Even her earliest books contained complete thoughts related to a theme. The themes she focused on from November to May included the girl and her animals, rainbow stories, and adventures and travels from her life. Often she would elaborate on a theme as she continued to write. . . . Katie's sight vocabulary included the words "the," "cat," and "dog," and by May it also included "of," "book," "day," "to," "today," "mommy," "daddy," and the names of some friends. She experimented with the spelling of many words that she uses, such as "dear," and "journal." Katie's invented spelling uses consistent rules. She has the initial consonant-vowel-consonant in "rab" (rabbit), and both syllables of "spr" (supper). She uses vowels as markers and often uses an initial vowel but not always the correct one. She occasionally represents long vowel sounds with letters such as: o in "om" (home) and ramb$o$ (rainbow); e in at$e$ (auntie) and pt$e$ (pretty). Most consonant sounds are represented. The format in which she writes includes horizontal and vertical placement. . . . Katie can write complex sentences with prepositions and prepositional phrases. Katie uses pronouns and matches them correctly to her verbs. Her nouns and verbs also match. . . . Katie writes to convey information (i.e. addresses and events), to keep a personal record, to entertain herself and others, and to communicate with others about her feelings. . . .

Marcy's first draft of a biographic literacy profile for Katie provides us with some insights into the potential of such an approach to assessment. Marcy knew Katie because the little girl attends the school in which she is principal. However, she had not spent the year observing Katie's literacy behaviors, and she had no notes from the time when Katie had worked on the construction of these texts. Marcy relied solely on Mary's descriptions of Katie's writings and upon the examples contained in the portfolio of work that Mary had brought into the institute. But what Marcy knew, as did the teachers in her school who had already begun recording their observations of children's literacy behaviors in their classrooms, was that this was still a "thin" account. If they had been able to base the process of portfolio analysis upon their own disciplined, firsthand observations of Katie as she reconstructed the functions, uses, and forms of written language, then the detail (thick description) generated by such observations would greatly have increased the possibility of providing relevant support and instruction for Katie as she learned to read and write in school.

However, there were many other teachers in the institute that summer who had not yet begun to systematically observe and keep notes on the early literacy behaviors of the children in their classrooms. For them, the opportunity to construct a "first draft" of a biographic profile made them want to meet Katie and observe her as she used print "to convey information . . . to entertain . . . and to communicate her feelings." For it made visible to them that although the profiles they were constructing might be idiosyncratic in their form and expression—highly dependent in fact upon their own education and training—the patterns in Katie's writing reoccurred in similar ways across their own individual, "archeological" reconstructions of her early literacy development. The following excerpts illustrate how these teachers created recognizable images of Katie as a young reader and writer:

> (1-a) In November, at home, Katie spontaneously wrote a series of four books about a girl and her pets. She wrote the words one per line, from the top to the bottom of the page. The first book went back to front, the next three went conventionally front to back. Each book was a story written in complete sentences.
> (1-b) Kate has a strong sense of theme. Her books focus on a single topic: "The girl walking with her cat, her dog, and her rabbit." When she writes in a different genre she writes in a consistent fashion. She uses her writing for varied purposes.
> (1-c) Katie can carry a theme through several individual pieces; each

time she does, she elaborates on her ideas (e.g., stories about a girl walking animals).

(1-d) She uses one word per line, complete thoughts per page with pictures describing text.

(2-a) Over the course of seven months Katie has composed in a variety of genres. Personal narratives, journal entries of daily events, and fictional stories are examples of these collected from home and school.

(2-b) Katie is using a different style for her journal. She tells events of the day, using herself as the protagonist, and she writes from her own point of view.

(2-c) Katie writes about important people and animals in her life. She writes an autobiographical sketch in her journal.

(3-a) When Katie composes she uses a combination of illustrations and words. Her illustrations mirror her text and are integral to it. When she writes, "The GRL WT TO BAD The CAT WT TO BAD TO The DOG WT TO," she has each of her characters in their beds smiling from the page.

(3-b) Drawings correspond directly with the text.

(3-c) Katie writes with meaning and her illustrations mirror her text.

(4-a) Katie uses rules that she has learned, that she has access to, and that she has invented.

(4-b) In December and January Katie often wrote her stories left to right across the paper. She is using vowel markers: *a, o,* and *e.* She is including complex critical features in her invented spelling: ram*b*o for rain*b*ow, A*T*E M*N*A for Aun*t*y Mo*n*ica.

(4-c) Katie attends to dominant (critical) sounds in words (e.g., SPR for supper). Her spelling is rule governed by her own set of phonetic rules.

(4-d) Katie knows about vowels and uses them as markers . . . Katie seems to be aware of some critical features of words (e.g., *RAMBO* for rainbow, *SPR* for supper).

At the end of the day the teachers and administrators shared the profiles that they had written and, as they listened to each other, they made further notes. No one had a complete picture, and no one ever would, but between them they had created a sketch of Katie's early literacy development that no diagnostic or standardized test could ever achieve.

The impact of having written such biographic literacy profiles is clearly evident in the statements made by the teachers and administrators who are beginning their second year in the Project. Recently, Brenda Eaves, who is teaching an entry class, spoke in clear terms about the difference the profiles are making: "I've been taking notes in my classroom for years, but when you don't put them together, you don't get the whole picture. The notes are not enough. You just miss so much." Then she added, "We don't need to accept tests anymore and we can articulate why we don't need them." As we talked, Brenda said that for her one of the most important differences that the profiles were making was not one that she had anticipated. "I'm feeling a whole lot better about communicating with parents," she explained. "The profiles really help me to communicate what kids are actually doing."

In another conversation, Mary Benton, who is the reading coordinator in the school in which Brenda teaches, talked about the "spillover" into her school. While Brenda had spoken of the effect of the Project on parent-teacher communication, Mary talked about some of the other effects that the Project was having on the daily lives of both teachers and children. She said that as the teachers entered their second year of participation in the Project, many of the conversations that she was hearing were about the changes they were making *across the curriculum*. "The Project has created a forum," she said, "for us to discuss kids beyond the profiles. We're talking about how we've changed. How we're looking at kids differently. *The more you look, the more you see.* The math committee is talking about developing math profiles. We're no longer just looking at reading and writing. I think what we're moving towards are biographies of children's learning in school."

Essentially, what was happening in this conversation, and in many other conversations that are taking place as we meet to discuss the Project, is that we are changing minds—*our* minds. We are the ones who are changing. We are "playing" our experiences of working in holistic/process classrooms in which instruction is based upon our assessment of *children's observable literacy behaviors* against a backdrop of our own and other educators' experiences of using standardized and diagnostic methods of assessment and teaching. There is a continuous interplay between our past and present experiences as we try to place ourselves in the much larger arena of what is happening in education both at the national and the local level. In Washington, President Bush spoke of the need for more "accountability" within the system, and at the same time, in a local paper, there is a report of a school district in which "*all of the student population* has been tested for special education needs" (Gospodarek, 1989). The newspaper report states that children have been "earmarked," "coded," and "segregated," placed in "modified" classrooms, "resource" rooms, or in "rainbow park" so that they can receive the special services, the various kinds of "therapy," that their "conditions" require. The article also states that children whose needs cannot be met by the district are to be sent to a place called "Children Unlimited Inc." An apt name it seems, for within our medicalized education system there are an unlimited number of children whose needs are not being met by "the system."

The major question driving the Biographic Literacy Profiles Project is "What happens when we base instruction upon our observations of children?" In the October 1989 issue of the *Anthropology Newsletter* Jeffrey Shultz writes:

> We have focused on societal and cultural influences on schools and processes of classroom interaction without knowing a great deal about what role the learner plays in all of this. More needs to be known about teaching, learning and schooling from the *perspective of the learner.* [emphasis added] (p. 10)

Shultz then adds:

> [I]t is important to examine what our knowledge of classrooms, schools, culture and society has to say about the preparation of teachers. Specifically, how would a teacher education program based on this knowledge differ from more traditional programs? (p. 10)

Without any grand plan, but through reflexive research and teaching (Barnes, 1976), and by asking ourselves how we can base instruction upon our observations of children, I think we have gained some understanding of what happens when both teachers and administrators try to view teaching, learning, and schooling *from the perspective of the learner,* and we have also gained some insights into the ways in which teacher education programs based upon this knowledge would differ from the more traditional programs that are presently offered in most colleges of education.

TEACHING, LEARNING, AND SCHOOLING FROM THE PERSPECTIVE OF THE LEARNER

To understand schooling from the perspective of the child it has become essential for us to try to understand the social organization of children's everyday lives. Their lives, in other words, need to be viewed within the larger social, cultural, and political contexts, both visible and invisible, that determine what and how they learn both in and out of school. We must be "side by side" as we think of children

(Figure 3–1). It means beginning with individual children, metaphorically standing next to them, trying to imagine the world from their individual and shared perspectives. It means asking:

- What's happening?
- What's going on?
- How do these children create order out of the complexities of their everyday lives?
- How does this child construct and use language?
- How does this child learn to generate problems as well as solutions?
- How does this child become a member of a community of learners?
- How does this child theorize about doing?
- How does this child lead others in problem-solving situations to arrive at workable solutions?

When teachers ask these questions, their classrooms change. Even holistic/process teachers with years of experience notice the difference.

At the second Institute that took place in the summer of 1989, teachers and administrators who had been participating in the project for one year met to share their experiences, advance their own work, and begin working with a new group of teachers from their respective schools. Much of our time was spent in observing ourselves in complex problem-solving situations—observing the ways in which we, as learners, generate and reconstitute problems through the use of the social, symbolic, technical, and material resources at our disposal, and then go on to invent new procedures and arrive at instrumental solutions. Some teachers and administrators participated in the collaborative problem-solving situations, while others observed and took notes, which were later shared and analyzed by all those who participated in the Institute. In this way, we advanced our own understanding of the social construction of cognitive tasks, while at the same time the teachers new to the project had an opportunity to think about the possibilities of establishing classroom environments in which they could observe children engaged in *solving the problem of problem-solving literacy.*

Later that day, the second year Project teachers, who had been observing, note taking, and writing profiles for the past year, met in small groups with the first year Project teachers. As they looked at

FIGURE 3–1   Sharron Cadieux side by side with Jeffrey (photo by Deborah Sumner)

portfolios of children's work, they talked about *teaching from the child's perspective*. Listening to them talk provided another level of verification for the legitimacy of the direction that the Project had taken through the previous year. Each month, as I had visited these teachers in their classrooms, specific concerns (based upon actual experiences) had been discussed, and later these concerns became the focus of the afternoon group meetings that we held in each of the schools. Our experiences in working together troubleshooting problems and developing clearly thought-out practical solutions have eventually led to the emergence of what we have since come to regard as the objectives of the Project. In presenting these objectives, I will try to include some of the questions that were asked and the answers that were given at the second Institute, which was recorded for me by Helen Schotanus of the New Hampshire State Department of Education, so as to document the processes of change that all the teachers participating in the Project experienced.

SEEING THE PROJECT THROUGH ITS OBJECTIVES

One: Learning to Observe Children's Literacy Behaviors

"It's a change of mindset," a teacher explained. "I notice different things—what children can do rather than what they can't do." The only "rule"—one that I have jokingly said is carved in granite—is that we focus upon children's *observable literacy behaviors*. We are watching children as they develop personal understandings of literacy that are both socially constructed and individually situated in the practical accomplishments of their everyday lives. There are no linear, predefined, or artificially isolated skills to be ticked off on some reductionist "scope and sequence" chart or checklist. The teachers and administrators participating in the project have made what is essentially a paradigmatic shift. They are making the connection between the ways in which children in their classrooms both *learn* and *use* language. Their observations are providing them "with insights not only into the complex and seemingly chaotic ways in which individual children's reconstructions are encoded and processed into coherent patterns of symbolic relationships, but also into the equally complex and chaotic ways in which their symbolic inventions are transformed into functional forms that they use in classroom and everyday settings" (Taylor, 1989, p.193).

The paradigmatic shift that has taken place in the ways in which the teachers and administrators think about literacy is creating "new perspectives on reality" (Doll, 1989, p. 65), which require that we learn to look at children's literacy behavior in different ways, and this, in turn, affects what we see. Our task is to try to describe children's personal understandings of the forms and functions of written language that they develop as they participate in the problem-solving environments that we create for them. To achieve this aim, it is essential that teachers are supported in their own explorations of the many functions, uses, and forms of written language, for we cannot observe what we have not learned to see.

Characteristics of Family Literacy

In the Biographic Literacy Profiles Project, we began by examining the multiple interpretations of literacy that have been generated by ethnographic studies in family, community, and school settings (Heath, 1983; Taylor, 1983; Taylor and Dorsey-Gaines, 1988; Taylor and Strickland, 1988).

The following are characteristics of family literacy:

1. Some rituals and routines of written language usage appear to conserve family traditions of literacy, while others appear to change the patterns of the past.
2. Patterns of family literacy are constantly evolving to accommodate the everyday experiences of both parents and children, and the introduction of a younger sibling can lead to systematic restructuring routines.
3. Many of the literacy experiences that occur at home take place as parents and children go about their daily lives.
4. On many occasions, the act of reading is not the focus of attention, and the print has no intrinsic value. The "message" is embedded in some other event, useful within the context in which it was written or read, but otherwise appearing to be of little importance.
5. Many of the deliberate uses of literacy found in family settings occur when moment-to-moment uses of literacy are in some way lifted out of context to become specific events that are the focus of attention.
6. There are times when reading and writing become deliberate acts, when the text becomes as important as the message that it contains.
7. At any one time multiple interpretations of a literacy event are possible, and the possibility of different interpretations are created over time.
8. For each family member participating in a literacy event, the occasion is both socially constructed and personally interpreted through the interplay of the family members' individual biographies and educative styles.
9. Both moment-to-moment and deliberate uses of literacy can be social events or solitary endeavors.
10. Whether solitary or shared, deliberate or momentary, literacy is a complex, multidimensional phenomenon.
11. When both parents work or when there is a single working parent and time is at a premium, the moment-to-moment and specific uses of print that occur when a parent is at home full-time with a child will diminish.
12. However, literacy can become a key element in the ability of some families as they attempt to juggle all of the schedules, rituals and routines, and time constraints that are a part of their daily lives.

In our explorations of the functions, uses, and forms of literacy, these characteristics of *family* literacy have become directly relevant to our observations of literacy in *classroom* settings, for although none of the participants would suggest that literacy in the one setting is the same as literacy in the other, there are characteristics that are common to both. The notion of conservation and change in the transmission of literacy styles and values is directly relevant, as is the idea that many of the ways in which we use literacy in classroom settings occur at the margins of awareness, in moment-to-moment uses of reading and writing that only come to our attention when for some reason the act of reading or writing becomes a deliberate act, and therefore a specific event. Sensitivity to such patterns of literacy have become immensely important as the teachers in the Project have tried to create collaborative learning environments in which, if we stand side by side with individual children, there are multiple meanings for any literacy event that occurs in the classroom setting.

Similarly, in such classrooms, it is essential that teachers learn to observe the dynamics of both shared and solitary literacy experiences. Thus we have become comfortable in talking about a plurality of literacies of practical complexity, chaotically patterned into personal and shared configurations, and even though no two configurations are exactly the same we can describe the social organization of the configurations and also the types and uses of literacy that form the patterns that we observe.

Types and Uses of Reading

The following list describes the different types and uses of reading, one form of literacy:

1. Confirmational: Reading to check or confirm facts or beliefs, often from archival materials stored and retrieved only on special occasions.
2. Educational: Reading to fulfill the educational requirements of schooling; reading to increase one's ability to consider and/or discuss political, social, aesthetic, or religious knowledge; reading to educate oneself.
3. Environmental: Reading the print in the environment.
4. Financial: Reading to consider (and sometimes make changes to) the economic circumstances of one's everyday life; reading to fulfill practical (financial) needs of everyday life.
5. Historical: Reading to explore one's personal identity; reading to explore the social, political and economic circumstances of

one's everyday life; reading conserved writings that create a permanent record of one's personal or family history.

6. Instrumental: Reading to gain information for meeting practical needs, dealing with public agencies, and scheduling daily life.

7. Interactional: Reading to gain information pertinent to building and maintaining social relationships.

8. News related: Reading to gain information about third parties; reading to gain information about local, state, and national events.

9. Recreational: Reading during leisure time or in planning for recreational events.

10. Scientific: Reading to gain information about or develop new understanding of the natural or physical sciences.

11. Technical: Reading to gain information using the different symbolic forms of technological communications (computer, fax, virtual reality); reading to advance one's understanding of the functions of such technologies.

12. Other.

Types and Uses of Writing

Similarly, writing has many types and uses. It can be:

1. Autobiographical: Writing to understand oneself; writing to record one's life history; writing to share life with others.

2. Creative: Writing as a means of self-expression.

3. Educational: Writing to fulfill the educational requirements of school and college courses; writing to educate oneself.

4. Environmental: Writing in public places for others to read.

5. Financial: Writing to record numerals, to write out amounts and purposes of expenditures, and for signatures.

6. Instrumental: Writing to meet practical needs and to manage/organize everyday life; writing to gain access to social institutions or helping agencies.

7. Interactional: Writing to establish, build, and maintain social relationships; writing to negotiate family responsibilities. (The writer envisions or knows his or her audience and writes to the addressee.)

8. Memory aids: Writing to serve as a memory aid for both oneself and others.

9. Recreational: Writing during leisure time for the enjoyment of the activity.

10. Scientific: Writing to develop new understanding of the natural or physical sciences.
11. Substitutional: Reinforcement or substitution for oral messages; writing used when direct oral communication is not possible or when a written message is needed to create a record (e.g., for legal purposes).
12. Technical: Writing to gain information using the different symbolic forms of technological communications (computer, fax, virtual reality); writing to advance one's understanding of the functions of such technologies.

Thinking about the types and uses of reading and writing enables us to focus upon the social processes through which individuals and groups of children create literacy configurations that are functional in their everyday lives. Observing children as they use reading and writing in classroom settings has emphasized how important it is that we gain some understanding of literacy as a problem-solving activity, so we have incorporated into our observational framework recent research on problem solving in the workplace and other everyday settings (Carraher, 1986; Carraher, Carraher, and Schliemann, 1985; de la Rocha, 1985; Lave, 1985; Lave, Murtaugh, and de la Rocha, 1984; Scribner, 1984).

Literacy in Problem-Solving Activities

When we use print in classroom settings there is continual interplay between the activity and the setting. The activity and setting are mutually dependent—the one does not exist without the other. Using social, symbolic, technological, and material resources, students and teachers can:

1. Recast (reconstitute) problem–solution relationships.
2. Examine variations in procedural possibilities.
3. Discuss contradictions in interpretations of problem–solution relationships.
4. Depart from literal formats through the reorganization of tasks.
5. Develop least-effort strategies.
6. Arrive at "instrumental" (purposeful) solutions.
7. Theorize about "doing."
8. Lead others in problem-solving situations.
9. Invent new procedures.
10. *Generate problems as well as solutions.*

From this perspective, the problem-solving context exists in the dialectical relationships that are established between the activity and the setting. This proposition is both consistent with and supportive of the idea that children's personal understandings of literacy are both socially constructed and individually situated in the practical accomplishments of their everyday lives. The visual representation in Figure 3–2 allows us to imagine how such complex processes might interact. It is designed to suggest a kaleidoscope of patterns and shifting formations of such infinite variation that they cannot be depicted in fixed form. It is not a model in the traditional sense of the word. Instead, it is presented as a frozen image of the possible global patterns of the locally chaotic problem-solving relationships inherent in learning to use written language in everyday life (Taylor, 1989, pp. 191–92).

The characteristics of effective problem solving presented in Figure 3–2 lead us to the proposition that learners learn by solving situationally specific problems through the intellectual use of social, symbolic, technological, and material resources at their disposal. Thus, teachers need to construct environments that support such activity. This is done by providing opportunities for children to create multiple solutions to a problem. In this way children come to rely on nuanced judgments made in situations where there is often a high degree of uncertainty. Awareness of such complexity is essential if teachers are to observe and support children as they learn to organize their own problem-solving activities and become successful participants in non-routine problem-solving situations.

If we pause for a moment and reflect upon the first three ways in which project participants are learning to look at literacy, it is evident that *the kinds of information that we are obtaining from such observations bear little resemblance to the kinds of information currently assessed using traditional, standardized measures.* This paradigmatic shift is demonstrated, for instance, in how a child uses, in a complex back-and-forth matter, a reference text to construct her own book about dinosaurs (see Chapter 2 for an in-depth analysis). Rather than repeat that story, let's step lightly and play with the "Tuck-in Service" flyer (Figure 3–3) that was found taped to the glass door of a dormitory at a nearby college.

Undoubtedly we could fill several pages describing the insights into literacy that this flyer represents. The writer assumes a shared history with the students who might read the flyer, and she or he is hoping to capitalize upon (conserve) the rituals and routines of family literacy experienced by other students in the dorm. Thus, if we were present, we would be able to observe and describe some of the ways in which the event of storybook reading in the college dorm appeared to be socially constructed and personally interpreted through the in-

FIGURE 3–2   Problem-solving activity chart

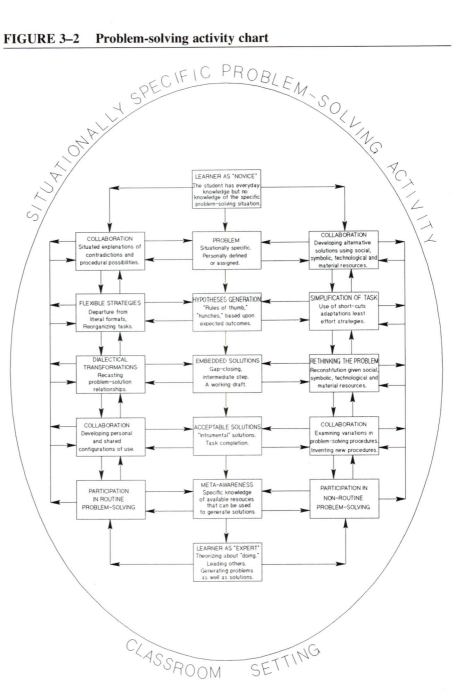

FIGURE 3–3   "Tuck-in Service" flyer

When's the last time you were tucked in your bed, given cookies and milk, and read a bedtime story?
Your right ... too long ago!
Sign Up Now ... For only $2.00
You can have this luxury service!

SIGN-UPS ... Wed thru Friday
                October 19th - 21st
      Lunch : Dinner at Prospect!
What a deal... what a Treat!!

terplay of the participants' individual biographies and educative styles.

We could also analyze the information presented in the flyer to gain some understanding of the types and uses of literacy that were utilized by the writer in the construction of the text. We could state that the flyer was a substitute for an oral message, and was written to fulfill instrumental as well as work-related needs, and to fulfill financial requirements. It is an example of environmental print that we can imagine reflects the autobiographical experiences of a writer who in turn appears to assume the biographical experiences of the readers.

We could continue musing on the types and uses of reading and writing reflected in the flyer, but let's move on and consider what it tells us about this situationally specific problem-solving activity. Since students are perennially short of cash, we can imagine that the writer has examined many procedural possibilities for stopgap solutions to alleviate this problem. In this particular situation, it is easy to appreciate the mutual dependence of the problem-solving activity and the setting. The writer needs money, students are away from home and miss their families, and thus the writer, as problem solver, arrives at an instrumental solution.

These descriptions of the dynamics of the "Tuck-in Service" literacy event are mostly inferential. But imagine the information that could have been gained if this activity occurred in a classroom with a teacher observing the event. This is essentially what is happening in the Biographic Literacy Profiles Project. Teachers are observing children in complex problem-solving situations, and they are using their understandings of a plurality of literacies to describe the interrelated complexity of such events.

Characteristics of Symbol Weaving

We could add another level to the analysis of the flyer in Figure 3–3 by discussing the "symbol weaving" (Dyson, 1986) that is taking place as the sad-eyed, thumb-sucking, teddybear-clutching person at the top of the flyer invites the reader to respond to the question "When's the last time you were tucked in your bed, given cookies and milk, and read a bedtime story?" Exploring the connectedness of multiple symbolic forms is an important feature of our observations of children's reading and writing behaviors, as we try to describe the many forms of symbolism used by children as they engage in situationally specific literacy activities. Newkirk's (1989) explorations of the interrelationships between pictures and texts has proved particularly helpful, and we are trying to counter the currently dominant way of thinking about other forms of symbolic representation as subservient to text. Newkirk states:

> Although we pay lip service to the idea that a picture is worth a thousand words, we don't really believe it. It's the thousand words that really interest us. Once the golden age of drawing has passed (around the second or third grade), art gives way to a predominantly, if not exclusively,

word-centered school culture, and children no longer allocate informativeness between the two systems. (p. 65)

Newkirk questions this "word-centered" approach to symbolic representation, and we in the Project share his concern. Our world is filled with graphic images, different ways of knowing, that we must learn to describe. A book that has become an important symbol of this need for a broader perspective on print is *Show Your Tongues* by Gunter Grass. In this diary, "a stunning document in words and drawings," Grass recorded his experiences of living in Calcutta.

What is so extraordinary about this achievement is that the words Grass wrote are integral to the visual images portrayed in the illustrations that appear at the beginning and end of the book. His writing forms the landscape, gives depth to the drawings, adds shadows to the faces and cracks to the walls. For me, it is one of the most socially significant examples of symbol weaving that I have so far encountered, just as the illustrated poems of William Blake are artistically/linguistically significant and Benoit Mandelbrot's *The Fractal Nature of Geometry* is scientifically significant. In the Project, we have used *Show Your Tongues* to legitimize the importance of creating environments in which children have the opportunity to use multiple forms of symbolism in the learning situations that they encounter. Our observations of print in everyday settings support the need we feel to extend the ways in which we think about the symbolic representations constructed by children. The more we focus our attention upon their productions, the more convinced we have become that our classrooms must be multimedia centers that encourage the exploration of complex symbolic systems.

Yesterday, when I had finished writing this section of the report, I telephoned Mary Benton and read to her what I had written about the characteristics of family literacy, the types and uses of literacy, and problem-solving literacy. Then we talked about the beginning of the Project, when teachers often focused almost exclusively upon sound-symbol relationships. They were familiar with the patterns, and they were comfortable describing the variations that they saw in the ways in which children invented their own patterns of the relationship and then reinvented the more traditional forms. Their detailed understandings of the ways in which children reconstruct sound-symbol relationships and invent the syntactic structures of various forms of texts are tremendously important, but there is so much more to literacy than these traditional skills. As the teachers spent more time observing children, they became increasingly aware of

some of the more complex relationships that children are establishing
as they problem-solve literacy. "Is this what's happening?" I asked
Mary. "What about sound-symbol stuff? It's certainly one of the important ways in which we're looking at children's construction of
written texts, but where does it fit? What happens when you observe
a child?"

Mary was quiet and after a few moments of silence I jokingly
asked her if she was "still there." "I'm thinking," she said and then
hesitated: "I don't know how to say it." But after a few more seconds of silence she explained that for her it was crucial to have a
solid understanding of graphophoneme concepts, but not let that be
the focus. "It's all there," she continued, "but not in the sense that I
am consciously pulling it apart. I'm trying to leave behind me all that
training that views sound-symbol relationships as a linear progression
of skills that all kids acquire in the same way. I'm not looking for
what children can't do with some checklist in my head." Mary
laughed as she tried to explain. "I'm going for everything, letting
what I see take on its own shape, watching until I see. Understanding
how each child learns and uses graphophonemic concepts comes only
after seeing how these are used in combination with other concepts
and strategies." She paused again and then concluded, "I think if I
went in with a structure broken down into types and uses, or graphophoneme patterns, I just wouldn't see what was happening. I'd be
too busy trying to find specific things. Going back and looking at what
I was writing at the beginning of last year—it's incredible what I see now
that I couldn't see then. The way in is to look at sound-symbols and
then it goes beyond—I think it's even gone beyond any notions of literacy. Observing kids is about us changing our thinking."

**Two: Learning to Develop Note-Taking Procedures to Record
Observations of Children Reading and Writing**

At the second Summer Institute in 1989, many of the discussions that
Helen Schotanus recorded for me were of the conversations about
note taking that took place between teachers who had participated in
the Project for a year and the teachers who were just beginning to
participate in the study. When one new teacher asked if there was a
system for note taking, she was promptly told that "there is no one
way to do it. No cut and dried how-to." Teachers talked about
"catching what is happening as it happens—otherwise you may lose
it" or "writing exactly what a child is doing over a longer period of
time—up to ten minutes." In one conversation a teacher said, "Writ-

ing is easier to take notes on than reading because with writing there is a product. How do you see reading?" In another conversation a teacher talked about "reaching all the children" in her class: "Some children demand more of one's time. Others demand very little and are easy to overlook."

Similar interactions have taken place in seminars when Project participants have talked about the research. Teachers ask, "Don't you have a note-taking system?" "A set number of children that you observe each day?" "Specific times when you observe and write?" "A list of skills that you write about?" At such times there is usually a Project teacher who jumps in and says, "We are each developing our own note-taking system. A system that works for me might not work for you. It depends on how you organize your classroom, and on your own literacy configuration—how you use print." The underlying assumption on which the Project is founded is that teachers are professionals in their own classrooms and do not need prepackaged ways of writing down what they see as children work together reconstructing the functions, uses, and forms of written language. In fact, we do not believe that observational teaching and instructional assessment can be packaged, for this is problem-solving teaching. On many occasions I have heard teachers say that the observations that they make and the notes that they write, as they work side by side with the children, cannot be separated into "strategies" and then added to the ways in which they teach. The observations they make and the notes they write are constitutive of ways in which they teach. For them teaching is learning about children as they develop original and authentic ways of using print to solve problems on their own and with friends, and as they use their creativity and ingenuity to develop insights and learn to theorize (talk about) the construction of invented and standardized forms of written language.

This fall (of 1989), during my visits to the classrooms of the Project teachers, I have been particularly interested in furthering my understanding of the note-taking procedures that they are developing. For just a few short minutes I watched Martha Dahl take notes as she worked with one of her kindergarten children. They were quick jottings, small things to remember, from the moment she talked with this particular child. What fascinated me were the many different types of notes that she was unobtrusively constructing and how the different types of notes that she made actually became a part of the instructional context in which she was working. I asked Martha if she would share some of her notes. The following are examples that she sent.

Several of the notes are written on an observational form that I
put together at the beginning of the Project. Martha uses just the top
section of these forms and, like other Project members, she has
adapted the format to suit her own particular needs. Indeed, some
teachers have never used the form, while others have combined reading and writing—a change I would make myself if I were using the
form today. Here is the first example of Martha's notes:

> *Writing:* Journal   Kitty (10-11-89)
>
> *Comment:* Story Language!
>
> *Anecdotal Description:* "Suddenly a leaf fell right into her hand. It was a
> yellow leaf—and she took it into her Mom." (Picture has a girl, apple
> tree, dog (?) and *yellow* leaf coming down.)

Martha is particularly interested in the language that her students use
as they talk about their writing, produce an invented reading, or give
a standard reading of the texts that they construct. From the comment that Martha made on this record it is clear that what she wanted
to remember was the language Kitty was using as she produced an
invented reading of her text.

The next example was written on a Post-it note. (Most of the
teachers use Post-its as they are easy to carry in a pocket and can be
pulled out and used at a moment's notice.) Martha wrote a verbatim
account of Kitty's personal narrative.

> Once upon a time I cut my toe some blood came and daddy came to see
> what was the matter. He called our next door neighbor and they came
> with Melanie and they took me to the doctors where they had to give me
> stitches and Aunty Betsy came and I slept on the way home. The End.

Martha attached to her notes a copy of Kitty's written account of this
oral rendition, an important step, for Kitty was able to read this text
(Figure 3–4). Further, this allowed Martha to learn not only about
Kitty's use of written language to create a personal narrative but also
about how she reconstructs sound-symbol relationships.

At a group meeting, Martha showed me how she could reconstruct the text, and she talked about the illustration in which Kitty
had drawn herself crying and her toe being cut. Today, on the telephone, Martha said, "The thing that impressed me was that she had
written the piece at home and she brought it into school to share with
me. She knew exactly what she had written, and a lot of the text was
right there. She could make sense of her invented spelling as she
read." We talked for a while about the writing Kitty does. Martha
said that based upon her observations she thought Kitty "was in tran-

FIGURE 3–4   Kitty's written story

sition. Sometimes what she says goes along with what she writes and sometimes it doesn't. Sometimes it seems really important to her that the sounds go with the writing, but not always."

Another note was short and to the point. On a Post-it Martha had written: "HSO [house] from another's journal. Then she said, 'This is my journal.'" The Post-it was left in the journal so that Martha could refer to it when she was conferring with a parent or working on her biographic profiles. "Most of the children don't mind if I leave a note in their journal. Some children would prefer that I didn't, so then I date and keep them."

Another type of note occurs on one of Martha's writing forms:

Writing: Journal   [Child's Name] (10-11-89)

Comment: Had written: A ① LOY
                                    EV

Anecdotal description:
Reading what she had written "I love you"
[Child]: "But I don't know how to write you"
MD: "How could you?"
[Child]: Thought for a while—"U!"—wrote U

Here was another form of note taking: Martha recording small snatches of her conversations with the children in her class. This gives her some idea of the ways in which she is creating opportunities for them to problem solve language as well as how they actually go about it. When I read this section to Martha she added, "It also gives me an idea if the action taken was self-initiated or taken as a result of working with me." Martha is clearly trying to learn more about the "grey zone" between what individual children can do on their own and what they can do with the support of a teacher (Vygotsky, 1978).

This approach to note taking allows us to understand the different ways in which the children in Martha's classroom are constructing texts as they write in their journals and the ways in which Martha is learning about each child's reconstruction of written language during the time when the children work in their journals. In other words, the notes point to global patterns that are locally unpredictable.

Writing: Journal   [Child's Name] (10-11-89)

Comment: Writing—"Someone is riding a motor cycle"

Anecdotal Description: Stuck
MD: "Maybe you could write about part of it? How about motorcycle?"
[Child]: "Okay"
MD: "What do you hear?" [Child]: "T? How do you make a T?" (Looking through alphabet cards) Found I—"I think this is a T."
MD: "Is it?"

[Child]: (Ask Martha)
MD: "See if you can find a T?" Looked thru and found *Ii* and *Tt* [Child]:
"One of these is a T"
MD: "Which one is it?"
[Child]: Pointed to T. Then wrote T and said—"that's all I hear in
motorcycle"

Writing: Journal   [Child's Name] (10-11-89)

Comment: Looking at letter cards to see how to make letters *N* and *K*—
can spell words beginning/ending sounds unsure of how to make letters,
enjoys looking thru cards for letters—says all letter names.

We could describe this last brief jotting as an analytic memo in which
Martha puts together an observation with some of the characteristics
of this child's writing that she has identified in some of her other
observations.

In the following example Martha produces a similar kind of note
when she includes some of her own problem solving (in the comments section) as well as the problem solving of the child (in the anecdotal section):

Writing: Journal   [Child's name] (10-11-89)

Comment: [Child's name] puts the letters in the space where he hears
them in the word. Doesn't necessarily write from beginning to end—but
gets them in the right space.

Anecdotal Description:
[Child]: "I'd like to write the whole word of snake." Had written
[Martha didn't have time to finish]
MD: "What else do you hear?"
[Child]: "A *T*."
MD: "Where?"
[Child]: "In the middle—is this the middle?"—moved over a space—
"No it's at the end!" Then wrote a *T* at end of space.
MD: What else?
[Child]: "*A*"
MD: "Where?"
[Child]: "In the middle"
Final writing: T iRTA SAT (I saw a snake)

In this note Martha presents an interpretation (working hypothesis/in-
formed opinion) of the ways in which this particular child is reconstructing the form of written language and then backs it up with a detailed description that illustrates how she arrived at the interpretation
that she presents in the comments section.

In all of these ways and other note-taking procedures Martha adds to the information that she has collected about each of the children mentioned here and, over a period of days, notes are written about every child. Keeping detailed notes provides Martha with an opportunity to learn more about the many complex ways in which each child in her classroom is learning to reconstruct written language. She is convinced that it is worth recording when a child draws a picture of her baby sister; writes her name from right to left, *N L T K;* and then reads "Kaitlyn." Martha also feels that it is worth recording the conversation that followed the event, in which she said to the little girl, "I don't know how to write Kaitlyn," and the child responded "Just look up here. I wrote it—see?" and studying the letters from right to left she read, "K–T–L–N." At this point, as I am reading the draft of this report to Martha on the telephone she interjects, "What I thought was so wonderful was her confidence in her own ability to write. I was feeling that I didn't know how to spell Kaitlyn and she felt confident enough to show me how she had spelled it."

Kathy Donovan, another second-year Project teacher, began her teaching career in special education and now teaches a class of first- and second-year children. When I visit her classroom it always takes me a few seconds to find her. The children work in small groups or on their own. There are invariably many activities taking place in the classroom, and Kathy is usually working with a few children on one project or another. Kathy uses a variety of note-taking procedures to capture the many ways in which the children participate in the daily life of the classroom. In a large binder Kathy keeps a separate section to record each child's particular ways of becoming literate.

Last year, during the writing workshop, Kathy wrote her notes on labels that she transferred to each child's page in her binder. The following examples are taken from the writing workshop record of one child ("K"):

> 11-30   "My birthday" added *a* while oral rdg. "I had—chocolate cake" "Oh I forgot the *a,* can I put it in?"
>
> 1-18   *A–N–D* spells *and*
> Don't forget D [child's name]—conversation between D and K. D seeking correct spelling.
>
> 1-18   "When I'm done with all my little stories I can put [them] in a chapter book."
>
> 1-26   "I want all my stories about *The Princess and The Mitten* published into a chapter book."

3-3 *she* consistently spelled *sey*
—word boundaries established
—sight words: *I my me* and *to*
—beginning, medial final sds
—short vowels present
—story sequenced
—working on not starting sentence with *and*

Kathy continues by recording a series of stories that K wrote and the comments that she made as she worked on them, such as "This is true! I'm going to put nonfiction on the bottom!" Other comments that Kathy makes focus upon K's writing strategies ("involves reader as audience 'and you would too I bet'"), upon the language K uses ("'good gracious' expression used"), and upon the way in which the writing activity was accomplished ("collaborated with A. Read orally and each took character part. Will be writing chapters. Discussed next events").

Kathy also keeps a log sheet for the writing workshops on which she records the key words that are taken from each child's writing and logged in their dictionaries. Thus at a glance Kathy can see the words that a particular student is using in his or her writing:

10-2	10-3	10-4	10-5	10-6
A: toad	fabulous	super	spider	animal
J: climbed	wanted	policeman	sign	Halloween
R: chameleon	seaweed	tooth	roller coaster	home run

The books that each child reads are noted on a "reading group conference record sheet." Kathy keeps a separate sheet for each child so that during the course of the year both Kathy and each of her students have a pretty good idea of which books have been read and what progress has been made. When conferring with Kathy the student summarizes the story and then chooses a page to read to Kathy. Then the student is asked to rate the book *E* for Easy, *M* for Moderate, or *C* for Challenge. Kathy circles the response and then she underlines what she feels is the level that the book represents. This allows her to check whether her own perception is "side by side" with the child's perception of the book. Kathy also has a section called "Response/Comments." Here she writes a description of the discussion with a particular child or the child's verbatim comments—for example, "I picked it because I thought it was funny. I liked the monkey part."

Kathy also collects information about the individual children in her class as they organize their daily life in school. For example, there is a "Lunch Count and Attendance" form that the children fill in themselves and then one child is given the responsibility of checking the information. Children sign up for their lunch and also for snacks, and the names in the various categories (hot lunch, snack juice, snack milk) are counted and the numbers entered at the bottom of the form. Kathy says this particular form provides her with a wonderful opportunity to observe the children in her class as they work together. She can make sure that everyone has what they want for snack and lunch and, because there is a category called "All Set," where every child writes his or her name, the form doubles as an attendance record.

At group meetings the teachers often compare note-taking systems and procedures and adapt their own system to accommodate variations on some of the other forms that they encounter. Some ways of collecting information come from texts such as *In the Middle,* in which Nancy Atwell describes taking the "Status of the Class." Sue Caswell, a third-grade teacher, who has just joined the Project, uses this procedure during reading and writing. She has encouraged other teachers to experiment with this quick way of recording the reading and writing activities of every child in the class. Sue says, "It only takes two to three minutes and then you have a record that you can use as you're working on a profile. You know immediately how long the child spent working on the project, and it gives you a good idea of the topics that interest them." Lee Proctor, another teacher, said she thought she would try this approach in her first-grade classroom as she wanted to find a better way of keeping track of her students' work.

While there are many different ways in which information is being collected, the process continues to evolve and changes are constantly being made as each teacher tries to find his or her own way of capturing the information that they need to construct biographic profiles of the children in their classes. For those teachers having difficulty incorporating note taking into their daily routine, often a simple adjustment is all that's necessary. When I first visited Bob Magher, who teaches third grade and joined the project this year, he quickly mentioned his problem with note taking. Then he was off to be with his class, talking about their writing and arranging to meet with children who were ready to confer. Bob sat at a table with a group of students who took turns reading and discussing the stories that they were writing. Bob took notes as each student read his or her text; then he used his notes as a basis for his contribution to the discussion that followed. He then gave his notes to the student on whose work he had been commenting. The student was free to use the comments (or not) in constructing a further draft. "What happens to the notes when the student has finished using them?" I asked. Bob smiled and said that once the student had used them they were probably thrown away. We talked for a while about the importance of the notes and of stapling them, plus any written comments made by other students, to the draft that had been discussed. Then once the piece was finished the stapled draft and the final version could be kept in the student's portfolio and used later by the student and by Bob as they reviewed the progress the student was making. Bob has adopted this way of collecting the notes that he was already making. As the year progresses he will modify the procedure so that he can use this important information when he is writing biographic profiles.

Three: Learning to Write Descriptive Biographic Literacy Profiles

The notes that Helen Schotanus wrote at the Summer Institute begin with a comment by one of the teachers who was joining the Project: "It was scary seeing what a person in the Project did last year." Leigh Walls responded by stating that "writing and composing, just thinking and pulling thoughts together took time." Leigh qualified what she had said by adding, "It took two hours each time I wrote about a child." The excerpts from some of the biographic profiles that are presented here reflect the amount of time that teachers take to write them. Disciplined and systematic observation and note-taking procedures create opportunities for teachers to construct detailed ethnographic accounts from the perspective of the learner. Such in-depth analysis requires slow and deliberate consideration on the part of the teachers who are writing them. The profiles that follow illustrate the developing literacy configurations of children from kindergarten through fourth grade, while at the same time they are suggestive of the particularity of the ways in which the teachers are working to construct these profiles. All of the profiles were written during the 1988–89 academic year except for the one written by Bruce Turnquist, who just joined the Project this year. Katerina's profile is the first biographic account that Bruce has written.

Leigh Walls: Excerpts from Tom's Biographic Profile

May/June: Tom's high interest in books has continued. He has clear favorites, especially among our "big books" and he requests those often. He listens carefully at story times and his predictions of what might happen next are always reasonable in the context of the plot, and frequently accurate as well, even when he has never heard the story before.

Tom understands that written notes are a way of communicating with those who are not close by. A month or two ago, he demonstrated concern for a classmate who was ill by asking an aide to write "I hope you are better soon" so that he could copy it and send it to his friend. More recently (5/12) he attempted to write (independently) a letter to his Aunt Pat. He brought a paper on which he had written: "V F M T" and said, "I want to say '*I hope you come soon.*'" We sat down together and he wrote: "I H O P U K M 2 N," needing help only in identifying the letters which made the "h" and "u" sounds. When he was writing, he reached the end of the line so he returned to the left side of the paper to finish his sentence, showing an understanding of left-right progression in written English:

V F M T
N
I H O P U K M 2 N

He then addressed the envelope, writing: "T O" from memory and "P A T" with a little help with the short "a" sound.

In his journals, Tom continues to draw many houses and trees. However, many of his pictures have become more involved. He demonstrates an understanding of perspective in these pictures; when his house is in the foreground, his school is small and in the background. As he explained to me, "That's the school. It's so little because it's so far away!" (5/19). He spent more than a week on a single page, making black line drawings of each kind of monster (ghosts, vampires, etc.) in a book about "monsters from the movies" which a friend had taken out of the library (Figure 3–5). He was intrigued with trying to draw every single monster and concentrated more on the art than the writing; however, he was willing to label some of the pictures when asked to do so. He wrote "M N S T r S" for "monsters" (with the help of a friend on the form of "r"), "V M P" for "vampire" and "K q" for "grandpa" from the tv show, "The Munsters" (6/1 and 6/6). He is very "tuned in" to his own writing. The day he wrote "S S M △ B B S S" for "This *is my babysitter's*" he commented, "There's 1,2,3, *S*'s!" (5/26). Another day, when he wanted to write "house," he said, "I hear *s* but that's at the end." So he wrote "A" followed by "S," showing an understanding of the importance of the sequence of individual letters if they are to properly represent the sounds of spoken language (5/25). Left on his own to write his page of our book about riding the horse, Big George, on our trip to the Owens' Farm, he wrote: "I L K B G J" for "*I like Big George.*"

Sharron Cadieux: Excerpts from Vanessa's Biographic Profile

September: Vanessa loves to write in her journal. She hears many sounds and can record them as labels on her own if asked to do so (B—

FIGURE 3–5 Tom's monster drawing

butterfly; bPL—little puppy dog, in reverse order). However, she is not satisfied with labels. She loves to tell stories. She adopts a story-telling voice and uses story language. (Another little puppy caught a butterfly, snap, snap, in his paws.) She wants her stories to be written down but is not yet able to use invented spelling to write a sentence on her own. If I repeat her sentence for her one word at a time, she will write a beginning sound for each word. (L P S N L L i A b ! —The little puppy was in love with an angel dog.) She is aware of punctuation. (She added the exclamation mark on her own.) Every page in her journal was concerned with the puppy, so she can carry an idea over several pages. Each page was a different episode or unrelated adventure in her puppy story.

November: Vanessa did not choose to write in her journal often this month. She preferred to draw separate pictures on a variety of paper types, often cutting them out. She wrote very little except for "B O O" and "M o M." Once she pretended she was a nurse and prescribed rest for me. At my suggestion, she wrote her recommendations in a booklet she had made. She used scribble lines in a left-to-right motion to represent cursive writing.

March/April: Vanessa wrote a great deal during these two months for a variety of purposes. She wrote books about a duck, a sheep, an owl, a bunny, and a house where animals come and visit. Animals, the sun and the moon, and comments about the weather often appear in her stories (T λ E R A N A W S A G O N A A O A A—which Vanessa read as "The rain was going away"; S M A A N L M L S W T P T O T λ E A H S A—which she read as "Some animals went up to the house"). More complex sounds such as vowels and "sh" are beginning to appear (H E W S S A ᗡ—He was sad; W L E W S W K   W L E   F A D   W L E   A B S H —which she read as "While he was walking, well he found a bush"). She has a strong sense of story language as indicated by her story introductions (W S A P N A T M W R W S A b K—which she read as "Once upon a time there was a duck"; A F N L T A N A M O O M S N A A N A L M A—which she read as "In the light of the moon the owl sat on her branch." She had likely written something similar). She also wrote about learning to ride her bike. (I R D M E B K L B E E S F W S b   D A D S D, added N b I T O R M B K—which she read as "I rode my bike all by myself. 'It was good,' Dad said." Added—"and tipped over my bike.") She wrote notes—"I LOVE MOM + DAD; I LOVE Ʉ O Ʉ." She wrote about getting a new tooth. She then added O N A V in front of M i E T O T (my tooth), and went on to revise my tiny printing on the bottom of the page the same way. She drew a very detailed drawing of a tree (with green leaves) with sap buckets and dotted blue lines indicating the sap running from the tap to the bucket which she labeled "M P L S E A P"—maple syrup.

May/June: Vanessa wrote a long story about a baseball game which represented a totally different subject for her. There was a clear sequence of simple outline drawings which very effectively showed the actions and detail. She wrote many signs for the science area describing an item she had brought in and explaining if the kids should touch it or not.

One day she came in and asked for a picture of a monarch butterfly. I showed her a book that might have a picture. She took the book and went off to find it on her own. She is clearly comfortable with books. Looking at the picture, she drew an incredibly detailed butterfly and wrote I S O A A M N N K B R F L I—I saw a monarch butterfly.

She wrote several notes about teeth, including T λ E T O T λ F R E G V M M E P A N E S A—The tooth fairy gave me pennies; A N O T O T λ K M N A T O   A O L E T O T λ A K M A—a new tooth coming in, an old tooth coming out. She then wrote her name followed by an exclamation mark.

Vanessa knows a great deal about books and print. She can write. She can use most consonants to represent sounds she hears plus "sh" and "th." She is aware of the uses of vowels and can use long vowels correctly sometimes. She can use print for a variety of real purposes with great confidence. She has a wonderful sense of story and story language, which she uses very effectively.

Brenda Eaves: Excerpts from Donna's Biographic Profile

In September Donna's writing was of favorite things that she had seen with her family, often her grandmother. She quickly sketched out her idea and then explained what it was. Her pictures were of pets, flowers, and rainbows. They were usually all in one color. She did not seem comfortable in writing any accompanying text though she could tell you parts of the words she "would use if she wrote it down." . . . Donna was focused on the charts and books during shared reading time. She would join the reading when there was a word or phrase that she recognized.

In October Donna's writing became more detailed and she had a definite purpose for the things she was putting on the page. Some of her stories were several pages long and she talked of realizing that writing could "save" things for you.

In April Donna has worked to write one story. It is called *MY BAST FANSE*. What began as a simple story about having a few friends come over to visit has grown until most of the children in the class are coming to visit in succession throughout the day. To organize this Donna made a list of all of her friends and asked them if they would like to be included in her book. Once that was done she set up a girl-boy pattern and began writing. "ONE DAY SAME OND KAM AND NATK ON MY DOOR. IT WAS MY BAST FRIEND . . ." At this point there is a little door in the page that opens to reveal the friend. The next page tells what they do until another friend comes and the process begins again.

Donna continues to read in her choice time. She uses books and charts that she is familiar with and she has been attending more to the details of words. As she reads she talks about recurring letter combinations like "ing," "ea," and "tion."

In May Donna has continued to work on her best friend book. It has been a very difficult project to include all of the children but she has stuck with it. At first she wanted each child to follow the same pattern of activity (come to her house, play, eat dinner, and go home). Then she said that she felt that this would get boring for the reader and so she tried to think of different things for each child to do—eating lunch, playing ball, playing with dolls or sleeping over.

In between adding friends to her book Donna worked on pieces about animals and looked back at her other pieces. She wrote a book called *Book of the Week* in which she combined her love of animals and an idea to make our weekly paper folder funny. She wrote "BOOK OF THE ShEEP SHEEP ARE NISE PEKAZ THEY GEVE YOU SOADRES." Each animal was written about using a similar format and once the text was written Donna planned the publishing so that each page would look just right.

Lori Bresnahan: Excerpts from Sam's Biographic Profile

In December, Sam continued to swing back and forth between fiction and non-fiction, with a story about good guys and bad guys turning into a piece about why Indians had wars over land. His written vocabulary is growing, and he is making use of rhyming patterns to spell words (cat, hat, fat, that, bat, mat). This makes sense, as he has been reading and re-reading *Hop on Pop.*

In January, Sam began a story (which continued through February and March), "James and the Big Thing." This is his own version of *James and the Giant Peach,* which had been read to the class. He wrote his title on the cover of his new journal (commenting on having written all of the words correctly), and announced that the story was going to fill up the whole journal (which it eventually did). He wrote a dedication, ("To JaMes My FREND"). He talks a lot as he works on his illustrations, seeming to try his ideas out on the others in the group before he writes them down.

During his library time, he returns to read the charts and books that we have read during shared reading sessions. He has also spent a lot of time reading through the *Hop, Skip, and Jump Book,* which is a word book filled with verbs and pictures to illustrate each. When he read this aloud, he used much expression in his voice. He has also read *Bony Legs,* again providing a very expressive reading, proceeding word by word, self-correcting as necessary.

In February and March, the illustrations seemed to dominate the pages of Sam's journal. He still added text, but not to every page, and sometimes it was quite small, being hidden by the picture. He did plan ahead what would happen in the story though, commenting "I'm almost to the part when—." He added pages to his journal to be able to complete his storyline the way he wanted it, drawing the illustrations first, with the text added afterwards.

Mary Benton: Excerpts from Alex's Biographic Profile

March: Alex varies between a text-then-picture and a picture-then-text approach to creating his stories. He has a clear sense of what is going to happen next in his story. The pictures are used to support the text. Alex's revisions have changed from ones which were only for him as a writer (not being able to reread his own text changing a character from a wife to a mother because he could spell the latter) to ones which concentrate on expanding the details of the story ("He kicked and kicked and kicked" revised to "The soldier kicked and kicked and kicked at the door"). While writing he uses a great deal of information from his printed and verbal environment. He sometimes overhears an editing conference between a teacher and another student and then spontaneously finds appropriate places within his own text where he can apply the skill discussed. After reading several *Frog and Toad* stories, Alex began structuring his own writing with a lot of dialogue so that he would have an opportunity to use quotation marks. Alex's self-selections now include non-fiction and chapter books. He is choosing books because of their appeal to him, not because of the amount of text. When reading fiction he particularly enjoys stories which contain some kind of puzzle or humor. . . . When reading he uses a combination of strategies to determine an unknown word. He is less reliant on using the picture as the primary strategy and self-corrects more often. He is more aware of when his miscues interfere with the sense of the story and is willing to stop and reread to see if he can reestablish the meaning of the text.

Kathy Matthews: Excerpts from Chris' Biographic Profile

September: Chris' first entry in his reading journal seems to reflect his feeling about reading: "Reading is okay . . . but sometimes I'm not in the mood for reading." Given the chance to read anything he wishes, he generally chooses familiar stories that he has either read or listened to in first and second grade. When selecting a new book for reading, Chris opts for books that are similar in genre to others he has read, have recently been read aloud in class, or are stories written by a familiar author. He often spends quiet reading time searching for a book. Once he has made a choice he looks carefully at each of the pictures in the book before he begins reading the text. Chris' primary strategy for new text is to "sound out the letters." Sometimes he reruns the sentence if what he reads doesn't appear to make sense.

Chris' writing often reflects his interest, and, sometimes, his concerns. His first piece of writing, *The First Day of School,* indicates his awareness of, and his positive feelings about the ways the class is similar to and yet different from last year. He shares his feelings directly with his audience ("There's a new school getting built. It is going to be big. I can't wait until the new school is built. Can you? I can't."), and uses the text as a way to pay compliments to me. Chris' daybook often contains summaries of the day's events, reflections, and speculation about different issues. His entries are sometimes detailed, sometimes sparse. The conversational tone of Chris' reading journal and daybook as well as his occasional revisions for clarity and meaning suggest he is very much aware of his reader audience.

Chris titles the pieces he composes and includes a title page as well. He is careful to put the date on everything he writes. He uses periods with initials and writes with mixed use of upper- and lower-case letters. Instead of crossing out words when revising, Chris prefers to erase what he no longer wants. His penmanship is executed with dark, heavy lines with wide spacing in between the letters within a word as

well as the words themselves. He usually skips every other line when
writing on lined paper. Chris' spelling development is in the early
transitional stage. He uses standard spelling for many high-frequency
words and has assimilated structural concepts such as -*ING* endings and
plural *S* as well as these phonetic concepts: all regular consonants, final -
MP, all long, open-syllable vowels, the short vowels *I, E, A,* the
digraphs *CH* and *Th,* and the blends *BL, SL, ST, FR, DR, TR, TW, SC.*
Chris often writes syllables as separate words.

November: Writing continued to be an expressive outlet for Chris this
month. He spent a great deal of time composing a very personal piece
entitled "THE CAT THAT CHRIS FOUND IN HIS YARD." Beneath
the title he wrote, "Based on a true story." He also included a title page.
Chris uses clear, honest language in his dialogue to describe the central
conflict of this piece, i.e., naming the cat ("I said to myself, "Na! Na!
Na!" and went upstairs."). The piece begins as a third person narrative
based on real experience ("One day Chris found a cat in his yard."),
quickly becomes a first person account ("It is orange like Chris' other
cat, Duncan. I have to come up with a name for it."), and ends with
detailed descriptions of the cat's behavior ("When I am sleeping he
comes on my bed and lays on my face and bites my nose . . ."), which
convey his fondness for his cat. Chris proofread and edited this piece by
himself, adding periods at the ends of sentences and apostrophes to
show possession.

Chris used written language for numerous purposes this month. He
began writing in a learning log, wrote a brief report about our archaeological experiences, and wrote letters to classmates that included
puzzles and jokes. Chris appeared willing to take some risks. He wrote a
story with science fiction overtones, humor, and bizarre episodes that
seemed intended to simply arouse audience reaction. He shared this
piece with the class and was able to be open to their suggestions without
abandoning his own point of view.

Bruce Turnquist: Excerpts from Katerina's Biographic Profile

September/Early October: Katerina has worked on three stories: "The
Bear and the Mouse," "The Thing in the Forest," and "The Missing
Teacher." "The Missing Teacher" has gone through several drafts and is
still in the process of revision. Katerina takes conference information
seriously. For instance, Katerina's story about the teacher has him
losing all his clothes through theft in the night. He goes out to purchase
new clothes the next day. Other children pointed out that this would be a
problem, and that the teacher might get arrested. Katerina redrafted her
work and had the teacher go to bed with clothes and shoes on. Again,
the children thought this strange. Katerina placed the shoes on the floor,
and eventually in the closet. Katerina also revises on her own. She plays
with the details in her stories.

Katerina uses formula language to begin and end stories. Examples include "One day . . . ," "Once upon a time . . . ," and "They lived happily ever after. . . ." Most of her sentences are straightforward, and make syntactic sense. Many of her sentences are simple in construction, but she is beginning to use compound sentences and dialogue. Katerina's punctuation and capitalization fit to a close approximation of the standard. End punctuation is appropriate. Commas are used for a series of words. Quotation marks enclose dialogue. Katerina's choice of verbs is usually in the passive voice. She's beginning to use more adjectives for effect ("They were dripping wet.").

Katerina's writing is by no means limited to story writing. She is conscientious about keeping a Reading Journal and writes in it more often than is required. She writes about favorite parts of books, favorite characters, why she picked a book, and her opinion of a book. She often backs these statements up with a reason. (". . . My favorite character is Oscar. Oscar is pretty nice because he learns a lesson. The lesson is to stay around where he lives.") ("I thought this book was boring. Because there were words I didn't like in there and I didn't like the picture a lot either.") Katerina generally browses through the first page of a book to determine whether or not to pursue it. Her reading choices show variety with a mix from magazine articles on animals, to joke books like *Witcracks,* to folk tales, to favorite picture books. Most of her choices can be read in one sitting. She usually abandons "chapter" books after a couple of days. She enjoys using the listening center, and follows the text as she listens. She is currently using the center to read a "chapter" book, *Stone Fox.*

Katerina's uses of literacy show that she places great value on it. This is particularly true for her as a writer. She uses writing for social interactional purposes. For instance, she became enthusiastic about a Home-School Journal when her sister's class began using one. Having suggested it to her teacher and seeing no results within two days, Katerina created her own Home-School Journal and got her teacher involved in it. Katerina also uses writing for educational purposes. The back of a math homework paper will list the color coding she has used on the front as an explanation of the patterns she found. She has used her *LOGO* Log to do more than list commands. She describes what she has done at each *LOGO* session. ("I made square on the computer and I taught Nat how to use the LOGO and I think Ia'm doing good.") ("I made a double flag. It was neat.") These descriptions are Katerina's own idea. She proudly points them out to her teacher.

It is important to state here that even as I type these biographic accounts into my computer the teachers are changing the ways in which they are constructing them. Some of the Project teachers, who have spent a year writing profiles, are in the process of restructuring the task so that their profiles can reflect the multiple layers of information that they are collecting as they observe and take notes about the children in their classes.

Four: Learning to Increase Our Awareness of the Multiple Layers of Interpretation That We Are Incorporating into Children's Biographic Literacy Profiles

"You know at the beginning of last year I rejected your categories. They were confusing to me," Leigh Walls said a few days ago when I was asking her if I could include the profile of Tom in the previous section of this report. "But as the year went on what I was seeing in my notes fit." We joked a bit, remembering. Leigh said that for her the "category" that made the most sense focused upon the interrelationships between children's pictures and their writing, and then she added that she had just read an article published in *Early Childhood Research Quarterly* that examines the social uses of print (Schrader, 1989). Leigh said, "Their categories are similar to the types and uses of print that we are using in the project." I ventured that I thought she was reaching a time in her own development when she would be creating her own categories. Leigh laughed, "I already have," she said. "It's called 'the other' category."

We talked for a while about the way in which she was organizing her profiles this year. "I have to find a way to make it more manageable," she said, and she spoke of the time it was taking to write the profiles. She talked of taking her notes and the other information that she had collected and organizing it so that the biographic profiles would reflect the categories that we were using as we tried to think about the multiple layers of literacy activity that occurred in classroom settings. Leigh emphasized that she did not want to use the categories as a basis for classroom observation, and I agreed with her, "Then it would become just another checklist and the theoretical base would change. It would become an outside-in way of looking at children and we would be back into a 'medical model.' "

Like Mary Benton, of whom I spoke earlier, Leigh strongly believes in observing children and writing down her interpretations of what she sees. Kathy Matthews presented a similar point of view. When I spoke with her earlier this evening she said, "The thinking comes afterwards." Kathy is also trying to find a way to organize the information that she collects into a system of recording and reporting that makes sense within the framework that she has established in her own teaching. Kathy has been taking notes in her classroom for many years, but last year was the first time that she tried to synthesize the "data" that she had been collecting into some form of cohesive representation that would inform her own teaching and be given to parents, used by other teachers, and shared with the children themselves.

The problem that Kathy faced when she joined the Project was that she had been teaching the same group of children for two years, and she had too much information about them to produce a short paragraph each month about their literacy learning. The first profiles that Kathy wrote were three pages of single-spaced narrative—just for the month of September. "This kind of teaching is like an escalator," Kathy said. "The more you learn, the further up you go and the more difficult it is to get off." For Kathy, Leigh, and Mary, this is the year in which they will play with different ways of presenting the information that they are collecting, so that they can both make the process manageable for themselves and provide insights for some of the other teachers in the Project who have not yet reached a similar point in their own development. Indeed, for some of the teachers, taking notes is a challenge, and the profiles that they are writing still focus largely upon the development of sound-symbol relationships and syntactic structures.

It is important to emphasize here that the experiential differences that exist among the teachers have created an opportunity for us to establish a dialectical relationship which, through our collaboration, enables us to play with our own situationally specific problem-solving activities. These activities include:

1. Creating environments in which children can explore the functions, uses, and forms of written language.
2. Establishing notetaking procedures that reflect the practical complexity of the plurality of literacies occurring in these specific classroom settings.
3. Developing systems of analysis that reflect the multiple layers of interpretation that we are trying to incorporate in the biographic profiles that we are writing.

Consistent with the structure of the Project, in presenting our fourth objective I am going to add to and combine the information outlined in the first three objectives described so far. Thus the layering will be presented directly (explicitly) and indirectly (implicitly) in order to deliberately model the complexities of the process that we are trying to achieve.

1. Creating Environments in Which Children Can Explore the Functions, Uses, and Forms of Written Language.

In a chapter entitled "Thinking in action: some characteristics of practical thought," Sylvia Scribner (1986) reminds us that "the computer metaphor, dominant today, portrays mind as a system of symbolic representations and operations that can be understood in and of itself, in isolation from other systems of activity" (p. 15). Cautioning us about what I would call the distortions of anonymity that occur in such hermetically sealed studies, Scribner states:

> Researchers adopting this metaphor seek either to model mental tasks undertaken for their own sake ("recall a narrative," "solve this arithmetic problem") or to analyze individual mental functions (e.g., inference, imagery) abstracted from tasks and separated from one another. Whatever may be said about the value of this framework and these research approaches (and their accomplishments are recognized), they offer little possibility for probing the nature of practical thought. (p. 15–16)

The impact of research that "disembodies mental activity" (see Lave, Murtaugh, and de la Rocha, 1984) is clearly evident in the corpus of research studies that have been conducted in the reading field that focus upon eliciting information in totally synthetic laboratory environments or artificially structured classroom environments (see studies reviewed by Chall, 1989; also Taylor, 1989). Less evident are the effects of quasi-normative studies in which "context" becomes just another variable. And yet, as Lave, Murtaugh, and de la Rocha state:

> There is speculation that the circumstances that govern problem solving in situations which are not prefabricated and minimally negotiable differ from those that can be examined in experimental situations. (p. 67)

Studies in practical intelligence (Sternberg and Wagner, 1986) and everyday cognition (Rogoff and Lave, 1984) provide convincing evidence that mental activity is not context free (see also Carraher, Carraher, and Schliemann, 1985; Carraher, 1986). Thus we are left asking if the generic teaching of "skills" or the testing of—what? I no longer have any idea what "it" is that we test—have any relevance at all, except for the purpose of academic endorsement of what is essentially a political activity. If we shift away from the defective idea of generic teaching and learning that underlies this lucrative commercial enterprise and we localize education and try to think about teaching, learning, and schooling from the perspective of the learner, then we are no longer able to think about separating the activity from the setting.

Indeed, I would argue strongly that such a division has always been an illusion. Even on so-called "normed" tests the child's particular interpretation of the task is dependent upon the dialectical relationship that is established between the activity and the setting. The difficulty that occurs is that we cannot predict the individual child's response to the task. An example of a child's reaction to a standardized achievement test is provided by Don Graves, who recounts that in the Atkinson Study, a young boy kept putting up his hand, and in keeping with the standardized procedures for the administration of normed tests, his teacher kept signaling him to put his hand down. Eventually the child pointed to his test booklet and asked, "Who wrote this anyway? It doesn't have a voice."

Leigh Walls has shared another example of the difficulties that arise when there is no accounting for the perspective of the learner in standardized testing situations. Leigh spoke of a time early in her teaching career when she was teaching social studies in a junior high school. She was expected to administer the standardized tests used in the school, and on one occasion she watched as a junior high school boy zigzagged his way down the page, shading the boxes without looking at the questions. Leigh said it took him less than five minutes and he scored at the mean. What bothered Leigh then, and still bothers her today, is that the boy had difficulty reading. "He could not read the items on the test," she told us, and then she asked, "What was he learning?"

It is from this perspective that we have approached the task of constructing learning environments in which children can actively engage in the reconstruction of the functions, uses, and forms of written language. To quote Scribner (1986) again:

> The concept of the environment germane to practical problem solving is not a physicalist notion. Here "environment" includes all social, symbolic, and material resources outside the head of the individual problem solver. In this sense, activities such as seeking information from other people, "putting heads together" to come to collaborative solutions, or searching documents and looking things up in files, may be understood as extended and complex procedures for intellectual use of the environment. (pp. 24–25)

In the Project we often talk of the classroom "setting," and we use this term in similar ways to "environment" to mean individual and shared interpretations of the social, symbolic, material, and technological resources that make up the particular classroom. We also use the word "arena" to indicate the larger institutional framework which, in similar ways to the "setting," is made up of people using the symbolic, material, and technological resources at their disposal within the defined space of the physical plant called the school (Lave, Murtaugh, and de la Rocha, 1984). We do, of course, include family and community as constitutive of both the classroom setting and the institutional arena of the school. In the classrooms described in this section, family life takes place in classroom settings.

Our task then has become to gain insights into what Scribner describes as "the specificity of practical knowledge" and to gain some understanding of "the role of thought within a system of activity" from the perspective of the learner (1986). Standing side by side children with our heads together, we are trying to understand their learning based upon what we observe as they use the social, technical, symbolic, and material resources at their disposal. In the next few pages I want to explore what this means specifically for the participants in the Project.

Recently during a conversation that took place when the second-year Project members made a presentation of our work at the Maine Reading Conference, Lee Proctor said that she was keeping the first hour of her school morning "unstructured," and then she said, "The things I'm seeing I couldn't make happen." During this early morning unstructured time she sets them "the task of writing their news, and many of them start that when they first come in. I think they feel pretty much that they own it." In preparation for writing this section, I talked some more with Lee about what she meant by "unstructured" and she responded:

> I provide the time and the paper, and I visit with as many of them as I can. I spend a lot of time looking at their work when they've gone home. I look at the books they are reading, and I go through their folders just about every night. I find I can't keep that whole ball game going without a good idea about what they're doing. Initially, I'm just checking up on who's starting a book, who's finishing a book. I look at their logs. Their record is my record. It's a shared responsibility between us.

Lee is working with her students to create an environment or setting in which self-organization is constitutive of classroom life, recognizing in a similar way to Doll (1989) that the complexity of children's learning cannot be simulated in artificially structured classroom environments. As Doll explains:

> In retrospect, one aspect of self-organization we might have utilized bet-
> ter was that of the forced grouping of students. We placed them into
> groups of 2's and 4's because of my belief in the role cooperation and
> communication play in re-organization. Now I see we could have had co-
> operation and communication in a more varied, less forced mode. We
> should have *allowed* interaction and verbalization to occur, *not forced it*.
> Learning occurs on a number of levels and in a variety of manners—this
> is the nature of complexity. (p. 69)

Thus, in the Project classrooms, we are trying to provide opportunities for children to engage in problem-solving situations in which they
have participated in the organization of the activity.

In Sharron Cadieux's kindergarten classroom, the physical arrangement of the room is designed to encourage self-organization. At any
one time children may be actively engaged in a variety of learning situations, including playing in the housekeeping area. One day last
year, while Sharron was working with some children who were writing in their journals, children from the housekeeping area kept arriv-
ing with the telephone. "It's for you," they would say, and Sharron
would stop what she was doing and talk on the telephone. As the
morning progressed, the telephone "rang" continuously; each time, a
child would tell Sharron that someone wanted to speak to her. Finally, Sharron said, "Take a message." The child wrote a message
and gave it to Sharron. Other calls were received and more messages
were taken. Sharron put a notice board by the housekeeping area and
tacked the messages on it.

When I talked with Sharron about including this example of children's self-organization of a literacy activity being constitutive of the
classroom environments that we are trying to establish in the Project,
we had fun remembering that moment. "Kids would write messages
to each other," Sharron said, "and a lot of them could read them
back. They took messages for me. Once when we were reading them
back a child said, 'It's from Mr. Cadieux.'" I asked how long they
continued taking messages. "Eventually they lost interest in the telephone, but they had so much news to share that they began using the
notice board to write it down. If they had something to share they
wrote it down, and then they shared what they had written, and that
lasted a long time. Some kids used the notice board almost every day.
I think it was the sense of sharing information. They announced their
important news."

Sharron talked about the kinds of messages that the children wrote. She said that many of their messages serialized the events in their lives: "It's almost Julie's birthday party. Two days to Julie's birthday party. . . . Today is Julie's birthday party." Or, "I might get glasses. I might get glasses. Tomorrow I might get glasses. Today I might get glasses. I don't need glasses." Some of the messages were about events that were worrying individual children. For instance, one child wrote messages when her aunt gave birth to a premature baby, and the family was very concerned about the health of the baby. Sharron said, "When the baby reached eleven pounds, that was a big thing; she wrote an announcement and put it on the notice board." Sharron's children wrote notes about learning to ride their bikes and about having fights with each other, and when they gathered together they shared what they had written. If we stand side by side with Sharron and her children, we can gain some understanding of how they are learning about the many ways in which print can be used as a substitute for an oral message. Their interest in message writing and their self-organization of the activity underscores the complexity of the environmental setting that Sharron has established with her children.

Sharon Williams, a first-grade teacher, provided us with another example of the ways opportunities can be created for children to actively engage in the reconstruction of the functions, uses, and forms of written language. Sharon shared her class list with the teachers attending one of the group meetings we conduct throughout the year, and she said that she used the class list from the beginning of school in September "since all the children can find their name." Sharon explained that one of the ways in which they used the list was to record lunch and recess milk orders, and she pointed to a list to show us how the system worked. "*H* for hot lunch; *C* for cold lunch; *B* for lowfat milk, which comes in a blue container; and *R* for regular milk, which comes in a red container." Sharon talked about Sally, who was the first child "to record on our list," and she explained how she had asked Sally and another child to get the information they needed.

In writing up this account of the event that Sharon described, I telephoned her and she explained, "Both children had lists and they figured out how to use them." Then she added, "It's child structured and child figured out, and the task changes according to the children involved. Sometimes another child will join in and add his or her expertise." Going back to Sally, Sharon explained that Sally had sat across a table from the other child, and as the child called out a name Sally would find the name on her list and record the called-out re-

sponse from the child whose name had been read. The children figured out a system for themselves and it worked. At the group meeting Sharon said, "Sally felt confident and capable of doing this task."
Then she laughed as she told us that two weeks later the intern had
misplaced the attendance sheet and had gone immediately to the children's records to find out who was absent. "Our list has multiple purposes for both records and problem solving," Sharon concluded. In
Sally's biographic profile, Sharon wrote, "Sally is using print to organize and record information. She had the responsibility of recording
lunch and recess milk orders for a week, and she was able to use the
list of class names to accurately record all of the children's requests."

In Susan Sullivan's second-grade class, the children gathered together, and two boys moved to the front of the group and sat on
chairs facing the class. One of them was carrying a terrarium, and as
he sat down he carefully balanced it on his lap. He reached inside
and took out a red eft salamander. The boys had two of them. One of
the girls in the class had brought into school twenty of them that she
had caught in the woods with the help of her dad. The girl had given
two of the red efts to the boys, who had then made a terrarium for
them. "It was totally their own project," Susan said. "They went and
collected mushrooms and mosses. I had nothing to do with it except
that I showed them some books where they could find out about
salamanders."

Susan said that the boys took the terrarium, together with the
Audubon Field Guide to Reptiles and Amphibians, everywhere with
them. The two boys have been studying this book and another entitled *Reptiles* that they now shared. They talked about the red eft for
a while, and then the discussion shifted as the boys talked about the
book they had been studying, and one of them flipped through the
pages until he reached a page about turtles. They read and talked
about turtles for a while with the children sitting around them, and
then the conversation turned to rattlesnakes. The two boys looked
through the book together, somehow negotiating the turning of the
pages until they reached the page on which there was a picture of
several snakes—including a rattlesnake. They showed the picture to
the class. Then one boy read, not straight through the text, but relevant bits of information that they both wanted to share. Susan listened, and when he has finished reading she asked, "What does it
mean when it says rattlesnakes can strike?" A discussion followed,
and the boys alternated between looking at the book and talking with
the class. Eventually the class arrived at an acceptable explanation,

and they went on to discuss where the poison comes from. Children made suggestions. "It comes from the back of the throat," one child said. Others suggested the mouth, the teeth, and the tail. "How can we find out?" Susan asked, and the discussion continued, with most of the children agreeing that the best way would be to go and look in the library.

For a moment Susan talked with them about the library, and then the discussion was back to rattlesnakes, and Susan asked if rattlesnakes were useful. "There was a section in the book on useful snakes. I took it right off the page," she said. The children considered whether rattlesnakes were useful and if there were any positive reasons to have them around. The boy read from the text, and the discussion went back and forth between the information presented in the book and the information provided by the children, as they posed problems, developed hypotheses, and discussed possible explanations.

What happens in Susan's classroom underscores the importance of establishing with children environmental settings that enable them to explore the practical complexity of scientific knowledge. Susan said, "They get everybody interested and talk about it all the time. Right now they have a black-spotted salamander and they are working out what it means to be nocturnal. They took it out with them at recess and put it on some playground equipment and the salamander was distressed. They had a long discussion about why the salamander was not happy, and they have been trying to find out more about when they need to sleep and when they need to hunt."

At the beginning of this report we met Mary Yates, and I presented the biographic profiles that the teachers in the first Summer Institute wrote about her daughter Katie's literacy development. Mary is a second-grade teacher, and the following story was written by one of her second-grade children, Vicki. It is a story called "SUPR MOREO Brothrs." On the cover Vicki had drawn a small person, and inside a speech bubble she had written "to mare yats," and in another speech bubble "a good boook." Vicki had also written "by Vicki," acknowledging that she was the author of the book. Inside the story begins:

Moreo and Lawege
wint for a wock
in wrld one one
It was Hot so
Lawege tock
a swim

The prinses is in
trobol. what cinde
oof trobol the trols.

Lawege is in big
trobol whth
the dragan got [read "can't"]
Get bet up.

and got in to big
trobol and moreo
was in bigr

It was a canin but
He could not flut up
in the air.

yaaaww spines
are coming done

Lawege is in shock and
Moreo is history in
world 2 3

I'm olmost thare
to see the prinses.
Get a way big men
Dragan.

I Don't want to
be Lonch seid
Lawege thes
fling fish are

Jriving me crasey.
Ware is the prinses

ware Ther

Vicki explained that in the last picture Lawege and Moreo have saved the princess, and the turtle and "the guy who shoots the spines" have been caught. I asked Vicki who was holding onto the turtle and the spines and she said, "Just a person."

Mary said that when she talked to Vicki, she explained that she had started her story at world one one and finished it at world two three, because that's as far as she can go when she plays the Nintendo game. Thus we can say that it appears that Vicki is symbol-weaving as she works to create a story based upon the Nintendo game (Figure 3–6). It is interesting to note that when I have shown this story to researchers and educators, the immediate reaction is that they can't comment on the piece because they do not know the game. What we are learning in the Project is that such games are a part of the educational environment of the classroom, for children bring their technical expertise of playing video games with them when they come to school. It is clear that from the perspective of the learner, electronic games have both practical significance and theoretical relevance. This is not to suggest that the child has meta-knowledge of the theoretical and practical significance of advanced technologies, but simply to suggest that from the perspective of the child the technology is functionally important. Vicki provides verification of this perspective when she explains that her story is written in the worlds that she has visited when she plays the game.

Vicki's story could be described as archetypal in its construction, for it is a new copy of an old pattern, with a fairy-tale structure that incorporates a new technology into a traditional form. In the Project we are trying to learn from the children about this technology so that we can gain some understanding of the ways in which it has become a part of their daily lives. At the second Summer Institute, for example, we spent several hours discussing with Donna Parmenter a story

FIGURE 3–6   **Vicki's Nintendo story**

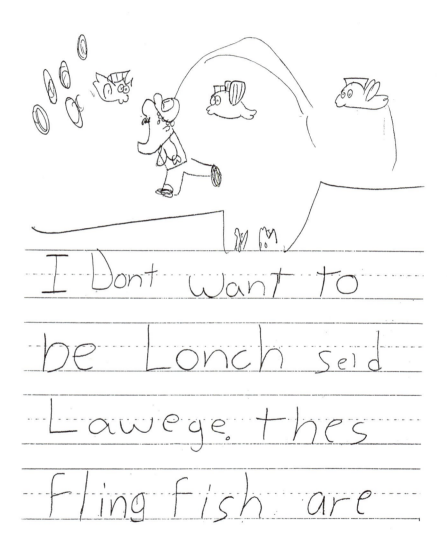

I Dont want to
be Lonch seld
Lawege. thes
Fling fish are

written by a boy in her class who was being evaluated by the child study team. We knew from observing and talking with him that the story was carried by the voice of a race commentator, and that he had incorporated elements from *The Road Warrior* into his text, in which the formation of letters served to illustrate the speed of the cars performing at a raceway as well as give a verbal rendition of the speed of the Mad Max chase. If you flipped the pages, the writing created the illusion of the increasing speed of the race.

A week after I worked as a participant-observer in Mary Yates' classroom, I visited Bob Magher's third-grade class and listened to Jeff read another Mario Brothers story during a writing conference with Bob and three other students. I present it here to emphasize that the children themselves are actively engaged in the process of incorporating new technologies into the classroom environment, and that the teachers in the project are sensitive to this development. Jeff gave his story the same name as the Saturday morning TV show "Captain N The Game Master," and above the title he had written "make-believe." The story was written in script and dated October 3, 9, 10, 12, 16:

> One day I was playing Super Mario brothers with Andrew and Bill when Andrew got hungrey so I paused the game and when I came back my game was unpaused and Andrew was gone. Billy was sitting the couch and breathing heavy. I asked him what happed he was talking to him and the game came unpaused and Andrew got sucked into it. Billy and I got up from the couch and I touched the T.V. I got sucked in too. Billy yelled, "Wait a second Jeff! I'm coming with you"! and he touched the screen and he came in too. I landed in the level 8-4. I saw Andrew then Billy almost fell on my head. I told Andrew and Billy to follow me we had to jump over pits of lava. Billy fell in one of them. He only has 1 guy left now. We made it to King Koopa. I told Billy and Andrew to run under him but not to pick up the ax. I had a case full of fire bombs I killed King Kooper I am going to save the real princess. We went to get her she told us we must save Pricess Zelda. She told us how to get to a warp zone that gets you all of the wepons and triforce and to the 9th palace and to Ganon. It is in the Castle Vania. And there is a warp zone to Castle Vania in the wall of the palce. We went in to the warp zone and ended up in Castle Vania. We saw Madusa I got the whip out of my pocket and whipped Madusa with it good I brought my paddle belt with me. I was tired I paused the game. I jumped out of the T.V. and got a drink then ["then" inserted] I went back in and unpaused the game ["game" inserted]. I kept whipping Madusa. I beat her we got to the

warp zone we went through it. Now we are in the nineth level. Ganon is
in the room right above us. "O.K. lets go guys'!' I shouted get the sivler
arrows out "Who is going to go in'?' I shouted. Billy and Andrew both
said at the same time "Not me"! "O.K. fine I will go". I said. I went in
to ganon You have to stab him four times then you have to hit him with
silver arowws. "Ouch'!' yelled Ganon I hit him with my sword once.
"Ouch'!' he said again 'cause I hit him. "Ouch"! he said again. "Ouch"!
he said. Now he is brown. I have to hit him with silver arrows "Bang" I
hit him once. "Bang" I hit him twice. "Bang" I hit him three times now
he is dead. I ran out to tell Billy and Andrew. "Billy, Andrew I beat
him"! "Come in let's go get the triforce"! "And save princess Zelda."
We ran in to the room where Ganon used to be I grabed the triforce and
ran in the door with Billy and Andrew. There's Zelda guys"! I shouted.
"Billy don't go there you'll get killed!" Billy was so excited he ran up
Zelda and in to the fire. "I warned him". "Yup, you did". said Andrew.
"Well it will be a long time before we see him again. He is dead we
won't see him until we die." "O.K. now Andrew you wait here I am
going to put out these fires." There finished. "Come on Andrew"! We
ran up to Zelda "I gave her one of the triforce. I gave Andrew one too."
We held them up above our heads. Then Zelda told us we have saved
H—— and the whole world of Nintendo Land. The End.

In a way similar to Vicki, Jeff was symbol-weaving the technological quests of video games ("You'll have to think fast and move even
faster to complete this quest!" Super Mario Bros.) with the images
and stories that result from the transposition of these games into a
Saturday morning T.V. show about Kid Nintendo. In addition, Bill
and Andrew are friends of Jeff's. Bob said, "The kids like to do that,
they incorporate each other into their stories." When all these elements are combined, the result is something between a child's version
of the *Canterbury Tales* and *Bill and Ted's Excellent Adventure*. Jeff
made his own story, incorporating his friends into a technological adventure that has many of the elements which can be found in traditional, even ancient, story forms.

The final example builds upon the questions raised about complexity
in classroom life and is connected to the ideas of symbol weaving in
problem-solving situations in which the children themselves have
participated in the organization of the activity. During the 1988–89
school year, Kathy Matthews' third-grade children studied the culture
and mythology of ancient Greece. Kathy has written an article about
her students' study of mythology (Matthews, 1990); at the beginning
of her paper Kathy describes the Greek festival, the culminating
event of their year of activity and study:

In our "amphitheater" that evening, two groups of children performed their own versions of the classic tales of Perseus and Persephone, using elaborate puppets that they had made. Guests wandered through the exhibits of the children's work, admiring the results of weeks of problem-solving and labor: Aaron's scale model of the Parthenon, Debbie's version of the Minotaur's maze, the wings Mike had built so that he could fly like Icarus, Jenny's life-like Pegasus perched for flight, embroidered tapestries of Athena, Prometheus, and Aphrodite, the twelve dioramas Chad and Amber sculpted in plasticene to symbolize the labors of Hercules, Matt and Nate's relief map of Ancient Greece, and our clay pots painted with classic Greek designs and seeded with Greek herbs. The guests talked with the children about their work, read the reports they had written, and feasted on traditional Greek fare including that classic bacchanalian drink—grape juice. (p. 40)

Kathy speaks eloquently of the "significance of the metaphors that myths have provided" and of the importance that mythology has played in the lives of children for thousands of years. During my visits to her classroom I became increasingly aware of the historical connection that Kathy was encouraging her children to make between their own lives and the lives of ancient civilizations. On my first visit to her classroom the students were creating visual representations of their own life histories, and my second visit coincided with the sorting of artifacts recovered during an archaeological dig. It took several minutes before I began to see what was happening. The children were working in twos and threes, sorting and classifying the objects that they had collected during the dig. Kathy was participating, clipboard in hand, examining objects shown to her by the children, listening to them, and discussing with them the classification systems that they were developing as they worked to create a record of their participation in the dig.

As a novice or neophyte, there has never been a time when I have visited Kathy's classroom that I have been able to walk in and just take notes. When children participate in the construction of their own environments, the task of the participant-observer, like that of the teacher, is to try to capture some of the practical complexity of the symbolic activity. What are they doing and how are they doing it? What kinds of negotiations are taking place? How do they arrange to work together? What problems are they trying to solve? What are they saying? What are they writing in their daybooks, journals, and learning logs? What are those diagrams? What are they drawing on those large sheets of paper? Is that a mountain that those children are painting? How is it constructed—with cardboard and glue? What

books are they reading? Are they studying geometry? ancient forms
of measurement? the origin of machines?

In *Order out of Chaos*, Prigogine and Stengers (1984) write about
the "irreducible multiplicity of representations," and although they
are not talking about classrooms filled with children, I am convinced
that the description applies. When we provide opportunities for children to participate in the construction of their own learning environments, their activities are structured into complex temporal patterns.
We can capture only a glimpse of what Prigogine and Stengers refer
to as "the wealth of reality, which overflows any single language, and
single logical structure" (p. 225). At the second Summer Institute, as
we had gathered together to discuss a problem-solving activity in
which we had all participated, Kathy tried to create a visual representation of what the participants said had taken place as they worked
together (Figure 3–7). "Do you think that the diagram reflects some
of what happened in your classroom as the children studied Greek
mythology?" I asked. Kathy replied, "I think there was as much
depth and breadth. It was certainly that complex." The diagram—and
Kathy's written analysis of the activity (Figure 3–8)—provides us
with just one interpretation of the practical complexity of a problem-
solving event, but perhaps it will enable us to imagine the multiplicity
of interpretations that are possible when self-organization is constitutive of classroom life.

*2. Establishing Data-Collecting Procedures That Reflect the
Practical Complexity of the Plurality of Literacies Occurring in
Specific Classroom Settings.*

Collecting information about children's learning depends upon the
classroom environment. If a child copies from the board:

> Tab is a sad cat.
> Tab has a pal.
> His pal is Mac.
> Mac is a rat.

there is not much to be learned (see Taylor and Strickland, 1989).
The task is curriculum (or basal?) generated and teacher defined.
From the perspective of the learner there is not much happening. The
child might passively copy or even rebelliously refuse to complete the
task. Either way we learn nothing about the ways in which the child
uses print in the self-organization of problem-solving tasks, nor of the
ways in which the child is problem-solving the construction of written texts. Conversely, as the "Tuck-in" flyer (Figure 3–3) serves to

FIGURE 3–7   Kathy's problem-solving diagram

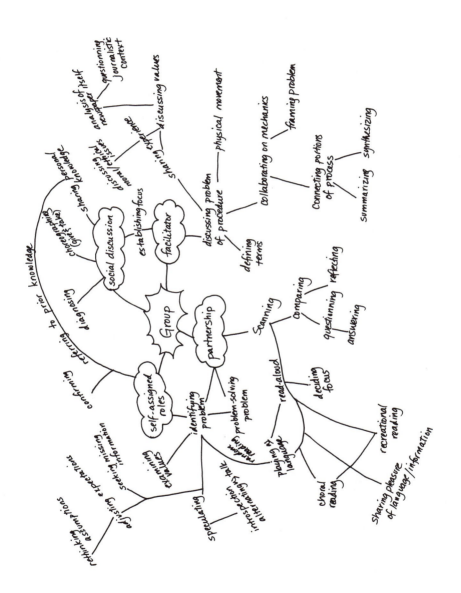

FIGURE 3–8   Kathy's analysis of the activity

Solving the Problem of Newspapers

Group dynamics— how group worked together
- partnership   ~ social discussion
- facilitator   ~ self-assigned roles

Approaches to problem of task
- identifying problem
- discussing problem of procedure
    - collaboration on mechanics of procedure
- framing problem
- problem-solving problem
    - connecting portions of process
    - defining terms
    - physical movement

Components of Problem-Solving
- reading aloud   ~ establishing focus
- silent reading   ~ decision-making re:focus
- choral reading   ~ diagnosing
- recreational reading   ~ summarizing
- re-running text   ~ synthesizing
- introspection alternating w/talk ~ hypothesizing
- playing with language   ~ speculating
- innovations on language   ~ sharing pleasure/laughter
- comparing texts   ~ choreographing (give & take)
- scanning   ~ answering

FIGURE 3–8   continued

Components (cont'd)

~ seeking missing information
~ adjusting expectations
~ rethinking assumptions
~ referring to prior knowledge
~ sharing experiences
~ expressing values

~ debating moral issues
~ analyzing newspaper quality
~ questionning journalistic content
~ reflecting
~ comparing
~ questionning
~ confirming

Note-Taking Issues

~ coping w/ task
  - defining terms
  - reviewing directions
  - group decision-making
  - dialogue re: procedure

~ ways of note-taking
  - running record
  - categorizing
  - focus on dialogue
  - inclusion of physical movement

~ personal difficulties
  - removing self (observer)
  - staying in observer's role
  - mechanics of group reading

illustrate, pieces of print generated in problem-solving situations can provide us with opportunities to build multiple interpretations of the functions and uses of text. When we have texts produced by children we can develop detailed analyses of their structural features (sound/ symbol relationships or syntactic patterns), but without systematic observation by the teacher we learn very little about the ways in which the individual children collaborated as they worked to develop hypotheses, simplify the task, or rethink the problem. Did they share personal knowledge? collaborate on mechanics? Did anyone speculate about the outcomes of the problem? adjust their expectations?

choreograph the discussion? How many drafts were made? notes? plans? What conversations took place as different symbol systems were incorporated into the text?

Neither dead tasks (workbooks) or inert texts (print without knowledge of production), are enough to create an adequate picture of learning from the perspective of the learner. And, while I would rather have the child's production than some simplistic ("asinine" is probably a better word) text copied from the board, the child's writing without notes written by the teacher still only provides a part of the picture. Portfolios are not enough. To understand how individual children actively engage in the reconstruction of the functions, uses, and forms of written language, we need to observe them at work. The observations that teachers make and the notes that they write are central to the process, and when the information generated through their systematic observation of children is combined with portfolios that contain notes, plans, and first drafts as well as final copies, then we have an opportunity to construct biographic profiles that reflect the literacy development of individual children and we can use these profiles to help us support and enhance the learning opportunities of every child that we teach.

"Take a message," Sharron Cadeiux said to one of her kindergarten children; the rest of the story you know. In her master's thesis Sharron writes:

> I had always encouraged children to explore writing for a variety of purposes (notes, signs, reminders), but did not make a concerted effort to include these in the child's writing folder on any regular basis. If I kept them at all, it was as an interesting glimpse at children exploring written language and its uses, not as an example of one child's understanding of the various functions of language. Taylor encouraged us to save all the little scraps each child wrote, pictures and "letters" they did at home to give to the teacher, examples of environmental print they could read, signs or lists resulting from play ("KEEP OUT" signs, menus, shopping lists), examples of spontaneous writing done at home if we could get them. All of these often indecipherable examples of children's understanding of the uses of print were to be carefully dated and included in each child's folder along with more formal examples of writing and teacher observations. By more formal examples of writing, I am referring to the journals and stories the children write using invented spelling following a writing process model. This is the type of writing I had monitored in the past almost exclusively. The notes, signs, and other products of play were noteworthy and validating examples of each child's writing development, but I did not make a concerted effort to make them part of the child's record of progress. . . .

I now view these writings, which usually find their way into wastebaskets both at home and at school, as indispensable glimpses into each
child's understanding about how print works. Such information is essential if we truly seek to begin at each child's level of understanding and
provide experiences to encourage growth from an individual perspective
rather than education based upon adult assumptions. (pp. 79–80)

Together with the examples of children's writing, and the reading
logs that Sharron collects and keeps in each child's folder, she also
records what she calls the "supporting information" of actual conversations between herself and a child and between children working together—what she refers to as the children's "explanations" of the
work that they are doing.

Sharon Williams was the second teacher whose classroom we visited in the discussion on creating classroom environments in which
literacy is used for authentic purposes. Two days ago (October 27,
1989) I received a letter from Sharon with more lists. The multiple
uses that her children devise for this simple list of names underscores
that the text is not enough. Sharon writes:

Dear Denny,

Here's another use of my class list. Last Tuesday we had indoor recess
and the children were playing a game with a score. A number of them
got lists to record the game. Here is one I collected. Another girl recorded scores on her sheet. I couldn't find that one. It was a throwing
game. Ms. Gurchin and I did not play. Evan won and you can see who
all played. . . . If I find the other list I'll send you a copy.

Sharon's comment about not being able to find one of the copies
is a relevant one, for as Sharron Cadieux notes, much of the everyday writing of children ends up in wastebaskets or as Project teachers
often remark, the writing is too precious to be given to the teacher.
Our task is to try to get *representative samples* that we can keep in
children's portfolios to use in analyzing their literacy development
and in building biographic profiles. Very often this means making
copies of the writing so that its communicative purpose is not inter-
rupted. On the copy of the game list that Sharon sent to me one of
the children had written "NOPLeYg" by her name and by the name
of Ms. Gurchin, and the score had been kept by making X's by the
individual players' names. Sharon included another class list with her
letter and this one had served to record the children's Halloween
masks. "Jack-o-Lantern" and "Frankenstein" together with an "or-
ental princess" and a "O O U O C U U U V" (happy clown) were
written by the children beside their names. If we add the way in

which Sharon told us Sally used the list to record snack and lunches, we have three very different literacy events taking place that require specific explanations of the children's participation (collaboration) in the dynamic construction of a self-organized problem-solving situation.

A single piece of paper might be used for multiple literacy events, and a single literacy event might lead to the production of multiple interpretations of the event. When David, a first grader in Lee Proctor's classroom, read *Cat on the Mat* by Brian Wildsmith, he spent several days making a model of the cat standing on the mat. Then, on October 16, he decided that he would write about it when he wrote his news. David wrote "I L C R O T H C A T / O N T H M T" (I like reading the *Cat on the Mat*) (Figure 3–9). Later, on the same day, David wrote, "I L C M C P R t S" (I like making projects) (Figure 3–10). David shared both the book and the model with the rest of the children in his class. After school he invited his mother into his classroom. She brought his young brother with her, and together they looked at the model and the book.

I had talked with Lee about the ways in which David interpreted Brian Wildsmith's book, and a few days later I received a letter with a photograph of David reading to his mother and younger brother. Lee wrote,

> I'm really intrigued with the observation of David's understanding of the Cat on the Mat text. When he looked at the word card "cat" on October 12, he read "Cat Sat on the Mat," and repeated this assertion when I asked him again. He then read "cat" for "elephant," and had no idea about "goat." When I helped him with these, he quickly caught on to the fact that the words on the cards were for the animals in the story, and so he guessed the remaining animal names. (Problem-solving, by using classification skills!)
>
> On October 16, he says/reads "cat" on the card and says, "I know what this is because I can spell "cat"; he then picks out and reads the cards for "sat" and "mat" (the cards are all facing up so he can scan the "universe"). Pointing to "goat" he asks, "What's this letter called?" When I tell him "g" he reads "goat." He asks "is this a d?" Then he reads "dog" . . . and this says 'cow.'"
>
> When I ask him "What helps you to read?" he says, "The first letters." I realize that part of the obstacle for him has been a problem with identifying the lower-case letters—an observation which informs my teaching.
>
> But letter identification is only a small piece of what he is working on. He has figured out something fundamental about the phonetic aspects of reading between October 10 and October 16, I think. He hasn't

FIGURE 3–9   David's "I like reading *The Cat on the Mat*"

needed to do this when looking at the book because here he reads fluently, using the pictures and his memory for the syntax. But the vocabulary cards lead him through a gray area of sound/symbol representations, helping him to both isolate single words from the aural stream, and to figure out what they are.

I guess this excites me because I have the sense of being able to glimpse through a window to "see" his process.

In her letter Lee focused specifically upon the ways in which David appeared to be developing some understandings of how sounds and symbols go together. On an earlier occasion we had also spent some time talking about the model that David had made of the cat on the mat, and Lee had sent a draft of a chapter she is writing for the book about the Project. Lee had marked the following passage with a red pen:

At one point in the winter, I began to feel that the projects did not constitute a sufficiently "literary" form of response, and the energy level which went into their making seemed pretty high for a reading period. And so I shut down the project operation, and instituted written responses to stories. But with this dictum, every aspect of the process seemed to flatten. The choosing of books did not seem to be as spontaneous. Indecision and wandering increased. Energy went to less con-

FIGURE 3–10   David's "I like making projects"

structive actions. Share-times were not as interesting. We needed a Class Meeting to air feelings about my removal of the project option. When we agreed as a group to add written responses, and retain projects also, the zest seemed to return.

These examples of the information we are collecting serve to emphasize the importance of trying to capture the complexity of the richness and diversity of children's literacy experiences in classrooms that encourage the self-organization of problem-solving activities. Sometimes it is the connectedness of a series of literacy activities surrounding a single event, such as reading a book; at other times it might be an odd incident that eventually leads to the discovery of a more general pattern. Since we have discussed Vicki's "SUPR

MOREO BROTHRS" story Mary Yates has become increasingly aware of the use of technology by the children in her classroom. During a telephone conversation Mary talked about a book about aircraft engines that one of the girls in her class had written that day. Mary said that the girl's father was an aircraft engineer and that when she visited his office she played with a computer-simulated aircraft engine. Mary said that the student explained that "by pressing the buttons she could move a pulley that pulled parts of the engine back and forth." The book the student wrote describes the differences between several aircraft engines. Mary has made a copy for the child's portfolio and written notes describing the conversation that she had with the child as they discussed aircraft technology.

If we try to synthesize the ways in which we are trying to "capture the complexity" of children's literacy development we can state that among us:

- We are collecting as many artifacts as possible of the different types, uses, and forms of literacy that occur in our specific classroom settings.

- We are including examples of "family literacy" (notes and stories written at home) and "recess literacy" in our collections.

- We are keeping daybooks, learning logs, reading logs, and journals as a rich source of information.

- We are ignoring artificial boundaries between scientific, mathematical, and social forms of literacy by paying particular attention to the collection of information that illustrates the ways in which children use the technical, symbolic, social, and material resources at their disposal.

- We are paying particular attention to situationally specific, self-organized situations in which print is constitutive of a problem-solving activity.

- We are incorporating examples of the ways in which children use multiple forms of symbolism in the learning situations that they encounter—both in and out of school.

- We are making sure that the work collected in children's portfolios is accompanied by detailed observational notes.

- We are making audio recordings of children reading (usually self-selected) books. Our aim is to make three recordings for each child (September–October, January–February, May–June).

- We are experimenting with the use of video recordings to capture specific literacy events so that we can explore with children what's happening as they participate in some self-organized problem-solving activity.

• We are taking still photographs of children collaborating on projects and generally participating in the literacy life of the classroom.

• We are keeping paintings, graphic productions, and three-dimensional structures together with observational notes and photographs of the activities.

• We are including any examples of the above that the children themselves want to add to their portfolios.

• We are making a separate record of each child's comments upon his or her own literacy development, giving special attention to the child's analysis of his or her literacy portfolio.

3. Developing Systems of Analysis That Reflect the Multiple Layers of Interpretation We Are Trying to Incorporate in the Biographic Profiles We Are Writing.

Describing the first chaos theorists, James Gleick (1989) writes:

> They had an eye for pattern that appeared on different scales at the same time. They had a taste for randomness and complexity, for jagged edges and sudden leaps. . . . The revolution in chaos applies to the universe we see and touch, to objects at human scale. Everyday experience and real pictures of the world have become legitimate targets for inquiry. (p. 47)

Although Gleick is writing about physicists and mathematicians, he could very well be describing the holistic/process teachers participating in the Biographic Literacy Profiles Project, for they teach from the perspective of the learner, and of necessity they have developed and continue to develop an eye for pattern, which enables them to see from multiple perspectives the practical complexity of children's symbolic activity.

When teachers join the Project we emphasize that they should "take it easy," learn to look and learn to see, try to make some notes about every child, and begin to collect data that can be kept in each child's portfolio. But we advise them not to try to write biographic profiles for every child, but rather, to write one or two, five at the most. It takes time to build a theoretical framework for observing children and even longer to learn how to observe. Even so, some teachers decide to write profiles for every child in their class. "How could I write them for some and not others?" a teacher will say. So in the end it is a personal decision; it is the teacher who must decide.

This year as we work together at our group meetings we are exploring ways of making the task more manageable. At one of our group meetings Leigh Walls, Sharron Cadieux, and Martha Dahl worked together. Each had brought with them their notes and the portfolio of one child. Their task was to help each other see more, to look in different ways, and to push each other's thinking. For a while I joined their group and listened to them as they worked. "We're taking notes on the notes," Martha said. They were reading the notes that Martha had written about a child in her kindergarten classroom. Although I never heard their exact questions, what they appeared to be asking each other was: "What's happening?" "How is this child constructing the forms of written language?" "How is this child using written language?"

I listened for a while. At one point Leigh said to me, "Although it seems like an extra step it really does make the process quicker." Then she added, "The structure came at the very end," and she showed me the grid that she had developed. Leigh's grid had ten "categories"—

1. graphics
2. oral description
3. sight words (subdivides into reading vocabulary and independent spelling vocabulary
4. invented spelling
5. types/uses of language
6. story structure
7. skills
8. problem solving
9. content-variety (sources/inspiration) and
10. —as you've probably guessed—other.

I know that in presenting these categories for Leigh she would want to make it clear that she is not using these categories to look at children in her classroom. They are analytic categories developed to help discover patterns in the notes she has written and the children's work she has collected. I want to emphasize that such categories are not intended to be used as a checklist. In the Project we often talk about the difficulties that arise when ways of studying and teaching children become packaged. I know I speak for many of my colleagues when I say that we are deeply concerned when process writing or holistic reading and writing practices are commercialized. Mass production changes both the philosophical and the theoretical foundations of holistic/process teaching and learning and therefore changes the practical intent. It is not possible to commercialize learning from the point of view of the learner.

For me, one of the most exciting developments that has taken place is how the second-year Project teachers have explored ways to make the process of writing profiles more manageable. Martha and Sharron teach in one school, Leigh teaches in another, Lee Proctor and Kathy Matthews are in different schools; yet they have all begun to devise ways of analyzing the information that they are collecting about the individual children they teach. Lee Proctor has developed a second grid. At the top of the sheet of paper she has written "Information for Literacy Profile," and beneath is a space for the child's name and the date of her analysis (later forms will provide Lee with the opportunity to compare her notes with the earlier notes that she has written). The paper is then divided into eight boxes—

1. type/use
2. content
3. graphics
4. structure
5. problem solving
6. spelling
7. sight words
   and
8. mechanics.

Kathy Matthews has developed a series of grids, including one she uses to record developmental spelling patterns. She has also added further areas for analysis for reading and writing; these include such categories as "cueing systems" and "self-evaluation."

At the group meeting when Leigh, Sharron, and Martha explored the possibilities of analyzing the information they had collected using the categories we had been using in the Project, there was also a whole-group discussion that focused upon the same topic. "There is no one way," Sharron Cadieux said. "I've found that whenever I come up with a system there is always an exceptional situation that doesn't fit." Leigh Walls continued, "This works for me but it might not work for you," as she showed the participants the small Post-it notes that she writes as she analyzes each child's work. One of the notes that Leigh had written was to encourage a child to begin writing on the left side of the paper rather than the middle. "Sometimes I write questions to myself," Leigh explained. "Other times I write down things that I want to work on with a particular child."

The variations between the working strategies that the teachers have devised are explored whenever we meet, and teachers often make a note to try a way of working that a colleague has described. But whatever the differences between us, there is unanimous agreement that when we are working out what's happening in a child's literacy development we begin by reviewing all of the information that we have collected.

"Pile it on the table" is something that I have said on more than one occasion. Start in September with the first piece. . . . Systematically sort the stuff. . . . Look at the information in the order in which it was collected. . . . Look for patterns . . . recurring themes . . . significant changes . . . jagged edges . . . sudden leaps. . . . Pick representative examples of the child's work and use them to illustrate the particular statements that you are making when you are writing his or her biographic profile. . . . Problem-solve the multiple ways in which individual children are using print and try to reflect upon the complexity of the process. . . . But whatever I say, the ways in which the profiles are developed depends upon the individual literacy configurations of the teachers who are doing the analysis, their own local interpretations of global patterns, developed intuitively as well as analytically, sometimes with difficulty, sometimes with ease. No two profiles that they write are ever quite the same. However trivial the information may seem on the surface, the details of each child's literacy development are noted, for we learn from children's uniqueness, and what makes them special makes teaching them worthwhile.

TEACHING, LEARNING, AND SCHOOLING: WHAT HAPPENS WHEN YOU MAKE A PARADIGM SHIFT?

Crucial Changes in Perspective

In "A New Way of Thinking: The Challenge of the Future," Sam Crowell writes,

> If we are to succeed in creating a new way of thinking, the focus must go beyond teaching practices. The structure of the school will be profoundly affected. The "school" cannot separate itself from learning. It is not merely a place or an organization; the school is teaching and learning. (p. 62)

Crowell's position is consistent with the definition of learning environments, settings, and arenas presented in the previous section of this chapter. However, knowing that the school is teaching and learning does not make it any easier for administrators and teachers. The power of teaching from the learners' perspective is that discontinuities between theory and practice are minimized—individual children become central to the educational process and decisions are made to support each child's learning. Betty Marston, a second/third-grade teacher, puts it this way: "We are interested in teaching children, but we are not interested in teaching them to fit into some mold." But the difficulty is that the system (state regulations, federal laws) is not set up to support teaching from the learner's perspective. At the national level our educational system is driven by what Steven Jay Gould (1989) refers to as "traditional hopes for progress and predictability" (p. 318).

We are not very good at dealing with the immeasurable contingencies of life and learning. We are expected to be accountable, and accountability is built into the system. We use standardized tests to make sure that teachers teach and children learn. At a recent conference a researcher told the audience that, in his state, merit pay for teachers was tied to the California Achievement Tests. How does this contingency affect teaching and learning? What pressures does such a policy put on teachers? How does it affect opportunities for them to teach and children to learn? And what about other contingencies?

In a recent report in *Science News*, Raloff (1989) reports:

> Children from low-income families who participate in the federally funded School Breakfast Program improve more on annual achievement tests than do classmates who qualify for the program but skip the school breakfast, new research shows. Though other studies have identified nutritional benefits from the subsidized breakfasts, this is the first to demonstrate the program's statistically significant impact on academic achievement. (p. 247)

Does this mean that in some states merit pay is tied to whether children are well fed? I apologize if it seems I am making light of a serious matter, but it is essential that, in presenting the effects of the paradigm shift taking place in the Project (and in many other projects across the country), we recognize that anomalous and paradoxical practices are inherent in the system and that traditional notions of progress and predictability might not be in the best interests of the children we teach.

To overcome the difficulties that individual teachers face as they try to make changes in the ways in which they work with the children in their classrooms, the institutional structure of schools has to change. Larry Cuban (1989) states:

> I fear that further disappointment lies around the corner unless policy-makers, practitioners, researchers see that patterns of instruction, uses of technology, and treatment of students are heavily influenced by durable organizational structures that must be fundamentally changed, if neo-progressive notions about schooling are ever to be fully realized. (p. 222)

The adjective "neoprogressive" bothers me but I do agree with Cuban that if we are going to change the way in which we teach then many durable organizational structures must be fundamentally changed. Kathy Matthews said that from her own perspective what the Project is really about is "changing the ways in which teachers are allowed to change." In the next few pages, through the voices of the teachers, administrators, parents, and children who are making them, I will present some of the changes that have taken and are taking place as we continually try to create opportunities for teachers to base instruction upon their observations of children.

Changes Taking Place from the Perspective of the Classroom Teacher

In her master's thesis, which focuses upon assessment, Sharron Cadieux writes:

> When I first returned to public education, I viewed assessment as a threat to how I wanted to teach. I wasn't using the school adopted basal reading program but had to give the end of the book tests. The first test I gave confirmed my fears. My students did not do well though I knew they were able to handle the concepts and certainly could read the words. Because they had not done the workbook pages they were ill equipped to take the test which followed the same format exactly.
>   So I adopted a more defensive strategy (like any "rational teacher" according to Lorrie Shepard, 1989). I showed my students how to function within the test format. If the test expected them to write numbers in front of sentences to indicate a sequential order, I found a workbook page with that format (one of many in a single workbook) and showed them how to do it. After that, they had no problem, though I had to devote a fair amount of instructional time to the process. (p. 67)

In a subsequent section of her thesis Sharron writes:

> In the past I felt that my approach to teaching was at risk if my students couldn't make the transition to decontextualized assessments. I no longer feel the need to "prove" that children can handle traditionally tested skills. I am moving from a defensive attitude toward assessment to a more constructive one. I feel assessment is valuable only if it pro-

vides insight into the child's knowledge and understanding of how language works. Such information can be used to guide a teacher's interactions with each student as well as document growth. One might argue that tests should be able to do these things, but they can't. The difference between tests and "assessment from the child's perspective" is both subtle and dramatic. The shift is from negative to positive, from what the child can't do to what she can do, from an adult's understanding of literacy to a child's understanding of literacy. For the first time I am beginning to feel hopeful that schools can move from an emphasis on the test to an emphasis on the child. (p. 85)

The position stated by Sharron is shared by most (I would say all) of the teachers and administrators participating in the Biographic Literacy Profiles Project. Like Sharron, many of the participants are experienced holistic/process teachers who have been striving for years to provide authentic learning experiences for children that (by definition) cannot be tied to the standardized programs and standardized tests that so many teachers are expected to use. The difficulty has been that they have needed a way to clearly articulate that the children that they teach are learning in far more complex ways than would be possible if they have been using the simulated teaching/ learning activities that are presented in packaged programs. Building biographic profiles based upon observations of children's literacy behaviors has helped the participants in the project to become more confident in their abilities to explain their students' growth.

Paradoxically, or perhaps ironically, as they have become more comfortable in presenting explanations of their teaching practices they have also become more accountable to children, parents, and administrators in the districts in which they teach. In the last year we have shared the Project with more than a thousand teachers and administrators through workshops, seminars, and classroom visits, and we have become comfortable addressing the questions that we are asked. Mostly we share our own experiences and, as you have probably already guessed, we try to make sure that we do not suggest that we have *the* answer or even that *an* answer, as such, exists.

Changes Taking Place from the Perspective of Educators Who Provide Supportive Instructional Services

Mary Benton and I spent several hours talking on the telephone trying to work out how we could describe the children who receive support from teachers who are members of specialized instructional services. The descriptors used in many schools and in the literature have pejorative connotations that we want to avoid. Mary works in classrooms with children who have been referred because they need a little more support than they can receive from their classroom teacher. Alex was one boy whom Mary worked with (see the biographic profile on p. 84). During the 1988–89 school year Mary observed Alex and several other children in their classrooms and she also read books and wrote stories with them in a one-on-one setting. The profiles that Mary wrote were used in combination with the biographic profiles that were written by classroom teachers.

Mary explained that her profiles are not really biographic because although she observes in the classroom she is not in the room on an ongoing basis. "If a child has been referred we have to address the reasons for the referral," Mary spoke deliberately, "but in your mind you have to keep it in perspective because if you become too focused on reasons then you are back into the old model." I asked Mary if I could write that on her first day back in school last September she got rid of all the tests that she used to administer. "Sure," she said. "I have committed myself. I don't have any tests so I can't test. I lived with those for too many years. They don't serve any purpose, and in the end I didn't know any more than I knew before. All you do is validate the numbers." Then Mary went on to explain by talking about a child who had been tested. "Before we started using profiles," she said, the child had been given eight different tests: Kaufman ABC, TOLD-P, EXP.O-WPT, WISC-R, Bender-Gestalt and Recall, PPTVT-R, and a Complete OT. "The recommendations told us nothing," Mary said. "If you use tests they just keep mushrooming. They don't provide the information—supposedly you'll come up with something, [but] you don't, so even well-intentioned people get caught into 'Well, one more test will tell us.'"

Mary then said she was in the middle of writing up a profile for a boy she had been observing who a doctor said "had" ADD (attentional deficit disorder). "We're hoping that when we show all this other stuff no one will think the label is applicable. I watched him for forty-five minutes as he wrote a story. He was completely focused on what he was doing. Hopefully we can show his family that. He focuses on lots of different things, listening to the teacher read a story, participating in group activities and in problem-solving situations. All he needs is to write more and to read more, and in his classroom he is doing that." Mary finished up the conversation by saying that the "catch-22" was what happened when a student was receiving special services through public law 94.142. "Then you have no option. You have to test."

Terri Apgar works with Mary Benton. She is the one who does the testing for public law 94.142. "You're boxed in," Terri explains. "There's no way around it at the present time." Then she added,

"The other problem is that you are time bound. You have forty-five calendar days to complete the evaluation. It's hard to watch the child and engage the child in meaningful activities within the time constraint." This is the first year of Terri's participation in the Project. She is working in Lori Bresnahan's classroom collaborating with Lori. "I've also written a profile of a child who falls under the federal umbrella," Terri said. She talked of "lightweight" testing and of the way she had devoted her energies to observing the child she was evaluating. "Our staff takes real good care of children so basically you know, but you still have to test. I wish I was allowed to do what I can do without all the constraints. I've worked and made lots of notes. I did a lot of observing, watching, trying to catch something. The profile presents a more positive picture and provides tons more information than the test results." Terri continued by saying, "The classroom teacher also developed a profile. They were very different, but you could see it was the same child." Like Mary, Terri then discussed the differences between the profiles that she is developing and the ones that the classroom teachers develop: "They're much more concentrated, one-on-one situations in both writing and reading." She talked about a child study meeting. "It's so nice to be able to say, 'Now let's talk about what he does when he picks up a book and actually reads it.'"

Changes Taking Place from the Perspective of the Principal

Ed Barnwell is the principal of two schools in the Project; you have met several of the teachers who work with him. In a paper that Ed has written on "Teaching, Learning, and Leading" he states:

> In our school's journey, we've been led by the children into new approaches to many aspects of our school from teaching to curriculum development to support services to school leadership. Through our efforts to become more responsive to children, we are fundamentally changing our school.
>
> A multi-billion dollar industry churns out teaching materials and resources. Most of it is norm-referenced according to author and publisher concepts of what can most reasonably be expected of similarly graded kids in Oshkosh, Galveston, Concord. . . . I am inherently suspicious of these materials, not that there is necessarily anything wrong with them (many, in fact, are excellent resources), but that they contribute to false assumptions about our student populations. It seems that by adopting normed, graded materials, it can too easily be assumed that there must be an appropriate match between the materials and the needs of most students. More insidious is the built-in expectation that the children should fit into the expectations of the program or leveled material. . . .

If success in first grade is defined by successful completion of a given set of materials, then we invite testing, screening, or opting children out of that context and into alternative programs with the well-intentioned aim of preventing school failure. If, however, we choose to measure school success in an individualized instead of group way, then we reverse the roles of responsibility—"failure" is then an institutional inability to respond to a child's need, not a childhood affliction. At our school, we are adopting a zero-failure attitude. Children can learn to different degrees, they can explore different interests, but they can't fail. We can fail by not providing the right environment or by not finding ways to reach each child. I think by shifting the burden of succeeding to the school we are becoming more respectful of diversity.

Later Ed talks about the teachers in the Project:

They know children can't be counted on to do what is expected based on group norms. They have the confidence and insights to make choices. These teachers aren't driven by test scores or the performance of other groups, including those they've had before. . . . They are striving to listen to what children's voices tell them. They are becoming less reliant upon others' notions of what ought to be. They are dedicated to helping all children succeed.

Peter Sweet, another principal in the Project, agrees with what Ed had written. Although there are some differences in their philosophies, there is much that is the same. Peter shares Ed's deep concern for teachers, and as we talked he voiced some of his own concerns. He spoke of his experiences as the principal of a school in which the teachers have been involved in holistic/process education for many years. Peter said, "As a staff we have set a direction and established a philosophy." He talked about the dedication of the teachers, but then added, "I'm concerned about teacher burn-out. One of the biggest difficulties is that teachers as professionals do not have control. They have less control of their professional lives than any other professional group. Everybody is an educational expert." Peter spoke of the steering committee for an upcoming conference on education. "There are twelve people on the committee and only one is a teacher. Change should be teacher initiated, teacher implemented, and teacher controlled. But teachers don't have the power."

We talked about the Project. Both principals and teachers have made many changes in class schedules to provide time for teachers both to work together and to work with me. However, the ways in which the institutions function within the much broader political framework of the system have not changed. Policy makers still require statistical proof that children are learning, as is evident by

NAEP's preparations for the 1992 nationwide testing of fourth-grade reading. Peter went on to talk of his own concerns about the lack of support from the State Board of Education. He spoke of the different philosophy of the State Board and the effect of the difference on community support (or lack of support) for schools. "It's much easier to get the support of parents than nonparents. But sixty-two percent of the adult population in the state do not have children in school." Peter then added, "For us it's getting to the point that they could make or break our school."

One more principal's voice adds to the complexity of the issues surrounding administrative support for and participation in the Bio-graphic Literacy Profiles Project. This is Cathy Hamblett's second year as a principal in a school that is continuing the process of creating a more holistic approach to education. Cathy said that because she was just beginning her career as a principal, she was probably more "parochial" than Ed or Peter. She said that it has been important to her that we have been "up front" in the Project by being clear that what we are trying to accomplish will "take years and years." "What is so important is that it's supporting teachers—giving teachers legitimacy as well as legitimizing children," she said. We talked for a while about Peter's concerns; I read to her what I had written. "A lot of the elementary standards are driven by numbers," Cathy said. "Very often the collection of statistical information drives funding. One of the biggest issues is that children have to be identified to receive special services." Cathy then talked about "local control": "In many districts it's a serious issue. Our school board supports process teaching."

We talked for a while, discussing the changes that Cathy and her teachers were making to support more holistic/process approaches to teaching and learning. Then Cathy said, "I think we have to show them that it can work at the local level and then share this with the state. Say, 'Okay, here is an alternative way of collecting information that tells us about kids learning.' We have to show them. Until then the state won't change." Listening to Cathy I thought about Peter, and I wondered if years ago he would have agreed with her. I think that Cathy is correct when she says that experience separates her from principals like Peter, who for many years have participated in and supported the teacher-initiated changes that have taken place in schools. For while Cathy is hopeful that the changes we are making might eventually lead to changes at both the state and national levels, Peter is not so optimistic. He says, "Teachers don't have the power to institutionalize change."

Complexity Theory and the Reorganization of Schools

The Biographic Literacy Profiles Project began with a single child for whom small errors in teaching and testing followed by repeated retesting had such a catastrophic effect that the school failed—afflicted by what Ed Barnwell refers to as "an institutional inability" to respond to the child's educational needs (Taylor, 1988; 1991a, 1991b). The first biographic profile was written for this child, and although the school that he attended did not take the descriptions of his observable literacy behaviors into consideration or use the information as a basis for his instruction in reading and writing, a group of teachers from another school became interested in the profile and asked if it would be possible for them to write literacy profiles for their first-grade children. One school participated in the early, tentative steps, which eventually led to the development and implementation of the research project in six other schools. At the present time 47 teachers and administrators and approximately 1,000 children are participating in the project, so I can write that although we were unable to change the system for a single child, a single child is changing the system. This is important, for at a time when so many of us are overwhelmed by the mass testing of children, which is mandated through federal laws and state regulations, this young child has taught us that "individual activity is not doomed to insignificance" (Prigogine and Stengers, 1984).

Essentially, the Project is about this child and the many other individual children who have taught us to seriously question the notion of objective reality by helping us make visible the complexity of symbolic activity in their everyday lives. We have learned that "scientific paradigms can exercise a strong influence on prevailing thought" (Prigogine and Stengers, 1984) and that the dominant societal and political educational ideology is driven by traditional hopes for progress and predictability that might not be in the best interests of children. Based both upon my own research experience and upon my participation in the Project, I would argue that we are irrevocably altering the lives of young children when we impose upon them our traditional aberrant theories and educational practices. Somewhere along the way we have forgotten that "the playground of contingency is immeasurable" (Gould, 1989) and that in the lives of young children we must learn to look at the ordinary and mundane events if we are to see the remarkably rich and subtle complexity of their symbolic behavior.

In *Seeing Voices*, Oliver Sacks writes, "It is all too easy to take language, one's own language, for granted—one may need to encounter another language, or rather another mode of language, in order to be astonished, to be pushed to wonder, again" (1989, p. ix). This is the purpose of our study. We are trying to push beyond our own training in the "objective" reality of the present educational system in order to be astonished by the irreducible plurality of functions and forms of language that children use in their everyday lives and, especially for us as teachers, in classroom settings. As we push each other to recognize the wonderful complexity and uniqueness of the symbol-weaving behaviors of children, we are also trying to build the professional expertise and specialized knowledge that will enable us to work with every child in ways that insure that "individual activity is not doomed to insignificance" within the classrooms and schools in which we teach. We have learned that to make such a shift in thinking is a slow process, and that we ourselves must engage in the situationally specific problem-solving activity of learning to teach from the perspective of the child. There are no "step-by-step" or "classroom-tested strategies" (as is suggested by a flyer for a writing program that I recently received in the mail)—just teachers and administrators dedicated to professionalism and with in-depth knowledge of the specific social, symbolic, technical, and material resources, the complexly patterned contingencies, that are constitutive of children's literacy learning in classroom settings.

Within this reflexive framework:

1. Teachers are encouraged to explore their own literacy configurations and to share the ways in which they use print in their everyday lives with the children that they teach.
2. Teachers are supported as they work to recognize their own expertise, and their professional opinions are supported when decisions are being made about the education of the children that they teach.
3. Teachers are provided with opportunities to increase their understanding of the ways in which children reconstruct the functions, uses, and forms of written language.
4. Teachers *work together* to explore their own literacy configurations, to share their expertise, to help each other develop new understandings, to share viewpoints on specific issues, and to construct biographic literacy profiles for the children that they teach.
5. Principals participate with teachers in the development of organizational structures that support the focus on teaching, learning, and schooling *from the perspective of the learner.*

6. Principals provide opportunities for teachers to receive ongoing support in their classrooms, at Project meetings, and in summer institutes.

7. Principals provide opportunities for parents to meet with teachers to learn about the project and to explore the way in which their children are learning about literacy as they learn to *use* literacy.

8. Principals themselves are actively involved in the construction of one or more biographic profiles, so that they have personal understanding of the practical significance of this approach to instructional assessment.

It is this collaboration—of teachers and principals—that has made the Project possible. Credit also needs to go to the local school districts for their financial support of the Project for, although the State Department of Education gave their approval, no money has been given to the schools and only limited funds have been made available for two three-day summer institutes and for six seminars to disseminate information about the project throughout the state.

Perhaps it may seem inappropriate to comment on this lack of support within the context of the presentation of the theoretical framework and practical significance of the project. But from the perspective of many of the teachers it is important, for they spend their own time on the Project, and participants have often stated that much more could be accomplished if monies were made available. We can only hope that eventually as more emphasis is placed upon the reorganization of schools, financial support will be provided at both the state and federal levels. In the meantime it is important to emphasize that, although State Department support has been limited, Helen Schotanus, the only consultant at the Department with the assignment of early childhood education and reading, has played a major role in the Project. She has organized meetings and supported us in many different ways and in such an unobtrusive fashion that I think we sometimes take her for granted. But it is Helen who works, side by side with us, and so often reminds us that a child's first experience in school should not be in a testing situation.

Complexity Theory and the Restructuring of Educational and Political Practice

In a recent article in *Education Week,* Rothman (1989) writes that the governing board of the National Assessment of Educational Progress is "entering one of the most emotional and diverse debates in education . . . [as it is] creating objectives for its 1992 fourth-grade reading test." Rothman quotes the chairman of the NAEP panel as stating that "getting an agreement will take quite a lot of palaver . . . [as] primary-grade reading is probably the stage of reading that is most controversial in America (p. 7)." Rothman then illustrates the controversy by quoting the opposing views of two prominent reading researchers: should we be testing word-recognition skills, or using a test that would "minimize the gap between what readers do when they read and what they do on the test (p. 7)." I would argue that this is the wrong controversy, for these two opposing views do not represent the views of many educators, both researchers and teachers, who find the suggestion that "fourth-grade reading" can be tested to be scientifically indefensible and, speaking for myself, politically reprehensible. For while we go through the palaver of finding an appropriate *reading* test, other democratic nations are seeking alternative ways of assessing *literacy*—based upon scientific evidence (and common sense) that clearly indicates that the complexity of children's symbolic learning cannot be categorized and then encapsulated in some test.

In *Assessment for Better Learning,* the report on assessment presented by the New Zealand Department of Education (1989), the following statement is made:

> In assessment of learning, it is doubtful that numbers or grades can be thought of as anything more than rough estimates of the things they seem to measure. All assessments of learning include subjective judgements and, as such, are inevitably liable to bias and error. The notions, for example, that IQ is an accurate measure of human thought or that a socio-economic index precisely defines the social condition of a family not only ignore this subjectivity but deny human uniqueness. We have no ruler for human thought and must accept the limits forced on us by this fact. (p. 9)

In this country, the National Association for the Education of Young Children also supports this position, and although some may say that the following excerpts from the position statement published by NAEYC (1988) applies only to younger children, I would strongly argue that it applies to all children. Childhood is not a coat that kids take off when they reach fourth grade. In *Testing of Young Children: Concerns and Cautions,* NAEYC states:

> Mass standardized testing of young children is potentially harmful to children educationally. Testing narrows the curriculum. Inevitably teachers teach to the test. Many of the important skills that children need to acquire in early childhood—self-esteem, social competence, desire to learn, self-discipline—are not easily measured by standardized tests. As

a result, social, emotional, moral, and physical development and learning are virtually ignored or given minor importance in schools with mandated testing programs.

Testing programs also harm children intellectually. Where test scores are stressed, the curriculum is often designed to ensure that children memorize facts and figures that can be easily addressed by a multiple-choice test. More challenging intellectual pursuits such as reading for information, composing stories, problem solving, and creative thinking are given less emphasis. But these abilities will be even more important in the future. Children need to learn how to learn, so that they are prepared to function in an ever-changing American society. . . . Standardized testing seldom provides information beyond what teachers and parents already know. The systematic observations of trained teachers and other professionals, in conjunction with information obtained from parents and other family members, are the best sources of information. (p. 9)

To move beyond the debate, it is essential that researchers and educators reexamine the "scientific" assumptions on which testing (irrespective of whether the tests emphasize word recognition or comprehension) is based. This means reevaluating the existing dominant theoretical framework, which is based upon notions of objective reality and inevitably leads to reductionism, and giving consideration to the development of a theoretical framework that acknowledges that our interpretations of language (and life) cannot be reduced to a series of competing logical structures or linear stage-theories. Prigogine and Stengers (1984) state:

In view of the complexity of the questions raised here, we can hardly avoid stating that the way in which biological and social evolution has traditionally been interpreted represents a particularly unfortunate use of the concepts and methods borrowed from physics—unfortunate because the area of physics where these concepts and methods are valid was very restricted, and *thus the analogies between them and social or economic phenomena are completely unjustified.* (p. 207, emphasis added)

The unfortunate consequences of the plagiarism of physical science paradigms for use in social science research is made evident by Turner (1989) in his re-analysis of the research studies that were used, and are still being used, in the reading field's "Great Debate" (see Carbo, 1988, and Chall, 1989). Turner writes of the "patched-up program evaluations," "randomized field experiments," and laboratory experiments, all of which have severe limitations, and many of which (I would say all) are fundamentally flawed. Again, it is the wrong debate. In taking paradigms from the physical sciences and applying them to the study of complexly structured human behaviors, we have had to resort to complicated simplifications, and these have resulted in the creation of pathologies—not in the lives of children, as is so often stated in our medicalized textbooks on learning, but in the ways in which we do science and study human learning.

The irony is that while the education field still uses the notion of objective reality, the physical sciences have long since abandoned the idea (Gleick, 1987; Johnston, 1989). Prigogine and Stengers (1984) write of the "irreducible multiplicity of representations," which they state:

> implies a departure from the classical notion of objectivity, since in the classical view the only "objective" description is the complete description of *the system as it is,* independent of how it is observed. . . . No single theoretical language articulating the variable to which a well-defined value can be attributed can exhaust the physical content of a system. Various possible languages and points of view about the system may be complementary. They all deal with the same reality, but it is impossible to reduce them to one single description. . . . The real lesson to be learned from the principle of complementarity, a lesson that can perhaps be transferred to other fields of knowledge, consists in emphasizing the wealth of reality, which overflows any single language, any single logical structure. *Each language can express only a part of reality.* (p. 225, emphasis added)

If we try to study and teach from the perspective of the learner, then the everyday lives of children provide practical demonstrations of the position held by Prigogine and Stengers. The diversity of complex social behavior demands that we acknowledge the multiplicity of representations that, even when combined in complimentary descriptions (biographic profiles) of children's learning, only capture a brief glimpse of the complexity of the symbol weaving that takes place in the problem-solving situations as children reconstruct the functions, uses, and forms of written language. If we look and then learn to see, perhaps at some future date we will come to realize the catastrophic effect that our traditional plans for progress and predictability have upon the lives of children. When we politicize learning and make state-by-state comparisons of reading achievement scores (Rothman, 1989), we leave administrators and teachers with no alternative but to teach to the test. Children's lives are altered, drilled, and skilled—the natural rhythm of their learning is changed to a solemn beat.

Writing about recent research on the heart, Browne (1989) reports that scientists have found that "a healthy heart must beat somewhat chaotically rather than in a perfectly predictable pattern." The caption reads, "A 'healthy heart dances,' but a dying one 'can merely march.'" In schools across the country children "merely march" as they try to keep in step with the perfectly predictable patterns of the deadly teach-test beat. But it does not have to be this way. In many schools teachers and administrators are working to keep children's learning alive. Often unrecognized, teachers are providing practical demonstrations that in public schools we can work from the child's perspective, and teachers can create classroom environments that support and enhance the literacy learning that takes place when children participate in the self-organization of complex problem-solving situations. In the Biographic Literacy Profiles Project we have already shown and continue to show that such teaching and learning is disciplined and systematic. We can cope with complexity, and we can use it to insure that children have the opportunity to participate in an educational community that will prepare them for the complexity of the learning situations they will encounter as they learn new dances and step out to a new beat.

POSTSCRIPT: TEACHING AS A SUBVERSIVE ACTIVITY

On September 16, 1991, I wrote the following memo to the members of the Biographic Literacy Profiles Project:

> In the last couple of years I think that we have begun to understand that the Biographic Literacy Profiles Project (affectionately known as "BLIPP") is as much about ourselves as it is about children. It is about teachers developing personal theories, about teachers using their practical knowledge and theoretical expertise, and about teachers recognizing themselves, and being recognized by others, as professionals in their classrooms, schools, and communities.
>
> Our realization that research by teachers is a significant way of knowing about teaching and learning is shared by Susan Lytle and Marilyn Cochran-Smith, who writes in a paper entitled "Teacher Research as a Way of Knowing" of the reconceptualization of *knowledge for teaching* that occurs when teachers are the ones who are doing the research. What follows are some key ideas from the paper written by Susan and Marilyn. They state:
>
> 1. We are arguing that we need to develop a different theory of knowledge for teaching, a different epistemology that regards inquiry by teachers themselves as a distinctive and important way of knowing about teaching.

    2. What is worth knowing about teaching would include what teachers, who are researchers in their own classrooms, can know through systematic subjectivity.

    3. In this different epistemology, teacher research, currently marginalized in the field, would contribute to a fundamental reconceptualization of the notion of knowledge for teaching.

Susan and Marilyn go on to write about teacher inquiry as a way for teachers to know their own knowledge, and they present six cases (stories) of teachers' explorations. Within this context Susan and Marilyn write of classrooms as *sites of inquiry.*

When we observe children and write descriptions of their observable literacy behaviors we are creating critical sites of inquiry in our classrooms and in our schools. This is what BLIPP is all about. Learning to observe children and then learning to construct descriptions of their observable literacy behaviors encourages us to look at ourselves and our personal and shared ways of knowing. It's amazing stuff when you stop to think about it!

It is now February 1992, and I have been rereading "Teaching Without Testing" and reflecting on the memos that I have written over the past few years to the teachers who have participated in the project. What impresses me most is the optimism of my writing. I really did believe that there was enough flexibility in the system for project teachers to work as researchers in their own classrooms. I know that the teachers believed this too. We were both disciplined and systematic. We based instruction on children's observable behaviors, we documented students' progress, and we accounted for the ways in which students were learning to read and write in school. They learned in authentic problem-solving situations that took into account the plurality of literacies that they would need to fully participate in American Society. Ours was a democratic ideal, theoretically grounded and practically situated, an "ad hoc-racy" whose practices were both excellent and equitable. We based instruction on what children could do, on our observations of their learning, and we tried to expand upon their understandings of themselves as learners. Above all we honored diversity, knowing that it was our combined interests, skills, and abilities that would enable children to work collaboratively in ways that would prepare them for the rapidly changing world of the twenty-first century.

If this seems to be a romantic picture, remember that we worked together at the time when the playwright Vaclav Havel became president of Czechoslovakia. It was a brief moment of unexpected opportunity. And so, as the Berlin Wall was chipped away, we chipped away at the dogma of standardized instructional practice and bureaucratic procedure that had ascribed pathological conditions to children, and that had forced many young people to drop out of the system. Bathed in the events that were taking place in the world, we began to think that the ideal of democratic education was within our reach. But as I said, it was a brief moment in time.

In every school district in which I am presently working there has been an increased interest in testing students. In one school district, the teachers were told that the Gates-McGinitie reading test would be administered to *all* students beginning with first grade. The teachers were not consulted about the decision. In this same school district, the decision was made that there were too many second-grade teachers, so one of the teachers was "redesignated" as a "permanent substitute teacher" one month after the beginning of the school year. Her students were divided up and sent to the remaining second-grade classrooms. In another school district, massive budget cuts mean that project teachers do not even know if they will have jobs next year. And in yet another district, the hiring of a new school superintendent resulted in a change in administrative policies and a new emphasis on teaching to prepare students for the California Achievement Tests.

The CATs became an issue for another school district when the State Board of Education denied the request of one of the project schools to continue working a four-day week. The four-day week (students' instructional time was from 8:00 A.M. until 3:30 P.M.) had been in place for ten years. One Friday a month was reserved by teachers for curriculum planning meetings and in-service education; on most other Fridays teachers went to school to participate in ad hoc meetings, to review students' work, and to plan events for the following school week.

Peter Sweet, who is principal of the school, told me that when the State Board of Education was reviewing their request to continue the four-day week, both teachers and parents had reflected on the benefits of the arrangement. Peter said that since 1985, *not one student* who had received the majority of his or her education at the elementary school had subsequently dropped out of high school. Every student had finished school! Teachers found there was more time for collaboration both with other faculty members and with students, parents overwhelmingly approved of the arrangement, and the community was supportive. The State School Board was provided with all of this information, and yet without visiting the school when classes were in progress, and without consulting the teachers (who include Mary Benton, Kathy Matthews, and Bruce Turnquist, whom you have read about in this chapter), the Board arbitrarily reorganized the school week because of the CAT results, which the Board felt should be higher. No consideration was given to the lack of emphasis placed on these tests by the school. The tests were administered solely as a state requirement that had to be fulfilled. The test results did nothing to enhance any instructional practices, so no emphasis was placed on their administration, and no relevance was ascribed to the test results by the school.

In an article on the school that was published in the *Principal* in September 1991, researcher Helen Featherstone asks if the shift to the four-day week transformed the school. She writes, "Is the fruitful use of free time an essential precondition—or a product—of change?" After participating in the Project, my answer is that "free" time is both a precondition and a product of change. Change takes place in schools when teachers work in environments in which they can identify problems and explore solutions. This takes time.

Ironically, as Helen Featherstone's article on the four-day week was published, the teachers and children returned to the school to begin a new year of five-day weeks. The effect on the teachers has been devastating. The day is fractured, and they have less time to meet. As one teacher put it, "People don't get together to talk anymore. The sense of isolation is really strong." From my conversations with the teachers in the school, it would seem that the biggest difficulty is that the State Board's decision (like so many recent decisions in project schools) challenges the teachers' professional identity. Decisions are being made that critically affect the ways in which they teach, and yet they themselves are not a part of the decision-making process.

In project schools across New Hampshire, decisions about the standardization of programs and student assessment are being made without the opinions of teachers being taken into consideration. Their voices don't count, so veteran teachers who have worked all of their professional lives to improve the quality of education for their students are talking about the futility of that commitment. One such teacher spoke of the "uncertainty" and of "feeling threatened." She said, "We are not being supported by the administration, and we've become locked into standardized tests that don't assess what we need to know about children." Other teachers talk of "survival," of "emotional exhaustion," of their "frustration," and of their lives being "out of control." Some schools are more affected than others, but as one teacher commented when she read what I was writing, "the scenarios are different, but the stories are basically all the same."

Like Peter Sweet, most of the principals of the Project have supported the teachers and children by taking an active role in the political decision-making process at both the local and state levels. At the present time, Cathy Hamblett is actively opposing the development of a statewide third-grade testing program. This week she testified before New Hampshire's House and Senate Education Subcommittees. She spoke to them of the ways in which teachers in her school worked with the children in their classrooms, and she spoke of the ways in which they are assessing children's learning. Later, Cathy talked of trying to act as a "buffer" between the teachers in her school and the policy makers who are making critical decisions that affect the ways in which children are learning in school.

The proposed statewide testing about which Cathy testified came to our attention in the summer of 1991. On July 8 of that year the New Hampshire State Board of Education sent a memo to the Commissioner of Education proposing that the reading skills of all third-grade children be tested. It is difficult to ignore the coercive language contained in this statement. The Board outlined its intentions as follows:

> Using in-house knowledge, The Governor's Task Force Report and the National Goals as anchors, the Department will be asked to issue a set of *rigorous* objectives. These objectives should identify *concrete areas of knowledge* and detailed description of skills that *must be* mastered by the completion of the primary grades, thereby insuring future academic success. (p. 2)

At the request of the State Board of Education, a task force was created to "develop a detailed plan and schedule of activities for a statewide assessment program" (Marston, 1992, p. 2, emphasis added). There were subcommittees on reporting results, on objectives and standards, and on assessment tools (which in the report of the task force was noted in brackets to be the subcommittee on tests). The task force recommended "mastery and performance tests" in reading, language, and mathematics to be administered to all third-grade children—which was the recommendation of the State Board even *before* the task force was formed. At a meeting held at the legislative offices in Concord on January 29, 1992, members of the task force presented their plan to the House and Senate Education Committees. Among the reasons that were given for the administration of statewide tests at the end of the third-grade year was that the test results could be used by school districts to identify children who needed remediation *before* they took the national tests in fourth grade.

Teachers from the Project are writing letters and testifying in an attempt to change the minds of the legislature, which, we are told, is quite likely to support statewide third-grade testing. The teachers know it will be an uphill battle to persuade the committees, because at the local, state, and national level testing has become a national fetish that, Michelle Fine argues, fills public talk, shapes public policy and inhibits public imagination (see Fine, 1990; 1992). Many of the children that have participated in the Project will pass the test, but many of the children with whom we work will not. As with other tests that are administered to them, the ways in which they learn will go unnoticed. They will be tested, then remediated, and then retested and re-remediated until they reach a point when they realize that they are excluded from participation in school, so they will drop out, disadvantaged by the social inequality of such a system.

Perhaps it is from witnessing at first hand what happens to children who do not "make the grade" on standardized tests that keeps teachers from returning to old ways of teaching. In a letter to me one teacher writes, "I don't want to return to the old safe way—the sequential skills taught in isolation, the small pull-out groups [of children] that all need the same treatment to fix their problems. I have been encouraged to think, to learn, and to apply what I have come to know." In a telephone call another teacher says, "Everything has changed, but I can't go back," and then talks about the new emphasis on basals and end-of-unit tests, which she refuses to use. She says, "I'm not afraid. I can substantiate what I'm doing. The training and philosophy work."

Last night I telephoned Kathy Matthews and shared what I was writing in this postscript. When I got to the piece about the four-day week, she said that she felt that it was important to add that while no emphasis was placed on the California Achievement Tests by the school, it *had* administered the Stanford Achievement Tests, which was one of the state criteria for monitoring children's progress. "The Board ignored the results of those tests," she said, "and focused on the California Achievement Tests instead." When I reached the end of the last paragraph Kathy commented, "It's hard to undo the thinking about children's strengths and start thinking about their weaknesses." Then, speaking specifically about the project, she said, "It's made a difference for us and it's made a difference for the kids, but given the ways in which educational decisions are made, the reality of making it work is overwhelming." Kathy added, "I'd finally reached a point where I could be the teacher I wanted to be. How can they make me regress? Would they ask a physician to go back ten years?"

At a project meeting that we held last year, one state official who had come to make a presentation commented that we should "go underground." I have often thought about this advice, especially when I listen to teachers and principals who speak of the changes imposed on them at both the state and local levels. There is no doubt that for some, teaching has become a subversive activity. But we still have not "gone underground." Our work continues. We are developing new note-taking procedures, new literacy analysis grids, and new ways of documenting the complexity of problem solving. We have focused our attention on literacy and the mental health of young children, and on developing biographic literacy profiles of children that illustrate the ways in which children who have been sexually and physically abused use print to help them cope with the uncertainties in their everyday lives. As we have focused on children about whom we are seriously concerned, we have found that even five-year-olds in kindergarten have literacy configurations that they use to help them cope with the critical events that have taken place in their young lives.

We are also focusing our attention on developing alternative assessment procedures for children who have entered the special education loop. Working collaboratively, we are collecting information about children as they participate in their regular classrooms. Our observations have become more focused and our note-taking procedures more intensive, but the process is essentially the same. Once these data are collected, decisions are made about other forms of data that may be required. We have made videos of children participating in specific learning activities, and we have made audio recordings of conversations, which provide children with the opportunity to reflect on learning tasks. Most important, we talk with children, we ask them about the ways in which they are learning, and we ask them about what help they themselves think they need. On several occasions, the data we have collected has been used by the school's child study team as they have considered whether or not to code a child. The results of these efforts have been mixed. Sometimes it is hard to convince a school psychologist that the difficulties a child is encountering are socially constructed, especially when the psychologist listens to an alternative assessment presentation and then dismisses it by putting the WISC on the table and saying, "Now let's look at the hard data." But still we have not given up, for on other occasions changes *have* been made that provide new opportunities for children to learn in school. This semester we are continuing to develop new procedures, and we are trying to present our findings in ways that make sense to other professionals who presently don't share our philosophy of children's learning. As Kathy Matthews says, "It takes an audience that is willing to listen."

Fortunately, there are some policy makers and educators who *are* willing to listen. In California, the State Department of Education is developing alternative assessment procedures for special education, and I have been talking with California policy makers about the teacher-researchers with whom I am working in New Hampshire. They have read "Teaching Without Testing," they are interested in instructional assessment, and they are exploring the possibilities presented by the ideas. In Hawaii, approximately 180 Chapter One teachers participated in an institute that focused on the ways in which we are collecting information about children. At that institute, Dr. Donald Enoki told the teachers that if change is going to take place, it is teachers who will make the changes. Dr. Enoki told the teachers attending the institute that they were "one of the educational system's most valuable assets." He said:

> Your role as teacher-researchers is extremely important. . . . No longer can we depend on what others have told us about our children's progress—the test makers, the test publishers, and the psychometricians. We know that only what classroom teachers have developed, taught, and assessed are the true and meaningful measures of what a student knows and doesn't know. (pp. 4–5)

What teachers do actually matters. Their ideas count. They are agents for change in our schools. However tough the situation, however subversive the activity becomes, trying to see the world from the child's perspective has changed our minds.

Our ways of seeing are democratic. Unfortunately, they are not bureaucratic. Except in rare circumstances, I no longer believe that it is possible to be both, because when it becomes bureaucratic the struggle is not about pedagogy, it's about power. About who controls the activities that occur in schools. About who controls who participates in American society. About who controls the power base of the twenty-first century. In a telephone conversation, Kathy said that what is happening is that policy makers are redefining public schools to keep control in a very few hands. The way to tighten this control is to institute more tests that both define the curriculum and restrict innovative practices at the local level (i.e., teacher research). Kathy says, "It's easy for policy makers to talk about innovation, but it would be difficult for them to let it occur." What Kathy says makes sense. To allow innovation to occur, policy makers would have to give up control and share with teachers the responsibility for what happens to children in school. They would have to live with the uncertainty of knowing that it is teachers and children who are the agents of change, who will be working together to create an educational system that is both excellent and equitable. Children who are poor and children of color would have a chance to succeed. Their voices would be heard. Children whose young lives have been damaged by life's circumstances would have the opportunity to recover. *All* children would have the opportunity both to define problems and to solve problems, and they would have the opportunity to work collaboratively with diverse groups of people in ways that would allow them to be a part of the democratic ideal.

It is now December 1992. The New Hampshire State School Board (an appointed, autonomous body) continues to insist on the development of a series of tests to be administered to third-grade students in New Hampshire's public schools. The State School Board has also decided to cut the minimum standards of education in the state. Because of the inequities in school funding (per-pupil expenditures ranges from $2,899 to $9,554), there is no doubt that children living in property-poor districts will suffer because of the Board's irresponsible actions. Project teachers have joined other teachers across the state who are protesting these cuts, but their voices go unheard. Judy Thayer (who was originally appointed by former governor John Sununu and is now the chair of the State Board) has made it clear that she considers teachers nothing more than a special interest group. She said, "They are special interest because they get paid by the system. They are people who have something to gain or lose by this proposal." It is difficult for me to imagine project teachers as a "special interest" group except as a group with a special interest in helping children. To paraphrase Pat Shannon, the struggle continues.

PARTICIPANTS IN THE BIOGRAPHIC LITERACY PROFILES PROJECT

Terri Apgar, Jody Baker, Ed Barnwell, Laurie Barr, Mary Benton, Debbie Boisvert, Lori Bresnahan, Sharron Cadieux, Linda Carter, Sue Caswell, Sally Codd, Martha Dahl, Kathy Donovan, Lisa Drogue, Brenda Eaves, Davita Fortier, Ruthanne Fyfe, Terry Grady, Cathy Hamblett, Betty Jack, Shirley Joyce, Marcy Mager, Bob Magher, Betty Marston, Kathy Matthews,

Karen May, Bonnie Mulcahy, Patty Nicols, Joanne Parise, Donna Parmenter, Sue Phillips, Prudence Potter, Carla Press, Lee Proctor, Helen Schotanus, Nancy Shute, Ann Marie Spack, Katherine Sullivan, Susan Sullivan, Peter Sweet, Bruce Turnquist, Leigh Walls, Linda Walsh, Sharon Williams, Regina Woodland, Nancy White, and Mary Yates.

We would like to thank the parents of the children in the six schools participating in the Project for their support and encouragement. We appreciate the opportunity we have been given to include examples of their children's work in this report. In presenting the biographic profiles, all names have been changed. However, on some occasions, when particular biographic literacy events are described, first names have been used with parental permission. We would also like to take this opportunity to thank the members of the local school boards for providing the financial support necessary for the schools to participate in the project.

WORKS CITED AND PROJECT BIBLIOGRAPHY

1989. *Assessment for Better Learning: A Public Discussion Document.* Wellington, New Zealand: Department of Education.

Atwell, N. 1987. *In the Middle: Writing, Reading, and Learning with Adolescents.* Portsmouth, NH: Boynton/Cook Publishers.

Barnes, D. 1992. *From Communication to Curriculum.* Portsmouth, NH: Boynton/Cook Publishers.

Brown, R. 1989. "Testing and Thoughtfulness." *Educational Leadership* (April):31–33.

Browne, M. 1989. "Heartbeat Predictability Is Worse than Chaos." *New York Times* (January 17):C9.

Cadieux, S. 1989. *Assessment in a Process Oriented Classroom: Practice, Dangers and Potential.* Unpub. Master's Thesis, Antioch College, New Hampshire.

Carbo, M. 1988. "Debunking the Great Phonics Myth." *Phi Delta Kappan* (November):226–40.

Carraher, T. 1986. "From Drawings to Buildings: Working with Mathematical Scales." *International Journal of Behavioral Development* 9:527–44.

Carraher, T., D. Carraher, and A. Schliemann. 1985. "Mathematics in the Streets and in the Schools." *British Journal of Developmental Psychology* 3:21–29.

Chall, J. 1989. "Learning to Read: The Great Debate Twenty Years Later—A response to 'Debunking the Great Phonics Myth.'" *Phi Delta Kappan* (March):521–38

Coles, G. 1987. *The Learning Mystique: A Critical Look at Learning Disabilities.* New York: Pantheon Books.

Crowell, S. 1990. "A New Way of Thinking: The Challenge of the Future." *Educational Leadership* (September):60–63.

de la Rocha, O. 1985. "The Reorganization of Arithmetic Practice in the Kitchen." *Anthropology and Education Quarterly* 16:193–98.

Doll, W. 1989. "Complexity in the Classroom." *Educational Leadership* (September):65–70.

Duckworth, E. 1987. *The Having of Wonderful Ideas and Other Essays on Teaching and Learning.* New York: Teachers College Press.

Dyson, A. 1986. "Transitions and Tensions: Interrelationships Between the Drawing, Talking, and Dictating of Young Children." *Research in the Teaching of English* 20:379–409.

Enoki, Donald. 1992. Introductory Remarks Made at a Chapter One Four-Day Institute. Honolulu (January).

Featherstone, Helen. 1991. "The Rewards of a Four-Day School Week." *Principal* (September) 71(1)28–31.

Ferreiro, E. 1984. "The Underlying Logic of Literacy Development." In H. Goelman, et al., eds., *Awakening to Literacy*. Portsmouth, NH: Heinemann.

Fine, Michelle. 1990. "The Public in Public Schools; The Social Constriction/ Construction of a Moral Community." *Journal of Social Issues* 46(1)107– 19.

Fine, Michelle. 1992. "Deconstructing the 'At Risk' High School Population: Public Controversies and Subjugated Non Controversies." In R. Wollens, ed. *Children at Risk*. Albany, NY: SUNY Press.

Gardner, H. 1985. *Frames of Mind: The Theory of Multiple Intelligences*. New York: Basic Books.

Geertz, C. 1983. *Local Knowledge: Further Essays in Interpretive Anthropology*. New York: Basic Books.

Genishi, C. 1985. "Observing Communicative Performance in Young Children." In A. Jaggar and M. Smith-Burke, eds., *Observing the Language Learner*. Urbana, IL: IRA/NCTE.

Gleick, J. 1987. *Chaos: Making a New Science*. New York: Penguin Books.

———. 1989. "Chaos." *Teacher Magazine* (September–October):46–49.

Goelman, H., A. Oberg, and F. Smith, eds. 1984. *Awakening to Literacy*. Portsmouth, NH: Heinemann.

Goodman, K., P. Shannon, Y. Freeman, and S. Murphy. 1988. *Report Card on Basal Readers*. Katonah, NY: Richard C. Owen Publishers.

Goodman, Y., D. Watson, and C. Burke. 1987. *Reading Miscue Inventory: Alternative Procedures*. Katonah, NY: Richard C. Owen Publishers.

Gospodarek, Fran. 1989. "Conway School Board Hears Special Ed. Report." *Carroll County Independent*. (September 20)A8.

Gould, S. 1989. *Wonderful Life: The Burgess Shale and the Nature of History*. New York: W.W. Norton.

Graves, D. 1984. *A Researcher Learns to Write*. Portsmouth, NH: Heinemann.

Green, J. and C. Wallat. 1981. *Ethnography and Language in Educational Settings*. Norwood, NJ: Ablex.

Greene, M. 1978. *Landscapes of Learning*. New York: Teachers College Press.

Griffin, D. 1988. *The Reenchantment of Science: Postmodern Proposals*. Albany, NY: State University of New York Press.

Hall, N. 1987. *The Emergence of Literacy*. Portsmouth, NH: Heinemann.

Hansen, J., T. Newkirk, and D. Graves, eds. 1985. *Breaking Ground: Teachers Relate Reading and Writing in the Elementary School*. Portsmouth, NH: Heinemann.

Harste, J., V. Woodward, and C. Burke. 1984. *Language Stories & Literacy Lessons*. Portsmouth, NH: Heinemann.

Hawking, S. 1988. *A Brief History of Time: From the Big Bang to Black Holes*. New York: Bantam Books.

Heath, S. 1983. *Ways with Words*. Cambridge: Cambridge University Press.

Hiebert, E., and R. Calfee. 1989. "Advancing Academic Literacy Through Teacher's Assessments." *Educational Leadership* 46(7):50–54.

Holdaway, D. 1979. *The Foundations of Literacy*. Sydney: Ashton Scholastic.

Ianni, F. 1989. *The Search for Structure: A Report on American Youth Today*. New York: The Free Press.

Jervis, K. 1989. "Daryl Takes a Test." *Educational Leadership* 46(7):10–15.

Johnston, P. 1987. "Assessing Process, and the Process of Assessment, in the Language Arts." In J. Squire, ed., *The Dynamics of Language Learning*. Urbana: IL: ERIC, 335–357.

Johnston, P. 1989. "Constructive Evaluation and the Improvement of Teaching and Learning." *Teachers College Record* 90(4):509–28.

Juliebo, M. and J. Elliott. 1987. "The Child Fits the Label." *Elements* 19(1):19–21.

Langness, L. and H. Levine. 1986. *Culture and Retardation*. Boston: D. Reidel.

Lave, J. 1985. "The Social Organization of Knowledge and Practice: A symposium." *Anthropology and Education Quarterly* 16:171–76.

Lave, J., M. Murtaugh, and O. de la Rocha. 1984. "The Dialectic of Arithmetic in Grocery Shopping." In B. Rogoff and J. Lave, eds., *Everyday Cognition: Its Development in Social Context*, pp. 67–95. Cambridge, MA: Harvard University Press.

Lieberman, L. 1984. *Preventing Special Education for Those Who Don't Need it*. Weston, MA: Nob Hill Press.

Lytle, Susan and Marilyn Cochran-Smith. 1992. "Teacher Research as a Way of Knowing." *Harvard Educational Review* 52(4):447–74.

Mandelbrot, B. 1977. *The Fractal Geometry of Nature*. New York: W. H. Reeman.

Marston, Charles H. 1992. A Framework for the New Hampshire Assessment Plan Executive Summary. January 15.

Matthew, K. 1990. "Responding to the Call." In N. Atwell, ed., *Workshop 2: Beyond the Basal*. Portsmouth, NH: Heinemann.

Meek, M. 1986. *Learning to Read*. Portsmouth, NH: Heinemann.

Mehan, H., A. Hertweck, and J. Heihls. 1986. *Handicapping the Handicapped: Decision Making in Students' Educational Careers.* Stanford, CA: Stanford University Press.

Newkirk, T. 1989. *More than Stories: The Range of Children's Writing.* Portsmouth, NH: Heinemann.

Newman, J., ed. 1985. *Whole Language: Theory in Use.* Portsmouth, NH: Heinemann.

Opie, I. and P. Opie. 1959. *The Lore and Language of School Children.* Oxford: Oxford University Press.

Oransu, J., R. McDermott, A. Boykin, and the Laboratory of Comparative Human Cognition. 1977. "A Critique of Test Standardization." *Social Policy* 8(2):61–67.

Polanyi, M. 1983. *The Tacit Dimension.* Gloucester, MA: Peter Smith.

Prigogine, I. and I. Stengers. 1984. *Order Out of Chaos: Man's New Dialogue with Nature.* New York: Bantam Books.

Raloff, J. 1989. "In-school Breakfast Improve Test Scores." *Science News* (October 14):16,247.

Resnick, L. 1987. "Learning in School and Out." *Educational Researcher* 16(9):13–20.

Rogoff, B. and J. Lave, eds. 1984. *Everyday Cognition: Its Development in Social Context.* Cambridge, MA: Harvard University Press.

Rose, M. 1989. *Lives on the Boundary: The Struggles and Achievements of America's Underprepared.* New York: The Free Press.

Rothman, R. 1989. NAEP Board Is Seeking a Consensus on Reading." *Education Week* (September 27):7.

Sacks, O. 1989. *Seeing Voices: A Journey into the World of the Deaf.* Berkeley: University of California Press.

Schickedanz, J. 1986. *More than the ABC's: The Early Stages of Reading and Writing.* Washington, DC: National Association for the Education of Young Children.

Schrader, C. 1989. "Written Language Use Within the Context of Young Children's Symbolic Play." *Early Childhood Research Quarterly* 4(2):225–44.

Schultz, J. 1989. "Unit News, Council on Anthropology and Education, the Future." *Anthropology Newsletter* 30(7):10.

Scribner, S. 1984. "Studying Working Intelligence." In B. Rogoff and J. Lave, eds., *Everyday Cognition: Its Development in Social Context,* pp. 9–40. Cambridge, MA: Harvard University Press.

———. 1986. "Thinking in Action: Some Characteristics of Practical Thought." In Steinberg, R.J. and R.K. Wagner, eds., *Practical Intelligence: Nature and Origins of Competence in the Everyday World.* New York: Cambridge University Press.

Shannon, P. 1989. *Broken Promises: Reading Instruction in Twentieth-Century America.* Granby, MA: Bergin & Garvey Publishers.

Shepard, L. 1989. "Why We Need Better Assessments." *Educational Leadership* 46(7):4–9.

Sloan, D., ed. 1984. *Toward the Recovery of Wholeness: Knowledge, Education, and Human Values.* New York: Teachers College Press.

Sternberg, R., and R. Wagner. 1986. *Practical Intelligence: Nature and Origins of Competence in the Everyday World.* New York: Cambridge University Press.

Taylor, D. 1983. *Family Literacy: Young Children Learning to Read and Write.* Portsmouth, NH: Heinemann.

———. 1988. "Ethnographic Educational Evaluation for Children, Families, and Schools." *Theory into Practice* 27(1):67–76.

———. 1989. "Toward a Unified Theory of Literacy Learning and Instructional Practices" *Phi Delta Kappan* (November):184–93.

———. 1991a. "From the Child's Point of View: Alternate Approaches to Assessment." In J. Roderick and J. Green, eds., *Developing Context-Responsive Approaches to Assessment,* NCRE. Urbana, IL: NCTE.

———. 1991b. "Family Literacy: Text as Context." In James Flood et al., eds., *Handbook of Research on Teaching the English Language Arts.* New York: MacMillan.

Taylor, D. and C. Dorsey-Gaines. 1988. *Growing Up Literate: Learning from Inner-City Families.* Portsmouth, NH: Heinemann.

Taylor, D. and D. Strickland. 1989. "Learning from Families: Implications for Educators and Policy Makers. In J. Allen and J. Mason, eds., *Risk Makers, Risk Takers, Risk Breakers: Reducing the Risks for Young Literacy Learners.* Portsmouth, NH: Heinemann.

Teale, W. and E. Sulzby. 1986. *Emergent Literacy: Writing and Reading.* Norwood, NJ: Ablex.

1988. *Testing of Young Children: Concerns and Cautions.* Washington, DC: National Association for the Education of Young Children.

Turner, R. 1989. "The 'Great' Debate—Can both Carbo and Chall Be Right?" *Phi Delta Kappan* (December): 276–83.

Vygotsky, L. 1978. *Mind in Society.* Cambridge, MA: Harvard University Press.

Wolf, D. 1989. "Portfolio Assessment: Sampling Student Work." *Educational Leadership.* 35–39.

4

EARLY LITERACY DEVELOPMENT AND THE MENTAL HEALTH OF YOUNG CHILDREN

It is the intimate and necessary relation between
actual experience and education that we must
come to understand.

W e were standing around a table sharing the biographic literacy
profiles of the children in our classrooms for whom we were
especially concerned. On numerous occasions teachers attending
BLIPP summer institutes had demonstrated in practical ways the
depth of their theoretical understanding of what it means to learn
about children's early literacy development from the child's point of
view. But when you learn about language in this way, you also learn
about life, and some children's lives are so fragile that the experience
becomes one of sharing in human tragedies that in many ways we are
powerless to change.

We were meeting a few days after the end of the school year, and
for some teachers it was too soon for them to talk about what had
happened during the year in the lives of some of the children with
whom they had worked. They stood back from the table, arms folded
as if to shut out the accounts that were being given of the struggles of
other children whose devastating life stories had critically affected
the ways in which they learned to read and write.[1] Some teachers
cried. None of us were prepared. Our professional lives did not provide us with the protective shield that we needed to cope with the life
experiences of the children from whom we were learning.

It was not that their life experiences were new to us, because
there have always been children in our classrooms who have been
sexually or physically abused, or who are suffering from fetal alcohol
syndrome, but the more we have learned to look the more we see.
Problems that remained hidden in an exercise on a workbook page
become visible when children are given the opportunity to develop
their own literacy configurations by using print in ways that make
sense to them in their everyday lives. Moreover, the problems seem
to be increasing in complexity. In our classrooms there are children
without homes who come to school from shelters, and children who

during their fetal development were affected by their mother's crack-cocaine or heroin addiction. In addition, many children are malnourished and are growing up without adequate medical attention. But for the most part, we still continue to separate what happens to them in their everyday lives from what happens as they learn to read and write in school. Children and language are disconnected, lives that are lived are cut off from words that are spoken, and the topic at issue is arbitrarily transformed or recreated so that our attention is focused on the task of simply reading words.

The problem that we face in education is that we often seek immediate and simple solutions to complex problems. These quick-fix solutions are often presented as packaged "methods," "programs," or "techniques" for instruction. But unfortunately, as Ferreiro (1990) so aptly states:

> The tradition of all these "pedagogical gadgets" is behavioristic. These instructional materials are produced, organized, and administered with the idea that adults can control the learning process, that they can decide when it is time to start learning, what is easy to learn and what is difficult to learn, what is "readable," what is "teachable," and what is the right order for presenting stimuli. (p. 24)

It is from this behavioristic approach to early literacy development that Adams (1990),[2] in a book commissioned by the U.S. Department of Education to fulfill a congressional mandate, writes:

> If low-achieving students can be brought up to grade level within the first three years of school, their reading performance tends not to revert but to stay at grade level thenceforth; if we fail to bring students' reading to grade level within those first few years, the likelihood of their ever catching up is slim, even with extra funding and special programs. (p. 27)

For those educators who accept this proposition, getting the stimuli in the right order becomes of paramount importance. As Adams states, for "children who enter school with next to no relevant knowledge about print . . . mastery of the symbol-sound relations will require more study" (p. 239). The trick, as Adams presents it, is to provide "the right amount of practice" (p. 239). But unfortunately, as Adams also makes abundantly clear, there is no consensus, even among the proponents of this traditional approach to the study of early literacy development, on the right order in which to introduce sound-symbol relationships (p. 245).

Adams herself presents an excellent example of the lack of consensus when she writes about the different approaches to the teaching of symbol-sound relationships adopted by various programs. She explains that while many programs focus on consonants first, in some the initial focus is on vowels, and that within this latter group of programs some focus on short vowels first, while others begin with long vowels. Adams goes on to explain that beginning with consonants creates difficulties because some consonants (for example, *b, d, p, t*) cannot be elongated or even spoken without the support of a vowel sound, and that beginning with short or long vowels presents other difficulties. For example, she notes, "In most words, the 'long' sound of a vowel is signaled by relatively complex but only semireliable spelling clues" (p. 247).

Such word-splitting machinations do nothing more than create an artificial complexity that makes no sense whatsoever in *real* classrooms where *real* teachers help *real* children to read and write. In classrooms, teachers and children find themselves in an infinite number of learning situations, and these situations are constantly changing. Much of what affects early literacy development is not covered or even mentioned in books on literacy. This is most certainly the case for the research studies that form the basis for Adams' analysis of early literacy development. The critical life-changing circumstances of the everyday lives of young children such as those that are faced by the teachers attending our Summer Institute on literacy are rarely mentioned. Language and life are separated. Children are labeled low-achieving, slow-learning, learning-disabled, normal, nonmainstream, culturally mainstream, and, in some texts, low income prereaders. What is a low income prereader?

In studies of reading and writing that so often begin with words, children are unknown, and the circumstances of their everyday lives are unspecified. Lost in anonymity, their faces are masked by categorized conditions on which educational researchers have focused their attention. Under these circumstances, teachers have no way of speaking about literacy and the lives of children. But what happens if the child is unmasked? What happens if instead of beginning with *words* teachers are given the opportunity to begin with the *child?*

Meet Nicola, a kindergarten child.

NICOLA: A BIOGRAPHIC LITERACY PROFILE OF A KINDERGARTEN CHILD

The following portrait of Nicola is a biographic literacy profile documenting a year of her life. It is long and detailed, necessarily so, for there are no percentiles that can document the complexity of her

early literacy development and there are no labels that can ade-
quately describe the role that literacy plays in her everyday life. The
ways in which Nicola is learning to use print calls into question the
invariant, linear, cognitive models of reading that ignore the everyday
lives of children. By juxtaposing Nicola's biographic literacy profile
with the highly misleading pronouncements of the reading psychologists favored by Adams, what becomes clear is that their theoretical
explanations of reading development do not hold up when applied to
a single child.

Sharron, Nicola's teacher, began in a quiet voice.[3] "Nicola is a
child that I had in my kindergarten class this year. And she is a child
who was sexually and physically abused by her father." Sharron explained that Nicola's father was no longer in the picture, and that
when Nicola began school is September she was living with her
mother and her mother's boyfriend. Sharron told us that Nicola
called her mother's boyfriend "Daddy." She paused, and then as she
spread Nicola's work out on the table she told us, "Partway through
the year that daddy left and that was a major upheaval."

Looking at the papers on the table Sharron said, "At the beginning of the year I really wasn't focusing on any literacy development.
I was focusing on trying to contain the situation. She would strike out
against the children. She would push and shove and call them names
and things like that. She came in the middle of September, and it
wasn't until I sat down in the winter and looked through all her things
that I realized how much she focused on print."

Sharron elaborated. "In the beginning her drawings were not
very representational." She put an example of Nicola's early work on
the table. It was a mimeographed sheet of paper, dated September
12, 1989, on which Sharron had reproduced "When I am at school I
like to ———." There was a crayon mark and a primitive person
drawn beneath it. In the bottom left-hand corner Sharron had written
"play in housekeeping," which was what Nicola had said to Sharron
as they talked about what she liked to do at school. Linking Nicola's
experience of place with the literacy activity, Sharron said, "This is
'When I'm at school I like to play in housekeeping.' That was where
she anchored herself. She was always in the housekeeping area, generally playing alongside other children, interacting in a very superfi-
cial way with the other children."

We talked about writing. Sharron told us that Nicola could write
the letters in her name.[4] But, she explained, Nicola "was never quite
sure how to put them in order." Sharron then added that Nicola began
to use the print in the classroom and that "later on she was able to

find a place where her name was and copy that." Sharron showed us
the pieces of paper that she had collected on which Nicola had written her name. Then she opened Nicola's journal and flipped through
the pages so we could all see the entries Nicola had made. "She
didn't choose to write in her journal very often," Sharron said, "but
she wrote in lots of other ways, and she wrote a lot at home and
brought things in." Sharron placed another example of Nicola's writing on the table in front of us and continued, "She wrote on whatever
she could get. This says 'I made it for you.' You see? These are her
drawings. This is actually one of the rare times when she attempted
to draw people." Sharron pointed at the figures. "This is me and my
husband."

I asked Sharron if Nicola had met her husband, and Sharron told
us that she hadn't.

Kathy, another teacher in the project, asked, "How old was Nicola when she was abused? Had it been recent or earlier in her life?"

Sharron replied that it was about two years before she had come
to school.

Kathy said, "So she was probably three?"

Sharron nodded; then, placing another piece of paper, dated September 28, 1989, on the table, she continued. "This is a picture" and
"That's a house," she said, reading her written account of what Nicola had told her as she had shown Sharron her work. Sharron read,
"I writed it," and then explained, "She wanted me to read it, and I
asked her what it said and she said, 'I don't know.'" Then Sharron
drew our attention to the "very letterlike characters" and added,
"She wrote that way a lot, with a few real letter kind of forms coming
in." She placed another piece of paper on the table. "This says, 'God
Jesus please come with me.'"

Summarizing September and October, Sharron said, "In the fall
she brought lots and lots of things from home, or from wherever she
got them," and then she drew a contrast with the work that Nicola
did in her journal. Placing the journal on the table Sharron said,
"This is her journal. As I said, she didn't do a lot in her journal."
She flipped through the pages. "Her pictures are," she hesitated,
"very gross motor kinds of things. But she would label them and she
would tell me generally what they were." Sharron illustrated her
statement by showing the teachers one of Nicola's drawings. Nicola
had told her that the picture was of a foot with letterlike forms superimposed on top of it. Sharron had written exactly what Nicola had
said: "It says, 'It's a foot.'" Sharron turned through the pages, stop-
ping occasionally to elaborate on Nicola's drawings and writings. She

talked about one page in the journal, dated November 16, 1989, on which Nicola had drawn four recognizable flowers and had written the letter *F* (Figure 4–1). "I had shown her how to make an *f* for *flowers*," Sharron said. Turning to another page she said, "Someone had brought in a letter stencil, which she liked a lot." On other pages, Sharron commented, "That's 'a house,'" and on another, "That's 'a carpet.'"

Sharron put the journal aside and returned to the pieces of paper that she had collected and kept in Nicola's portfolio. She said that Nicola was involved in many other literacy events such as bringing in notes that she had produced at home and papers that she had found. Sharron showed the teachers one such piece of paper. It was a mimeographed list of children's names on which Nicola had made a list of letters and letterlike forms in such a way that they resembled a list of words (HnM, HBnn, PBnn). "She had apparently picked it up in the school yard," Sharron explained. "It was some child's paper, and she filled it in with her letters. She said, 'I made it for you.' And when I asked her what it said, she said, 'I made it. That page doesn't say anything. I just wrote it.' But she filled the whole thing in."

Following her comments on Nicola picking up papers that had been discarded in the playground, Sharron returned to the social events that took place in the classroom. "There were lots of complaints from the other children," she said. "And also from parents because she took things." Sharron paused, as if reliving events that had taken place. "Things were very important to her," she said. "One day I was helping her on with her raincoat, and she had a marker and a post-it pad in her hand, and she said, 'They're mine,' and I said, 'No, they're mine,' and she said, 'Okay.' I mean, she didn't really have any idea that that wasn't appropriate."

Sharron moved on. She placed a paper on the table. On it was drawn a sharklike fish with jagged teeth and fins. Again Sharron had written in pencil on the paper exactly what Nicola had told her when she showed her the paper: "This is a fish. It doesn't say it. It don't say nothing." "She didn't draw it," Sharron said. Then she added, "But she said she did."

"So someone drew it for her," I said, and then I asked if it was someone at home or at school.

Sharron laughed. "Well she didn't tell me that because she said she drew it."

For a moment we all laughed. Then Sharron continued. "This one says, 'It's a foot,' and she's got letter forms." Sharron flipped

FIGURE 4–1   Nicola adds a newly learned letter to her drawing

through several pages of Nicola's work. "She keeps going. She does this a lot, very quick things on lots of pages."

I asked Sharron if Nicola was seeing a counselor or a therapist. Sharron nodded. "The speech and language specialist," she said, "came in at the beginning of the year, and worked the first quarter for half an hour a week with all the kindergarten and first-grade class-rooms, and as a result of that started working with Nicola for two half-hours a week. That was all."

We talked of the support Nicola needed to help her cope with the critical events that had taken place in her young life. Sharron emphasized that Nicola's mother also needed support. She said, "Her mother was having a very difficult time in coping with life herself. In fact one time the speech therapist and I had called the mother to talk to her about Nicola." Sharron talked about what had happened when Nicola's mother came to school. "She was screaming at the top of her lungs so that other teachers came to see if we were okay. It was that bad. And it was because Daddy had left. The boyfriend had left, and she was venting her frustration on us. I mean, she wasn't yelling at us, but we were there to listen.

"There were no services in our school," Sharron continued. "We had a counselor for half a day a week who was booked." She talked of trying to get help for Nicola's mother through welfare, and of persuading her to call the family services unit. She added, "But there was something about the way they said that they wanted her to come in" that made Nicola's mother reluctant to do so. Sharron said they had asked Nicola's mother if she would like one of the school specialists to talk to them, but the answer was still no. In the end, Sharron said, "There were no services. No support."

A teacher wanted to know "What was the criteria for the speech and language? Was there something specific that keyed them to her?" Sharron answered that Nicola didn't have names for things. She said, "Something happened when the speech and language therapist took her one day and was talking with her about parts of the body. You know, her drawings of people are not very representational. They're like a circle with two eyes, which at kindergarten level is fairly unusual, and what came up was that she didn't know the [word for] fingers. Things like that. So that was a lot of what [the therapist] did. She worked on names of things. You know, 'These are fingers, arms, and elbows,' that kind of thing."

Again Sharron framed what she was saying by returning to Nicola's early literacy development. "But she was very aware of print," she said. She put another piece of paper in the middle of the table. It was a photocopy of an envelope that had been stamped and mailed on October 27, 1989 (Figure 4–2). On it Nicola had written many letters and letterlike symbols. There were *T*'s and *i*'s and *A*'s and *n*'s as well as other clearly distinguishable letters. "This is a note to the bus driver," Sharron explained. "She'd use anything to write on. When I asked her what it said, she said, 'This says *n*,' and it *was* an *n!*" To emphasize that Nicola had recognized the letter Sharron repeated what she had said. "It *was* an *n!*" Then she explained that Nicola was aware that "what she wrote down had to say something." She

FIGURE 4–2   A note to the bus driver

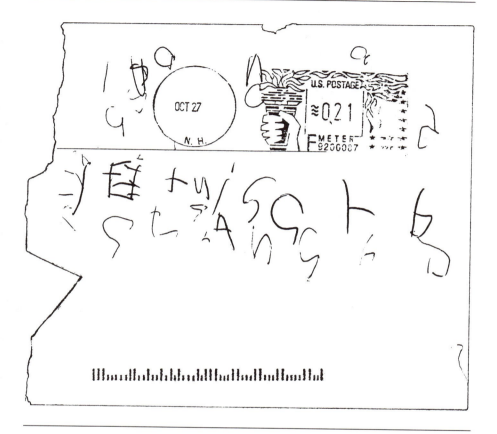

then surmised that perhaps this was the reason that Nicola used other children's writing and said that it was her own. Sharron showed the teachers another piece of paper and read her verbatim notes. "That's Peter and that's me and that's my dad and that's my mom and that's the sun." Sharron again told the teachers that Nicola had not drawn the picture but, she explained, "She added to it." Sharron went on. "Then another child dropped this picture and at first Nicola said, 'I made it.' Then she said, 'I found it.' And then the child said, 'Well!' and Nicola said to the child, 'Well, I had one.'"

Sharron moved on. "She liked the books at the easel," she said. "She would play school with the other kids, and she started to use the pictures to tell a story. At this time she wasn't in any way repeating the story line or paraphrasing it or anything like that." Sharron read from the notes, dated November 16, 1989, that she had written as she observed Nicola at the easel. " 'It didn't frighten me,' she said. 'I went into the darkness and I found something, a light.' " Sharron explained, "She was using the pointer and she was sweeping it under the print, and she identified the print." Sharron paused and again she summarized what she had learned about Nicola. "What became apparent to me was that most of her effort was on writing. It was on attempting to use some kind of print. She doesn't draw that often, and . . . what Nicola was doing was attempting to communicate. The characters become real letters. She can't name the letters yet, but all the letters are appearing." Sharron paused, and then went back through the examples of Nicola's work that she had laid upon the table. "In the beginning," she said, "they were much more scribblelike forms. But the letters become more and more frequent in the writing."

Sharron was back to the work in the portfolio (Figure 4–3). She read from the notes she had written: "That's my cat. I got a tiger cat and my brother got a grey one and my mom got a black one [Figure 4–3A]. That's the mouse [Figure 4–3B]." Sharron pointed at the mouse. The teachers focused on the work that was in front of them, and for a moment the room was quiet.

Kathy asked Sharron if she had any sense about the home environment and the role that print played in the home. Sharron said, "My sense would be that it wouldn't be very much. I mean in talking to Nicola's mom about reading and things like that she basically indicated that there wasn't time for things like that." Sharron then shared some of her own interpretations of the ways in which Nicola used print. She said, "Nicola was also very good about amusing herself, and I see writing as one way that she found to do that. Also, when she was writing she was quiet, out of the way, out of the path of whatever was going on around her."

"It helped her keep a low profile," I suggested.

Sharron nodded and said, "Which in her case I'm sure was a survival skill."

Kathy continued the discussion by adding, "She seems to have come into your room with a sense of [the fact that] writing can serve a purpose for people." She paused, then said, "I wonder if in fact you had any sense that she was given—of the things that she may or may not have been given—that there was always adequate paper and pencil available for her. I mean, she seems to know what you do with

FIGURE 4–3A   Nicola's notes

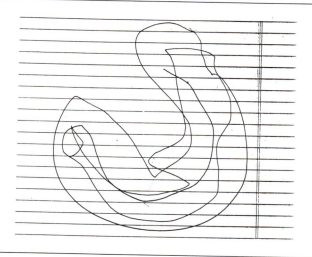

FIGURE 4–3B

envelopes and she seems to know—" Sharron continued, "She seems to be very good at scavenging things to write on." "Right," Kathy agreed, "and using them to write on. To create print somehow. So was a goal to entertain herself?"

The teachers picked up the threads of the conversation that was taking place between Sharron and Kathy, adding their own interpretations to the observations Sharron had made about Nicola's early literacy development. After a while I said, "It's becoming very clear in listening to you that literacy has become very much a part of Nicola's young life, and that the ways in which she is using print provides opportunities for working out how to support her in the classroom."

Sharron agreed and continued her presentation by talking about the ways in which Nicola participated in literacy activities that involved other children. "If I had suggested a class or group project, she was very enthusiastic about doing it. If we were in a group and the kids were pointing out things on a chart, she would point out something. Very often she would just point to it. Like in this instance she pointed to the word *kookaburra* without saying anything. But you know she was part of the group and she could point to that word." In the notes dated December 8, 1989, on which Sharron had based this statement, she had written down the words each child had said from the kookaburra chart that was on the easel. Nicola's name was a part of this list. Sharron had written, "Joining children in pointing out things on the chart. Points to *kookaburra*."

Sharron went on to describe other classroom activities that involved Nicola in print. She said, "The housekeeping area was the center where she spent most of her choice time." She pointed to some photocopies on the table (Figure 4–4). "These were in the housekeeping center as phone messages. She would fill them out and put the date on and she would put her name on the bottom and write who it was from and who it was to."

Sharron changed her pace and moved quickly through some of the later examples of Nicola's work that she had collected and placed in her portfolio. "This, by the way, is one of the first pictures of a face where there's features on the face. This was the very first face that she did that was a recognizable face. This was a sneezing picture kind of thing and underneath the tissue is a nose and a mouth." Sharron shifted her comments to the next example of Nicola's work. "This was in response to ten in the bed. You know, 'What would you say if you were on the floor?' and she wrote, 'Me sleep on the floor.'" Pointing at the printlike configurations, Sharron said, "She wrote that." The work was dated January 29, 1990. "She did very little in

Early Literacy Development and the Mental Health of Young Children

her journal at this time, but these are the kinds of things that she did. 'Mountains'—just letters. This says, 'Mommy, Nicola, Peter.' This was a Christmas picture." A teacher commented on the direction of Nicola's writing, and Sharron said, "Oh, yes. She printed left to right. Top to bottom. Little things in here are supposed to represent 'a tree, a carpet, a chimney, a present, a dolly,' and this is 'I write that.' She pointed to the picture, but she said 'it says "in the kitchen."' But you can see most of these are letter forms."

Sharron's excitement was catching. "She's moving along," I said. "You can really see—" Sharron, perhaps sensing that we were moving too fast, said, "She still would not be able to say consistently what an *n* was, if you asked her specifically what that letter was."

Sharron put a valentine card on the table and told us that Nicola had cut it out and given it to her. "It was not Valentine's Day," she said. "She had gotten them before. But she knew you were supposed to give them to somebody." She put another note on the table. "We had gone to the post office, and Mr. L— had shown us all around and he was very good with the children and we wrote thank-you notes and this was her thank-you note. She wrote, 'I like Mr. L—,' but the figure form was the most accurate she'd done so far."

Sharron put another photocopy on the table. "She made a puzzle," she said. "Other kids would make games at home and bring them in. She cut up a picture and brought it in and called it a puzzle." Teachers asked questions about the puzzle. Then Sharron continued by reading the notes she had written on another piece of paper: "'I touched a snake and it wasn't a rattlesnake.' I asked her 'When?' and she said, 'Today.' She brought in a bubble gum wrapper" (Figure 4–5). Sharron pointed at the writing on the wrapper, which she had photocopied and dated (February 19, 1990), "And she said, 'This says "bubble gum" and this says "apple bubble gum," and the other kids said "it's cherry."'" Sharron laughed, and the teachers, reading the wrapper, laughed with her. "Actually, it's 'strawberry,'" Sharron said. "But she knew it was supposed to say something about bubble gum."

Sharron spread several photocopies on the table. "This was something that I'd asked the kids to do. I asked them to pick a story and write and draw about the beginning and the middle and the end of it. In the beginning Nicola wrote, 'That's the pillow.'" Sharron explained, "She wanted *The House that Jack Built*. 'That's the pillow. That's the bed. They're sleeping.' We had done this story long before this, and she was basically looking at the book and using the pictures. My sense was that she didn't remember the story. But then in the

FIGURE 4–5   Nicola's bubble gum wrapper

middle section she said, 'Once upon a time the duck said, "Quack, quack, quack. Do you want to play with me? Yes I will."' So this is the first time that she has really shown me that she is really aware of story language. Then at the end she said, 'These are all the wedding parts—the earrings and everything.' She was into jewelry and stuff like that."

Several teachers asked questions. One teacher asked if the version of *The House that Jack Built* was the copy with "all the cut-outs." Sharron said that it was, and the teacher said she had guessed that it was from the way in which Nicola had written her story.

For a few moments the teachers talked among themselves about the developments that they were noticing in Nicola's literacy develop-

Early Literacy Development and the Mental Health of Young Children

ment. There was laughter and overlapping talk. Then Sharron continued by talking about Nicola's increasing interest in the charts that were displayed in her kindergarten classroom. When the children were reading the chart "Who Stole the Cookies from the Cookie Jar?" Sharron said that Nicola pointed at the words "Yes, you" and said, "That says 'cookie jar.'" Sharron went on to talk about Nicola's interest in one of the Big Books that were in the classroom. She read from the observational notes that she had written on March 12, 1990. "Reading *Mrs. Wishy Washy* at the easel she moved the pointer from left to right. "'Oh, lovely mud,' said the pig, pig."'" Sharron laughed, pleased with this development in Nicola's appreciation and use of print. "'Oh lovely mud,' said the cow. Then he jumped in it. "Oh lovely mud," said the duck. Then he walked in it. First went the cow. Then the pig in the tub. And then away went the cow. Away went the pig. Away went the duck. "Oh lovely mud," they said.'" Sharron looked pleased. She smiled and opened her eyes wide. "I mean—" she began, but she did not elaborate. There was no need. We all had some idea of how she felt and some understanding of what she wanted to say. Unable to remain quiet I said, "She got it!" "Yeah!" Sharron said.

Again the teachers talked among themselves and again Sharron brought them back to the progress that Nicola was demonstrating. "These are just some more responses to a group activity. She showed us a mimeograph dated March 13, 1990, on which she had reproduced for all of the children "If I had a —— for a pet, I would ——." Sharron pointed at the letters and letterlike forms that Nicola had written in the first space. "It was supposed to be a dinosaur." She then pointed at the second space, in which Nicola had written similar shapes and forms, and she read from the penciled notes that she had added to the page, "'I would bring it to my grandmother's.'" Then she emphasized that although the writing was unreadable in the conventional sense Nicola had been able to place her writing in the appropriate spaces and had therefore given some indication that she understood the format of this particular writing activity.

Sharron read from another copy (Figure 4–6). "This says, 'Mommy. Nicola. Peter. I didn't make Daddy because he's not in our family anymore.'" A teacher asked Sharron who Peter was. Sharron said, "Her brother."

"This is where she is really starting to put things together and make connections," Sharron said. She put a photocopy of a paper on the table on which Nicola had worked on April 20, 1990 (Figure 4–7). On it she had written across the top of the page nine very clearly de-

FIGURE 4–6   Nicola's family

finable capital *A*'s. These are followed by a mixture of *A*'s and less recognizable letterlike forms. In a line beneath the *A*'s were several *B*'s. The first two were hesitantly drawn and redrawn and then there was a circle, or perhaps an *O*. Next came another capital *B*, top-heavy but drawn more boldly than its predecessors, and last came an *R*-like shape, which was perhaps another capital *B*. Beneath the short line of *B*'s were two easily recognizable capital *C*'s. The first appeared to be carefully drawn; the second seemed to have been drawn more quickly, like a signature *C*. Beneath the *C*'s there was a *D* and a *p*-like *D*. Looking at the page of writing it is easy to imagine that Ni-

FIGURE 4–7   Nicola's letters

cola, having worked so hard at this production of letters, had ended
with a satisfying flourish of quickly drawn free forms, which create
the impression of several well-used signatures superimposed upon
one another. Sharron pointed at the line of A's. "She said, 'Them are
A's.' . . . I pointed to these and asked her what they were, and she
said, 'B's.'" Pointing at the C's, Sharron read from her notes,
"Those were 'K's,'" and pointing at the D's, she said, "and those
were 'L's.'" But "Them are A's" and "Them are B's."

After a few more pieces of writing from Nicola's portfolio Sharron came to a piece of paper on which there were thirteen lines of
print. Sharron talked about the fifth graders who visited her classroom and explained that they often wrote stories with the children in

her class. "The kindergartners told stories and the fifth graders wrote them down," she said. Then, reading the title, she continued. "And Nicola's story was a 'Bumble Bee Story.'" Sharron then read the story that Nicola had constructed with the fifth grader. "The bumblebee stings me. I feel sad and my mommy takes care of me. She puts salt on me. She puts a face cloth on me. She puts more salt on me and then I can go home to my own house. I play outside at my own house. I stay home at the rest of the day. I don't go back to grandmothers." For a moment Sharron was quiet. Then she said, "So she has a sense of being able to tell about something that had happened to her."

Sharron moved on. "This was Caitlin, one of her friends, and I showed her how to make a *C* and she was trying to make a *C* for *Caitlin*. This was the first time that she really—" Excited by the progress that Nicola was making, one of the teachers finished the sentence with "made the link!" "Yeah," Sharron smiled. "Because Caitlin was important and she wanted to do that for Caitlin."

Sharron looked at her notes. "I don't have this paper," she said. "I didn't save it. But we were making an alphabet book for *Grandmother's Trunk*. And on the *B* page she wanted to make a baby. And that was with some help." Sharron explained that other children in her room were also making the alphabet book creating lots of options for the *B* page. "So Nicola wanted to do a baby for *B*. And she wrote a *B*. She knew that it was supposed to be a *B*, and she wanted to know what other letters, and so I was trying to encourage her. I asked her, 'What else do you hear?', that kind of thing. And she looked at another child's work, upside down, who was also doing a baby and saw there was another *B*. And so she said, 'Another *B*.' And then she wrote one!"

Commenting on other pieces, Sharron said, "This was her favorite storybook character. This is the little pig and these are all the letter forms."

"They're really clear," I said. "It's like putting them into focus from the beginning."

Sharron went quickly through another group of papers. "She said, 'This is a girl' and 'numbers' and 'letters.' She was making different kinds of things. These are things from her alphabet book. This is 'gold' and this was a 'wagon.'" Sharron pointed out that Nicola "was still not interested in the drawing" and that she remained focused on "letters and letter forms." Sharron said that Nicola was really interested in "communicating through print" and, as if to emphasize the point, she said, "This was taking notes on a clipboard."

162

Early Literacy Development and the Mental Health of Young Children

Sharron always has a clipboard with her or on a table close by, and she uses it on a daily basis as she interacts with the children in her room and documents the ways in which they are constructing both the functions and forms of written language. Nicola began to participate in this activity. Sharron described how "she began taking notes of what the other kids were doing around the room."

Sharron had reached the last few pieces of work that she had put into Nicola's portfolio. She put a paper on the table that was dated June 11, 1990 (Figure 4–8). On it there was a round figure, a body and head in one, with clearly recognizable facial features, and with fat, round arms and legs. Beneath the rotund figure Nicola had written "E." Sharron pointed at the writing. "She said that it was 'me.' I asked her if she heard anything in *me*, and she said, '*S*.'⁵ I asked her if she could write it. So she wrote that." Sharron pointed to a letter that looked like an *N*. "So I said 'What's that?' and she said, '*S*.'" Sharron smiled. "Okay. So I asked her if she heard anything else in *me*, and she said, '*E*'! And I asked her if she could write that, and she did! Then this one [Figure 4–9] was a sun, and it is actually quite representational, far more than anything else that she has done before. And I asked her what she heard in *sun*, and she said—and I expected her to say 'C,' and she said, '*S*'!" Sharron began to laugh, and we all laughed with her. Sharron continued, her voice rising as she spoke. "And I asked her if she could write it, and she said, 'I can do *S*.'" Sharron summed up. "If you put the alphabet in front of her, by this time she could pick out about half a dozen letters and correctly label them. But she was also starting to make the connection between sounds and letters."

A discussion followed about Nicola's behavior in the classroom and the problems that she had to cope with in her everyday life. "It was very interesting," Sharron said. "During the last half of the year the overt behavior wasn't as noticeable. She rarely punched anyone or hit anyone, and when that happened it was usually a sign that things were falling apart. Like one day they came back from music and three kids rushed at me, you know, 'Nicola hit me,' 'Nicola punched me,' 'Nicola called me such and such,' and I said, 'What's wrong? What's happened?' And Mom was in the hospital and I didn't know it." Sharron then talked about a week when she had been away from school. "We had a male sub who was excellent. He'd been in the room before. He was an intern who had been in the school for a semester. But he had long hair tied in a ponytail, which is what, I guess, her father had, according to Mom."

FIGURE 4–8   Nicola's drawing of herself

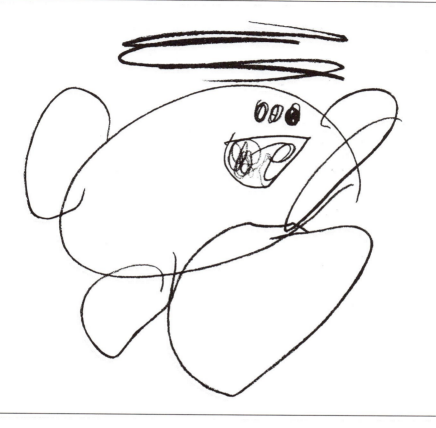

I asked Sharron if she meant Nicola's biological father and she
said, "Yes."

Sharron continued to recount what had happened in her classroom while the male sub was in the room. "She kind of freaked out.
And he looked over and there was Nicola and she had written all
over her face, and he was like, 'What do I do now?' And Mom came
in and she was all upset and she kept Nicola out [of school] until I
came back."

"She was out a good deal of the year," Sharron said. "She would
write on her dolls' faces, and there would be legs pulled off her dolls
and things like that." Reflecting on events that had happened, Shar-

FIGURE 4–9   Nicola's drawing of the sun

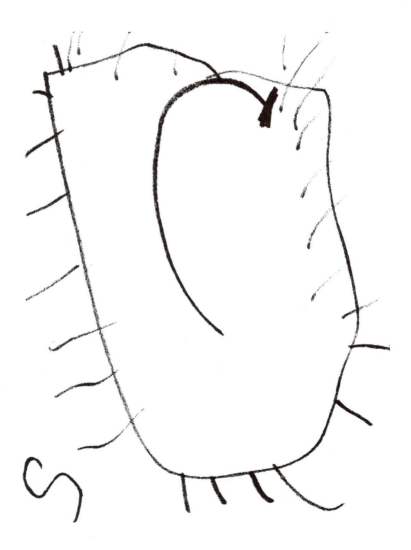

ron said, "Generally I discouraged things coming from home because it's a distraction. I don't want Ninja Turtles and things like that." She laughed; then, looking serious, she said, "But with Nicola it seemed so important. She was so tied to things. She would bring in dolls and doll clothes and things like that, and one day she took home half of the doll corner." Sharron laughed. "They were not really her things."

"How did you deal with it?" I asked.

Sharron sighed. "I called Mom and Mom said, "Oh yeah, she's been taking things. I don't know what to do about it." And so I talked about it being very important that she bring things back. And she still didn't bring them back." Sharron paused. "I wrote a note home. The things still didn't come back, and this was about a week later. In desperation," Sharron said she regretted it, but "I said 'Unless you bring the things back tomorrow you'll have to stay in at recess time.' And she didn't bring the things back. There. I said it. So now what do I do? And she stayed in at recess, which I thought at the time she kind of liked. And I thought, 'Well, this is totally defeating the purpose.'" Sharron laughed, and we laughed too. "But the next day the bag came," Sharron went on. "She brought them back. And after that I was able to use that as a threat and never have to follow through. It was something that worked."

We talked for a while about creating a structure and staying with the decision that is made.

Sharron told us, "She took other children's things home, too, and I got calls from parents. They're very apologetic. You know, 'I don't want to talk about other children but my child said Nicola took this and it's very important.' But for the most part the children played well with Nicola. I only had one incident at the end of the year. I had a child whose mother I had not heard from all year. But she said something about Nicola." Sharron spoke slowly as she tried to remember what happened. "I figure the situation was that I wanted them to work together. She said, 'My mom said I'm not supposed to talk to her.' That's the only time that anything like that came up, and the next day they were great friends again."

I asked Sharron what she thought might have happened to Nicola's literacy development if she had been in a classroom in which there was a program with a predetermined "right order" for the introduction of alphabetic symbols and sound-symbol relationships. Without any hesitation Sharron said, "I wouldn't have seen how important writing was to her, or how much she knew about the power of writing, or the forms and uses of writing. But also—I mean—the fact that she kept adding letter forms, as the year went on without formal instruction from me. She knew how to do that. But yet when we did the *Grandmother's Trunk* book, which was more specific, I really don't think she got much from that at all."[6]

We talked for a while about Nicola's self-initiated exploration, and of the ways in which she learned to use print in the ways in which she had seen it used. We also talked about her experimenting with print without any risks. "It's probably one of the least risky things in her life," I said. "For some children putting pen to paper is a very risky thing. But, perhaps, for Nicola—" We discussed again the idea that using print as a way of occupying herself. We also talked about the use of print as a way of self-expression.

Kathy said, "In some respects it's a vehicle, a way for Nicola to reach out to the world," and she added that Nicola made her aware of how critical print is to communication.

Sharron agreed and said, "In our classroom, kids brought things that they wrote at home, and that was what they shared, and Nicola was very anxious for attention and that was a way to get it."

Kathy said, "What really strikes me about this is that her early stuff is very much like a two-and-a-half to three-year-old child, and the progress that she made is the normal progress that you would expect a child of that age to make. So she's moving forward."

"She's making tremendous progress," Sharron said.

Kathy went on. "It's just that chronologically she has lost two— two and a half years of her life somewhere. But . . . the mandala with the legs coming out of it is just so typical, and the letterlike forms, the emergence of letterlike forms, is forward moving and very natural in many senses, but from the perspective of many educators it's at the wrong time in her life."

"According to the early reports, and according to her mother," Sharron said, picking up where Kathy left off, "as a result of the abuse by her father, she totally regressed . . . she was at a point and then she stopped talking."

Kathy asked what Sharron knew about the time when Nicola was abused.

"I did not talk about that a great deal with her mother," Sharron said. "She was fairly open about it. My sense was that [it was] the year that she was three. That year. Her mother mentioned things like her father threw her down the stairs. And because of that she didn't come to school sometimes because she had gone to see a chiropractor about her knees. Her mother was very concerned about her knees, and she said they were damaged as a result of being thrown down stairs."[7]

Again there was silence.
"So what happens next year?" I asked.
Looking troubled, Sharron said, "Next year she is going to be in
a contained situation with five other children. Special ed."

WHAT NICOLA CAN TEACH US ABOUT EARLY LITERACY DEVELOPMENT

In writing about "knowing letters," Adams refers to the research of
Chall (1967) and Bond and Dykstra (1967), who reported that a
child's letter knowledge is the best predictor of beginning reading
achievement. However, as Adams points out, in the following years
researchers found that teaching children the letters of the alphabet
did not result in any predictive advantage. Referring to the work of
Venesky (1975), Adams provides the following explanation:

> Perhaps, it was suggested, children who know their letters before enter-
> ing school come from homes where the right kinds of interests and activ-
> ities are fostered. Perhaps it was only that children who know their letter
> names before entering school have attained the proper level of cognitive
> development and emotional stability, have the requisite attention span,
> and have enjoyed proper interactions with adults. If this were so, then
> just teaching children letter names would be of no more use than making
> a fine cover for an unwritten book. (pp. 61–62)

Adams states that "[to] many, this conclusion was disheartening" (p.
62), and she goes on to give four different explanations that emerged
from later research on letter familiarity as a predictor of early reading
development:

1. The speed and accuracy of letter naming is an index of the thor-
   oughness or confidence with which the letters' identities are
   learned.
2. The speed of letter naming is an index of the automaticity or ef-
   fortlessness with which letter recognition occurs.
3. Comfortable knowledge of the names of letters hastens children's
   learning of sounds because it mediates their ability to remember
   sounds.
4. Many children basically understand the alphabetic principle before they have fully mastered—or even been taught—our language's set of letter-to-sound correspondences. (p. 63)

Early Literacy Development and the Mental Health of Young Children

So how does Nicola's development of letter knowledge fit the findings of the research studies that Adams uses in her analysis of knowing letters? Would Nicola be one of the children who would be considered as needing to be "brought to normal levels of fluency with letters and words through appropriate training" (Adams 1990, p. 65)? First, it is important to emphasize that while Adams gives the impression that researchers and educators have moved beyond explanations that suggest that children who know their letters before they come to school "come from homes where the right kinds of interests and activities are fostered" and "have enjoyed proper interactions with adults," these explanations are still accepted. Adams confirms this when she states, "Clearly affluence and leisure time bear on the richness of the cognitive experiences that a child might receive. After all the more one has, the more one can give" (p. 89). From this perspective one would expect Nicola to know very little about the alphabet and that if we were to test her letter knowledge using some standardized measure, our findings would almost certainly support that expectation. How wrong we would be.

Nicola knows a lot about letters. She came to school knowing the letters in her name, and she could reproduce these letters in random order and use them herself to write her name on her work. She used letters and letterlike forms to label her drawings, demonstrating her emerging understanding of the interrelationships between different symbolic forms. Her writing and her drawing connected the ideas that she wished to express. Nicola also used various combinations of letters and letterlike forms to write statements such as "God Jesus please come with me."

Gradually, as her kindergarten year progressed, letters predominated, although letterlike forms were still used, and combinations that were made up predominantly of letters were grouped in ways that suggested that she was using them to represent the shapes of words. In addition, Nicola began to name letters—for example, "This says *n*." She also began to make the connection between the sounds of language and the letters that are used to represent them—for example, when Sharron asked Nicola what sound she heard at the beginning of *sun* Nicola said, "*S*." Nicola also demonstrated her interest in the letters of the alphabet as she used a letter stencil. She covered many blank pieces of paper with carefully stenciled letters. She also practiced letters freehand: on one occasion she made a line of *A*'s followed by a line of *B*'s, several *C*'s, and a few *D*'s. Finally, by June, Nicola was using letters to represent words, and the words were also becoming more recognizable—for example, she wrote *E* for *me*.

This very brief summary of the ways in which Nicola invented and reinvented the letters of the alphabet leaves one wondering about the relevance of the research that Adams uses in her analysis of "knowing letters." What is most striking about the explanations that Adams provides is that they are all decontextualized. The emphasis is on learning letters as a skill that is separated from language in everyday life. There is no connection made between language and meaning, no hint that these letters are used to communicate. But Nicola tells us this. She knows that what she writes has meaning; she uses letters and letterlike forms to communicate. Her inventions and reinventions say something: "This says, 'Mommy. Nicola. Peter.' I didn't make Daddy because he's not in our family anymore." When she writes she tells us about her family: "That's my cat. I got a tiger cat and my brother got a grey one and my mom got a black one. That's the mouse."

In her notes Sharron wrote that Nicola "demonstrates awareness of using writing to record what people do." Nicola told her, "Whoever 'dooes' that I write it down here," and Sharron added that Nicola was talking about writing in her notebook. Again in her notes, Sharron wrote about Nicola's instrumental use of print when she is playing in the housekeeping area. "When using the phone message forms, she stamps the date and fills in the rest of the date, and the "to" and "from" spaces with letters and letterlike forms." Added to these emerging uses of print we might add that Nicola uses print for social purposes: "I made it for you."

On yet another level, Nicola shows us that even early in the year, at a time when her drawings were "gross motor kind of things" and her writing was made up largely of letterlike forms, she had some understanding that print carried meaning. At the easel she used the pointer, sweeping it under the print as she read, "I went into the darkness." Later, using the pointer she pointed at words and tried to identify them—for example, she pointed at a word and said, "Kookaburra." Eventually she was able to use the pointer to sweep under the print as she told a story: " 'Oh lovely mud,' said the duck." She could also dictate a story—for example, the "Bumble Bee Story"— perhaps recounting an event that had taken place, and doing so by presenting a sequence of events that eventually lead to a satisfactory resolution.

All of these observations of Nicola's early explorations of the forms and functions of written language are important, but what Nicola teaches us most of all is that writing is one of the ways in which she copes with the difficult circumstances of her everyday life. She has been raped, beaten, and thrown down the stairs. There is nothing proper about her childhood. However much her mother cares for her, however much time her mother spends with her, she cannot undo what has happened to Nicola. No one can. But we can insure that in school we do not assume that she is less likely to be a good reader because of her home circumstances or because she comes to school not knowing the letters of the alphabet. If Nicola were forced to work within the framework that Adams suggests, based upon her reading of the narrow band of research that she cites, Nicola would be an "other," practicing symbol-sound pairs, rehearsing skills, not communicating. Adams (1990) writes:

> Other children enter school with next to no relevant knowledge about print. Relative to their well-prepared peers, these children are likely to have less interest in these lessons and less appreciation of their point. We must therefore expect their learning to be slower and their patience to be slimmer. At the same time, however, mastery of the symbol-sound relations will require more study for these children. After all, some of them may still be having difficulty discriminating the letter shapes; their entering level of phonological awareness will be relatively low; and so, too, will their prior knowledge of letter-sound relationships. Much of the content of these lessons will be new for these children in detail and concept. As a consequence, it will be more confusing and harder to consolidate. Finally, in order for all necessary symbol-sound pairs to be learned well, each must be allowed sufficient practice and opportunity for evaluation. The implication, in short, is that the teaching of individual letter-sound correspondences cannot proceed quickly for these children. It must be spread over time. (pp. 240–41)

Adams footnotes Ausubel (1967) to support the idea that "sufficient practice" means "overlearning." The passage from Ausubel that she quotes includes the following statement:

> Overlearning, in turn, requires an adequate number of adequately spaced repetitions and reviews, sufficient intratask repetitiveness prior to intro- and intertask diversification, and opportunity for differential practice of the more difficult components of a task. Frequent testing and provision of feedback, especially with test items demanding fine discrimination among alternatives varying in degree of correctness, also enhance consolidation by confirming, clarifying and correcting previous learnings. (Adams, 1990, p. 239)

A close reading of Adams' text suggests that the ways in which children are taught depends upon the ways in which they live. Otherwise why cite research that shows that "low income prereaders can become fully proficient in splitting initial consonant sounds of words" (pp. 73–74), and why refer to such findings as "inspiring"?

Nicola helps us understand that such sociological confusion discriminates against groups of children. We cannot make assumptions about "low income prereaders," and we cannot assume that such artificially defined groups of children need to spend their time engaged in "intratask repetition prior to intro- and intertask diversification." If this were the case then Nicola would not be using print to help her get through the difficult life circumstances that have so deeply affected her, and Sharron would not have been able to observe and document Nicola's self-initiated explorations. Remember, Sharron said, "I wouldn't have seen how important writing was to her, or how much she knew about the power of writing, or the forms and uses of writing."

Exploring the small details of Nicola's early literacy development forces us to ask questions about the findings of Adams' analysis of the research studies that she refers to in *Beginning to Read*. Indeed, it is not only her analysis that is called into question but the research studies themselves. How is it possible for so many of these studies to wander so far from the realities of the ways in which children use literacy in their everyday lives? Adams provides one explanation when she states, up front, "Before you pick this book up you should understand fully that the topic at issue is that of reading words" (p. 3).[8] The book is not about children at all; it is about words—words that are dissected into component parts that children are then taught to reassemble, not in ways that make sense to the child, but in ways that make sense to the researcher. And if the researcher wants more information about children's abilities to perform these isolated tasks, the data is obtained through artificial training sessions. To give an example, in her examination of "phoneme manipulation tasks" Adams writes about Rosner's (1974) research as follows:

> Rosner tried to train kindergartners on the phoneme deletion task. The results? Even a whole school year's worth of training resulted in precious little progress. The exception was that the children became relatively proficient at deleting the initial consonants of words. (p. 72)

To give another example, in her discussion of "oddity tasks" Adams reports on the research of Bradley and Bryant (1983). She writes:

> [T]hey selected sixty-five of the children who had done most poorly on the oddity test and divided them into four groups. Children in the first group received forty individual tutoring sessions on comparing the beginning, middle, and final sounds of words. Children in the second group were additionally taught how these sounds were represented by letters of the alphabet. Children in the third group spent their forty tutoring ses-

sions learning how to categorize the words semantically (e.g., hen and pig are farm animals). Children in the fourth group received no special training at all. (p. 78)

Reflecting the research community's often unquestioning dedication to this form of empirical research, Adams calls studies such as these "valiant" and "exquisitely designed." But what if Nicola had been trained in one of these studies? What if she had spent her kindergarten year receiving instruction so that she could successfully complete a phoneme task? If this had happened, what effect would the training sessions have had on her literacy development? More important, what effect would the sessions have had on her emotional well-being? Would the interruption have been painful and costly to her creative reconstruction of the functions and forms of written language? How would such training affect her ability to use literacy in ways that help her cope with the difficult circumstances of her everyday life? Knowing the fragility of her existence, are we willing to take the risk? Are we willing to risk other children?

POSTSCRIPT: DECEMBER 2, 1992

Whenever I read a reference to Adams' *Beginning to Read* I think about Nicola and the many other children with whom I have worked who are discriminated against in her text. When children's learning is denied by researchers who prefer to conduct pseudoscientific experiments rather than spend time with children who can teach them about the ways in which they learn, it is time to speak out. It is of great concern to me that the references to Adams' text that I have read focus on "at-risk learners" and children from "lower-income families." For example, Cunningham and Cunningham (1992) note that Adams has expressed the concern that:

> [A]t-risk readers and writers will not learn enough from writing with invented spelling because of its indirect nature and because these students lack phonemic awareness and knowledge of letter-sound/sound-letter relationships. (p. 107)

Dixie Lee Spiegel (1992), writing about such print-specific skills as graphophonic awareness, includes a citation to Adams' text when she states:

> [W]e have evidence that not all children do naturally discover these conventions by themselves, especially children from lower-income families. (p. 42)

In this way reductionist research folds in upon itself, reifying ideas that have no basis in reality. The complexity of children's early literacy configurations is lost, and teachers are told that the only way to help them is to provide lots of practice at skill and drill exercises. Hopefully, Nicola's story will make visible the enormous penalty that children pay when they are forced to abandon their own ways of knowing by researchers and educators whose myopic ways of seeing disable and disenfranchise so many children.

NOTES

1.   It is important to emphasize that this is not meant to imply that children who suffer critical disruptions to their early childhood development are less likely to become literate. However, it is meant to imply that their literacy configurations are shaped in complex ways by the events that take place in their everyday lives.

2.   I have used Marilyn Jager Adams' book, *Beginning to Read: Thinking and Learning About Print,* because it is presented to policy makers, researchers, teachers, and educational publishers, as P. David Pearson clearly states in the foreword to the text, as "the most complete review, within a single cover, of our expanding knowledge of . . . issues and research in early reading instruction . . . [and] the processes involved in identifying sounds, letters, words, and meaning . . ." (p. 2). The text is published not only with the apparent approval of the federal government, but also with the apparent approval of the Center for the Study of Reading. Richard Anderson, the Director of the Center, states that "[the] book is destined to have a major influence on the teaching of reading" and that "although the book was written by a single author, Marilyn Adams, it is a project of the Center for the Study of Reading." Thus the scales are tipped and policy makers, researchers, teachers, and educational publishers reading the text might well be influenced by the official seals of approval. This is unfortunate, for the text should be freely debated. It is an important contribution to our understanding of the ways in which researchers have explored the early reading development of young children, how teachers have been taught what to teach, and how educational publishers have developed materials to fit policy makers' and educators' "program" needs. Although Dorothy Strickland and Bernice Cullinan began the debate in the afterword to the book itself, the afterword was not included in the one-hundred-page summary that was published by the International Reading Association. It is unlikely therefore that it will be read by many of those who consider and act upon the conclusions of the review. From my reading of the text it seems to me that what Marilyn Adams does is make visible the myths and stereotypes that are deeply embedded in the popular culture of reading instruction. It is from this perspective that I have used *Be-*

ginning to Read in my consideration of the early literacy development and the mental health of young children.

3. The portrait of Nicola was constructed from notes I have written, an audio recording that was made of Sharron talking about Nicola's literacy development, and copies of Nicola's work that Sharron had collected and placed in her portfolio. A draft of the portrait was shared with Sharron, and at that time several statements were modified and information was added.

4. When Sharron read an early draft of this chapter I had written that Nicola "knew" the letters in her name. Sharron pointed out that while she could write them, she could not say the names of the letters. Sharron said, "She could use them fairly effectively before she could name them."

5. Sharron pointed out, "What was really important was that this was the first time she isolated the sound and made *ess* and then said *S*."

6. Later, discussing the *Grandmother's Trunk* book, Sharron emphasized that what was significant about Nicola's lack of interest was that this was a more formal academic activity, which was designed specifically to teach children the letters of the alphabet.

7. It is important that we assume that Nicola's mother does all that she can to take care of her child. In my work with mothers who live in poverty, some without homes, and some suffering from alcohol and drug addiction, there has never been a time when I have doubted a mother's love for her child. Indeed, there have been many times when mothers have sacrificed their own well-being to insure the well-being of their children. Ieysha, one of the mothers who participated in *Growing Up Literate* (Taylor and Dorsey-Gaines, 1988), went without food for her children to eat. For two weeks she did not eat, but she still spent about thirty minutes each morning with her youngest daughter on her lap so that the little girl would have a good start to each new day. Ieysha had very little, but she gave a lot.

8. Chall (1990) presents a similar perspective when she states, "I got into reading through analyzing textbooks and writing for children and adults, and by studying what made them easier, harder, or more interesting to read" (p. 374).

REFERENCES

Adams, Marilyn Jager. 1990. *Beginning to Read: Thinking and Learning About Print*. Cambridge, MA: The MIT Press.

Ausubel, D. P. 1967. "A Cognitive Structure Theory of School Learning." In L. Spiegal, ed., *Instruction*. San Francisco, CA: Chandler.

Bond, G. L. and R. Dykstra. (1967). "The Cooperative Research Program in First-Grade Reading Instruction." *Reading Research Quarterly*, 4:428–444.

Bradley, L. and P. E. Bryant. 1983. "Categorizing Sounds and Learning to Read—a Causal Connection." *Nature* 301:419–21.

Chall, Jeanne. 1990. In "The Past, Present, and Future of Literacy Education: Comments from a Panel of Distinguished Educators, Part II." *The Reading Teacher* 43(6):370–380.

Cunningham, Patricia M. and James W. Cunningham. 1992. "Making Words: Enhancing the Invented Spelling–Decoding Connection." *Reading Teacher* 46(2):106–13.

Ferreiro, Emilia. 1990. "Literacy Development: Psychogenesis." In Yetta M. Goodman, ed., *How Children Construct Literacy: Piagetian Perspectives.* Newark, DE: International Reading Association.

Rosner, J. 1974. "Auditory Analysis Training with Prereaders." *Reading Teacher* 27:379–84.

Spiegel, Dixie Lee. 1992. "Blending Whole Language and Systematic Direct Instruction." *The Reading Teacher* 46(1): 38–44.

Taylor, Denny and Catherine Dorsey-Gaines. 1988. *Growing Up Literate: Learning from Inner-City Families.* Portsmouth, NH: Heinemann.

Venesky, R. L. 1975. "The Curious Role of Letter Names in Reading Instruction." *Visible Language* 9:7–23.

5

ASSESSING THE COMPLEXITY OF STUDENTS' LEARNING: A STUDENT ADVOCACY MODEL OF INSTRUCTIONAL ASSESSMENT

> To evaluate, we need to build descriptions of
> children as they participate in the social
> construction of their own environments. The ways
> in which we develop our explanations should be
> imaginative and intuitive, as well as analytic and
> well trained.

T he student advocacy model of instructional assessment is designed to support students' learning in an educational system
that strives to be both excellent and equitable. Above all the model
honors diversity, acknowledging that it is the combined interests,
skills, and abilities of students that will enable them to work collaboratively in ways that will prepare them for the rapidly changing world
of the twenty-first century. If such a student advocacy model were
adopted, students who learn in ways that do not meet traditional
school expectations would not be labeled. Students who are poor
would not be penalized. Students of color would have a chance to
succeed. Students whose young lives have been damaged by life's
circumstances would have the opportunity to recover. In this student
advocacy model, the emphasis is placed on gaining information about
the ways in which students learn, what they know, and what they *can*
do. The local knowledge of students and their families becomes important. Their ways of solving problems become the focus of attention, and supporting the ways in which they learn becomes the purpose of assessment.

The student advocacy model of instructional assessment rejects
the presupposition of human pathology that Skrtic (1991) states
serves as the special education field's "explicit disciplinary grounding."[1] Thus, the model necessitates a paradigmatic shift (Poplin,
1988a) away from reductionism[2] and reductionistic learning theory

(what students *can't* do) towards a constructivist perspective (what students *can* do). Poplin (1988b) writes:

> From a holistic/constructivist perspective, knowledge of disability, behavior management, sequentially ordered commercial materials, and tightly controlled direct instruction pale in comparison to knowledge of the student and the knowledge of how to design meaningful experiences around who they *are* rather than who they are not. (p. 415)

This paradigmatic shift in the ways in which educators think about students' learning requires them to metaphorically stand next to students and to imagine the world from the students' individual and shared perspectives. Individual teachers use their expertise to assume the role of the novice, the one who must find out how individual students know what they know, and how they have learned what they have learned. The following questions become important:

1. How does this student (do these students) cope with the complexities of their everyday lives?
2. How does this student (do these students) participate (collaborate) with others to accomplish academic tasks?
3. How does this student (do these students) construct and use written language?
4. How does this student (do these students) participate in complex problem-solving activities?
5. How can we, as educators, support and enhance this student's (these students') learning opportunities?

The approach is both disciplined and systematic. Most important, it places teachers at the center of the problem-solving process, to discover from the student's perspective how learning takes place. It is the teachers' expertise that creates significant ways of knowing (Lytle and Cochran-Smith, 1992) the local complexities of their students' everyday lives, the ways in which their students construct and use language, the ways in which their students participate in problem-solving situations, and how their students' learning can be supported in school.

Traditionally, the information that teachers have gathered about students is regarded as anecdotal, and the decisions that are made about whether or not students qualify for special education services are based on the psychometric evaluations of specialists (Mehan,

Assessing the Complexity of Students' Learning

Hertweck, and Meihls, 1986), who have limited (if any) experience of working with the individual students who are being considered for special services (Taylor, 1991). In this student advocacy model of instructional assessment, the observations made by teachers on a daily basis are what are considered important.[3] The systematic collection of information about students' learning enables teachers to advocate for those students who learn in ways that do not meet traditional school expectations. Further, the detailed documentation of individual students' learning enables teachers to determine which students could benefit from special services without overrepresentation or underrepresentation of any specific ethnic group.

The student advocacy model of instructional assessment has four overlapping and interrelated phases:

1. In the first phase, classrooms become "critical sites of inquiry" (Lytle and Cochran-Smith, 1991) as teachers and students work together to construct detailed and systematic accounts (portfolios) of the learning activities in which the student is involved on a daily basis.

2. In the second phase, teachers use their knowledge of individual students' learning to raise questions about students whose learning does not appear to meet traditional school expectations. During this phase, classroom teachers and teachers who provide specialized instructional services come together to discuss both the information that the classroom teacher has collected and the information that is contained in the student's portfolio. Based upon the detailed analysis of the data that the classroom teacher presents to the team, decisions are made about the gathering of further information. It is at this point that family members are encouraged to participate in the activities of what is called the "student support team."

3. In the third phase, the corpus of information gathered by the classroom teacher and by the teachers providing specialized instructional services is analyzed, and decisions are made about the types of support (social and academic, both at school and at home) that will best fit the student's needs. Based on these discussions, a student support plan is developed.

4. In the fourth phase, the student support plan is implemented, and the team meets on a regular basis to make adjustments to the plan based upon the ongoing collection of information by the team.

PHASE ONE: CLASSROOMS AS CRITICAL SITES OF INQUIRY

The student advocacy model of instructional assessment assumes that teachers will have the opportunity to make the paradigmatic shift away from reductionist learning theory towards a more theoretically grounded and practically situated holistic/constructivist approach that will provide opportunities for students to participate in authentic problem-solving situations. It also assumes that students will have the opportunity to actively construct meaning, and further that their interpretations of tasks and their solutions to the problems that they encounter will form the basis of instruction. Implicit in the model are the assumptions that:

1. Teachers cannot gain insights into the ways in which their students learn if they are trained simply to complete predefined tasks that present isolated skills and distort meaning.
2. Teachers can only gain insights into the ways in which students learn if they provide opportunities for students to participate *actively* in authentic problem-solving situations.

In the first approach, which is the dominant model of instruction in American schools, teachers have no alternative other than to check the list of predefined skills that a student is expected to master, and to remediate by reteaching those skills that a student has not learned (see Rueda, 1989; also Ruiz, 1989). The emphasis is on what students *can't do*. Not surprisingly, this approach fits well with the dominant psychometric framework of numerical assessment on which it is based (see Figueroa, 1989). In the second approach, teachers have the opportunity to use their professional expertise (theoretical grounding and practical knowledge) to gain some in-depth understanding of the complexities of their students' learning, by observing (or participating) as students use the social, symbolic, technical, and material resources that are available to find purposeful solutions to bona fide problems. The emphasis is on what students *can do*, and this constructivist approach fits well with our current understanding of the social construction of knowledge, language, literacy and learning, practical intelligence, and problem solving.

The student advocacy model of instructional assessment is a logical extension of current practices for teachers who are engaged in holistic/process teaching. In classrooms where students are actively engaged in the construction of fictional and expository texts, in mathematical problem-solving activities, and in the scientific exploration of known and unknown phenomena, teachers have clearly defined opportunities to observe, interact, and participate in the socially constructed academic life of their students. However, for many teachers, the information remains anecdotal. Momentary events take place and may be talked about, but then are quickly forgotten as other events take place and become the focus of attention. The student advocacy model provides teachers with the opportunity to develop systematic data collection procedures that will enable them to move beyond the limited value of haphazard, anecdotal accounts of students' learning.

Learning to Observe Students' Learning

To work within the framework of the assessment model, teachers will need time to develop the observational skills that they will require if they are to create records of students' learning that can be used as the basis for instructional assessment. The development of systematic data collection procedures is an evolutionary process, which is described in Chapter 3. In that account of instructional assessment, I emphasize that "we cannot observe what we have not learned to see." Teachers need time to learn to see what is happening when students work together on a complex problem-solving task. Again, the important questions are:

1. How does this student (do these students) cope with the complexities of their everyday lives?
2. How does this student (do these students) participate (collaborate) with others to accomplish academic tasks?
3. How does this student (do these students) construct and use written language?
4. How does this student (do these students) participate in complex problem-solving activities?

To make systematic observations of students' learning, teachers will need time to participate in in-service institutes, and they will need time in their schools to meet with colleagues to talk about both the observations that they are making and the data-collecting procedures that they are developing. Historically, the in-service institutes provided for teachers engaged in this model of instructional assessment have been designed to give teachers the opportunity to fundamentally reconceptualize their understanding of the ways in which intellectual activity is both socially constructed and individually situated in the practical accomplishments of their students' everyday lives (see Moll, 1990).

These institutes legitimize the recording of student activity that teachers have learned to disregard or not to see. For example, when a student is asked to construct an expository text, traditional educational standards and practices would focus the teacher's attention on the quality of the finished product. Even in holistic/process classrooms in which students confer with teachers and produce multiple drafts, attention is rarely given to the complexity of the problem-solving tasks on which the students are working. To expand upon this position further, consider the expository text constructed by Margaret, a first-grade student:

A Book
abut
Brontosaurus

This
Book
is
Dadcad
to
Kim
Roberts

I LOVe
Brontosa
it is
Nete

itwad abot
20 pons
+ abot
6 alfis

Thae Had
Small
brains

Thae Had
Loing
Tals

Thae
Had
Loing
Nags

Assessing the Complexity of Students' Learning

> Thae
> Had
> big
> bodese

Margaret's text reads:

> A Book about Brontosaurus by Margaret. This book is dedicated to Kim
> Roberts [name changed]. I love brontosaurus. It is neat. It weighs about
> twenty tons; that's about six elephants (Margaret's oral interpretation of
> the text). They had small brains. They had long tails. They had long
> necks. They had big bodies.

Betty, Margaret's teacher, had modeled for her students how to
find important information about dinosaurs in books. Then she had
asked her class to make a book about dinosaurs. In many classrooms
Margaret's book would be shared with the class, she would talk about
it with her teacher, and then she would be allowed to take it home,
and the occasion would be lost. There would be no record of her
writing; certainly there would be no record of the way in which she
constructed the book. In some classrooms, the book would be placed
in Margaret's portfolio, and when report cards were due to be sent
home, her teacher would use the text to write a few comments or to
make some required notations on a superficially redesigned checklist.
Some attention would be given to Margaret's ideas about dinosaurs,
and a lot of attention would be given to her developmental spelling
patterns and her use of writing conventions; but it is extremely unlikely that any attention would be given to the problem-solving strategies that she used in the construction of the text.

There would be no record of the book *The Monsters Who Died:
A Mystery About Dinosaurs* by Vicky Cobb, which Margaret used to
find information. What follows is an excerpt of Cobb's text:

> Everything about this beast was supersized! Paleontologists figure it
> weighed about 20 tons or as much as 6 elephants. It was named Bronto-
> saurus (bronto-SAWR-us), meaning "thunder reptile," because it must
> have made thunderous noise as it tramped over the ground. Did it live in
> water or land? The fossil footprints of the front feet only are evidence
> that the monster lived in water. Its hind feet probably floated along be-
> hind. Perhaps Brontosaurus lived in shallow lakes. The water would
> have helped support the tremendous weight.

Margaret managed to read the text with the help of her mother (a
volunteer in her classroom) and then with another adult when her
mother had to leave. She read sections of the text out loud ("It was

named Brontosaurus") and then she waited for the adult to read sections of the text she found difficult to read ("meaning 'thunder reptile'"). Margaret also skipped sections of text; she appeared to search for information to use in the book that she was writing.

Observing Margaret as she reads the dinosaur text and constructs her own book about the brontosaurus provides detailed information about the ways in which she is learning to read and write. Margaret demonstrates that she is engaged in a complex problem-solving literacy task. She *collaborates* (in this instance, with her mother) and *recasts the problem* (finds a way of using a difficult text about dinosaurs to create her own text). She *invents new procedures* (skipping chunks of text), and she *departs from the literal format* through her *reorganization of the task*. She also *develops least-effort strategies* to arrive at an *instrumental solution* (the construction of her own text). It is important to note that while she reads texts that include such words as *brontosaurus* and *elephants*, Margaret appears to be quite comfortable using her own interpretations of these words when she constructs her own text (*Brontosa* and *alfis*).

For Betty, Margaret's teacher, who works within a student advocacy model of instructional assessment, finding out how Margaret creates order out of complexities, constructs and uses language, and participates in problem-solving situations provides a framework for her observations. Teachers working within such a framework use their professional training and practical experience to find out how individual students take responsibility for (control of) their own learning. *Teachers learn to assume the role of the novice within the framework of their own expertise.*

Learning to Collect Information About Students' Learning

Once a stance of critical inquiry has been established by the teacher, decisions about what information to collect become straightforward. It is important for Betty to make a copy of Margaret's brontosaurus book before she takes it home. It is also important for her to make a note of the reference book that Margaret used, and to attach a copied page of the published text to the copy of Margaret's brontosaurus book. Finally, before the book is placed in Margaret's portfolio, it is important that Betty adds the notes that she has written, so that she can refer at any time to the information that she has collected and use it to gain some insight into the dynamic ways in which Margaret is learning to read and write (forms of written language), while *at the same time* Margaret is learning to analyze scientific evidence and use her analysis in the construction of her own reference text (functions of written language). Thus, when Betty asks the question "How can I support and enhance Margaret's opportunities to learn the forms and functions of written language?" she has the basis of an authentic assessment to guide her as she helps Margaret use what Margaret *can do* to advance her own learning.

In the student advocacy model of instructional assessment, constructing such records of each student's learning is central to the process. It provides teachers with the opportunity to support *every* student with whom they are working, while at the same time it provides them with the opportunity to raise questions about *individual students for whom they are concerned.* Andrew is one such student. Even before he entered a public elementary school, the decision had been made that he would experience difficulties in meeting school expectations. In Andrew's special education file it states that he was referred for a "learning disabilities evaluation due to difficulties that he experienced on the kindergarten screening." In the "Summary And Recommendations" the examiner writes:

> At the time of Kindergarten Screening Andrew could not state his age, address or phone number. Nor could he write hi [*sic*] name. He could not draw a picture of a person and appeared to have great difficulty following directions. At the time of this evaluation there is marked improvement in Andrew's overall ability to attend to the speaker. In addition he could state his age, address and phone number. He could also draw a picture of himself and write his name. Andrew still appears to have difficulty understanding what is said to him at times. For example on the McCARTHY SCALES OF CHILDREN'S ABILITIES when asked to name all the things he could think of that you wear he said "School clothes and pajamas." When and [*sic*] asked what else you can wear he responded "Because I'm so tired I go to bed." This is not an isolated incident. He gave a [*sic*] answer that was totally off base. As Andrew has been tested by the Audiologist and found to have no hearing problem it is the opinion of ths [*sic*] examiner tha [*sic*] his is a language problem. Andrew has beenevaluated [*sic*] by the Speech/Language Pathologist. . . .

What follows is the summary and recommendations of the speech and language pathologist.

> Andrew presents as a child whose understanding of language is below age level. His use of language is affected by his lack of understanding of

basic concepts, basic syntactic structures, and semantic concepts. Andrew's attention to tasks is affected by his inability to make good eye contact with the lesson or story within the classroom. This was noted during informal evaluation with this clinician. It is therefore recommended that Andrew receive speech and language services in order to improve his receptive and expressive language ability, and his pragmatics.

Andrew was in kindergarten when these evaluations were made. His family moved at the end of that year, and he entered first grade in a school in which the teachers were participating in the Biographic Literacy Profiles Project. His first-grade teacher, Nancy, working as a student advocate, began to observe Andrew as he participated in the activities taking place in his first-grade classroom. Andrew rarely spoke or made eye contact, but as the months went by, Nancy began to question the idea that he was suffering from a "language problem." Andrew was reading chapter books, and Nancy learned from his mother that he could read before he entered kindergarten. Nancy also learned that Andrew's journal drawings (often incomprehensible) were his personal representations of the Nintendo games that he liked to play. One such drawing consisted of grey pencil shading, which Andrew said was the move between one level of a Nintendo game and another level. Nancy also found that when Andrew was asked about the abstract representations that he was making of his Nintendo games, he could talk about the characters, the moves he was making, and, not surprisingly, how he got from one level to another.

By second grade, it was discovered that Andrew had a wry sense of humor that was evident in his interactions with his peers and in the way in which he approached academic tasks. His teacher, Maria, also began to appreciate the technical expertise that he displayed when using computers. To gain a more in-depth understanding of his use of this technology, she invited his mother to bring Andrew's Nintendo game to school so that she could observe him play the games that he so often wrote about. Maria said, "He taught me to play. I had never seen the machine. He had a hard time dealing with my slowness. He would tell me what to do and explain what I should watch out for. Even if I played every day I'd never reach the levels he can reach. Each new game he plays he learns the pattern. He thinks like that, he logs the information and cracks the code." Throughout the year, Andrew continued to display an intense interest in computer technology. He developed Logo programs, and he used a graphics program to write stories. The text in Figure 5–1 was written by Andrew at the beginning of his second semester in second grade. He wrote it without any assistance from an adult or from another student.

Andrew used a mouse to position the graphic of Peter Pan with the title of his story. He experimented for some time with the juxtaposition of the image of the boy and the title before he arrived at the configuration shown. Andrew then typed the first section of his story. When he reached "Wendy" he changed fonts several times before settling on the typeface for "FALLOW ME TO NEVER LAND." Returning to the original font, Andrew continued to write. He changed fonts again for "GO. GO. GO," experimenting again before choosing the elaborate typeface. As the work period drew to an end, Andrew quickly concluded his story. When Andrew talked about his computer text, he said that he was reading *Peter Pan* and that was why he had chosen to write a story about him.

At about the same time (February) Andrew also made a book about baseball (Figure 5–2). Andrew's baseball story is representative of his pencil-and-paper writing. Maria talks about the importance of the graphic images in the production of his texts. She notes that it is almost as if the ball is traveling, and she comments that a quick look will produce the effect of a video display in which a ball travels in an arc across the screen. Maria also talks about the interactive quality of Andrew's work. Very often when he's writing on paper he will add a verbal commentary to go with the text ("The green guy threw the ball").

Andrew plays with graphic images and weaves different symbolic forms together, and his use of computer technology adds unexpected dimensions to his handwritten work. All of these observations become important if his learning is to be supported in school.

At the present time, Andrew is a third-grade student in Maria's combined second- and third-grade class. Maria continues to make a detailed record of his observable learning behaviors, and she emphasizes the complexity of the literacy technologies that have become so important to him as he works to complete his academic assignments. But soon Andrew will be leaving Maria's class because his family is moving. Andrew will take with him the detailed record of his observable learning behaviors that Maria and the teachers providing specialized instructional services have constructed from their intensive analysis of the documentation contained in his biographic literacy portfolio. However, there is considerable concern for Andrew, as those who have worked with him know that it is highly likely that once again he will be identified as a student who has difficulty meeting school expectations.[4]

FIGURE 5–1 Andrew's Peter Pan story

THE ADVENTURE OF
PETER PAN.

ONE NIGHT. THE KIDS WERE GOING TO
BED. LATER ON. SOMEONE WAS ON THE
ROOF. THE KIDS WOKE UP.
I LOST MY SHADOW. HE SAID.
ITS PETER PAN. SAID JOHN.
IT IS PETER PAN. SAID MICHAEL.

WOW. SAID WENDY.

FALLOW ME
TO NEVER LAND.
YELLED PETER.
NEVER LAND. HERE WE COME. HA HA
HA. LAKTHED PETER.

GO. GO. GO.
YELED JOHN.
HERE WE ARE. SAID MICHAEL.
HERES THE UNDER GRUUND HOUSE?
SAID MICHAE. CAPTIN HOOK WAS
AROUND. PEPFRE FOR THE BATTLE.
SAID james hook. hook has died by
the croc. and never came back
again.   the End.

Assessing the Complexity of Students' Learning

FIGURE 5–2   Andrew's baseball story

the BASeBALL
FIeLD.

BU

ANDReW

Feb. 12.

BALLOU LIBRARY
BUENA VISTA UNIVERSITY
610 WEST FOURTH STREET
STORM ___ ___ IA 50588-1798

FIGURE 5–2   continued

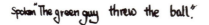

Spoken "The green guy threw the ball."

the blue JAY MAbE
A GOOD WACK·

Assessing the Complexity of Students' Learning

FIGURE 5–2   continued

FIGURE 5–2   continued

Summary and Conclusions

In the student advocacy model of instructional assessment, *systematic observations* and *detailed documentation* of students' participation in authentic learning activities create collaborative instructional frameworks that enable teachers to support their students' learning. The capturing of ongoing streams of behavior presents the greatest challenge. Placing copies of students' work in portfolios is not enough. Without the teacher's record of how the text was constructed there can be no authenticity of interpretation, and any attempt at systematicity is lost. Without observational notes we do not know who actually participated in the learning event, we do not know what was said, we do not know how the problem was defined, and we do not know what resources were used. To support students' learning, we need to know *how* their texts were written and *how* they accomplished the task. From this perspective, the classroom teachers are central to the instructional assessment process.

When teachers transform their classrooms into critical sites of inquiry, the transformation begins with themselves. Past experience suggests that teachers will encounter the most difficulties when they are asked to shift their focus from what their students can't do to what they can do. Teachers will need support as they learn to observe students who are actively engaged in problem-solving activities. They will need help in developing note-taking procedures that will capture the complexity of students' learning. They will need guidance as they work with their students to develop portfolios that will provide enough information for instructional decisions to be made. Finally, they will need assistance in determining how to support and enhance the learning opportunities of those students for whom they are critically concerned.

PHASE TWO: ASSESSING THE LEARNING OF STUDENTS FOR WHOM TEACHERS ARE CONCERNED

The student advocacy model of instructional assessment creates a framework for teachers to use their theoretical knowledge and practical experience to assess the ways in which individual students participate in academic activities in classroom settings. They have the opportunity to examine students' learning within a sociohistorical context. The combination of teacher's observational notes and the student's work, collected over time from September through June, creates an authentic record of the student's learning. It is this information that forms the basis of the intensive analysis that takes place when teachers focus their attention on students for whom they are especially concerned.

Learning to Conduct an Intensive Analysis of a Student's Biographic Portfolio

At a meeting of teachers who are working within a student advocacy model of instructional assessment, Sharron talked about Nicola, a kindergartener who had been sexually and physically abused by her father (see Chapter 4). Sharron spoke of the ways in which Nicola was creating order out of the complexities of her everyday life, learning to construct and use written language, and participating in problem-solving situations. Sharron began with a discussion of the ways in which Nicola was using print in September when she first entered kindergarten, and then, discussing the developments that took place in October and November, she began to build a biographic literacy

Assessing the Complexity of Students' Learning

profile (portrait) of Nicola. As can be seen from Sharron's account in Chapter 4, Sharron focuses on what Nicola *can do*. Small pieces of paper, a bubblegum wrapper, a torn envelop, become important. Nothing is regarded as trivial, and, as Sharron makes clear, for Nicola, learning to read and write is more than an academic exercise.

Sharron's systematic observations and detailed documentation of Nicola's observable literacy behaviors creates an opportunity for her to understand (develop significant ways of knowing) how Nicola (from the student's perspective) is learning to read and write. For example, educators often emphasize the importance of the child's knowledge of the alphabet and the child's appreciation of graphophoneme relationships. Based upon the data that Sharron has systematically collected, *without testing* it is possible to state the following about Nicola:

> Nicola knows a lot about letters. She came to school knowing the letters in her name, and she could reproduce these letters in random order and use them herself to write her name on her work. She used letters and letterlike forms to label her drawings, demonstrating her emerging understanding of the interrelationships between different symbolic forms. Her writing and her drawing connected the ideas that she wished to express. Nicola also used various combinations of letters and letterlike forms to write statements such as "God Jesus please come with me."
>
> Gradually, as her kindergarten year progressed, letters predominated, although letterlike forms were still used, and combinations that were made up predominantly of letters were grouped in ways that suggested that she was using them to represent the shapes of words. In addition, Nicola began to name letters—for example, "This says *n*." She also began to make the connection between the sounds of language and the letters that are used to represent them—for example, when Sharron asked Nicola what sound she heard at the beginning of *sun* Nicola said, "*S*." Nicola also demonstrated her interest in the letters of the alphabet as she used a letter stencil. She covered many blank pieces of paper with carefully stenciled letters. She also practiced letters freehand: on one occasion she made a line of *A*'s followed by a line of *B*'s, several *C*'s, and a few *D*'s. Finally, by June, Nicola was using letters to represent words, and the words were also becoming more recognizable—for example, she wrote *E* for *me*.

But this information is only a small part of what Sharron learned about Nicola. Throughout her analysis of the documentation, Sharron emphasized that Nicola's inventions and reinventions say something. Nicola knew that print carried meaning, and she used print in ways that were *autobiographical* (the Bumble Bee story), *educational* (reading *Mrs. Wishy Washy* at the easel), *environmental* (the bubblegum wrapper), *interactional* ("I made this for you," Valentines cards), *instrumental* and *substitutional* (writing phone messages), and *recreational* (writing to amuse herself) (see Chapter 3). Figures 5–3 and 5–4 present Nicola's ways of using writing and reading, respectively.

All of these interpretations are important, but from Sharron's perspective, working a student advocate within an instructional assessment model, the most important information that she obtained concerns the ways in which Nicola uses print to cope with the traumas that she has experienced in her young life. As we learned in Chapter 4, when Sharron was away from school the substitute teacher who took her place was a young male intern who had a ponytail like Nicola's biological father. Nicola was unable to cope. She wrote on her face and on her arms. She was so distressed that her mother came to school and took her home, and she did not return to school until Sharron came back the following week. Nicola expressed her anxiety (and grief) by writing on herself and on the dolls in the classroom. To keep out of the way, she occupied herself by writing on any piece of paper that she could find, and she reached out to other people through the writing that she did and then gave to them. Reading and writing helped her survive. *Before* she could read and write in the traditional sense and *before* her abilities would have registered on tests using traditional measures, Nicola had developed a clearly identifiable literacy configuration of exceptional complexity.

Within the framework of the student advocacy model of instructional assessment, the information that Sharron has collected and analyzed would be used to enhance and support Nicola's learning. Throughout the school year Sharron used this information to inform her instruction, but at the end of the kindergarten year, the child study team, operating within the old paradigm of special education, tested Nicola and made the decision to remove her from the regular classroom and place her in an intensive resource room for children who were judged to be unable to function in a regular classroom. Sharron said, "She wasn't at a point where she would reach grade-level expectations, and that was a problem for them."

Sharron's systematic collection of Nicola's writing and detailed documentation of her observable literacy behaviors is a practical demonstration of the importance of collecting data that can inform teachers about students for whom they are concerned. For Nicola, Sharron's portfolio provided an in-depth portrait of the ways in which she was learning at school and of the social contexts that were affecting her learning. Given the present regulations and the chronic inertia

FIGURE 5–3   Nicola's types and uses of writing

TYPES AND USES OF WRITING   Name: Nicola

Categories	Observations	Categories	Observations
Autobiographical	Dictated an account of an event in her everyday life (the Bumble-Bee Story)	Interactional	"I made this for you" Valentines cards
Creative	Writes to express herself "I writed it."	Memory-Aid	
Educational	Writes accounts of stories (the House that Jack Built) Fills in discarded worksheets found in the school playground. Writes in journal	Recreational	Writes to amuse herself (chooses to write)
Environmental		Substitutional	Writes phone messages.
Financial		Other	
Instrumental	Writes phone messages.	Other	

Assessing the Complexity of Students' Learning

FIGURE 5–4   Nicola's types and uses of reading

TYPES AND USES OF READING   Name: Nicola

Categories	Observations	Categories	Observations
Confirmational		Interactional	Receives phone messages written by other children. Reads the phone messages she writes to other children.
Educational	Reads close rendition of "Mrs Wishy Washy" at the easel. Goes to the easel and plays school with pointer. Participates in class readings of stories, poems & songs	News-Related	Reads news that she has written.
Environmental	Collects items such as the bubble-gum wrapper.	Recreational	Chooses to look/read books at choice times.
Financial		Scientific	
Historical		Technical	
Instrumental		other	

of special education, it was not possible for Sharron to make a difference beyond the confines of her kindergarten classroom. However, there are examples of classroom teachers and teachers providing supportive services who *have* been able to take the next step. They have used information collected in the student's instructional portfolio to raise questions that they have then explored through the collection of more focused documentation of a student's learning.

Learning to Use a Student's Portfolio to Raise Questions That Require the Gathering of Further Information

At the beginning of Bobby's fifth-grade year a student support team began working as student advocates on his behalf. At that time, Bobby was 11 years and 11 months of age, and the ways in which he was learning were a puzzle to his classroom teacher, Debbie, and to the teachers providing specialized support services: Mary B., the literacy educator, and Mary C., the Chapter One teacher.

At about the same time, Bobby's mother, who was concerned about his academic progress, requested a special education evaluation. Briefly, the school psychologist administered a WISC-Revised and interviewed Bobby. In addition, the special educator administered the Woodcock-Johnson Cognitive Battery–Revised (WJC-R), and the Woodcock-Johnson Standard Achievement Battery–Revised (WJA-R). The school psychologist stated at a meeting of Bobby's student support team, "We are talking about a child who is working in the superior range and the retarded range," and he added, "I wouldn't be surprised if there were some perceptual-motor difficulties."[5] In the report that was subsequently written by the special educator, the following summary and recommendations are presented:

> Bobby is not achieving commensurate with his age and ability in any of the academic areas noted above. The examiner recognizes that some of these gaps may be due to the amount of school Bobby has missed and his frequent changes of school. However, the examiner strongly suspects that Bobby has an educational handicap since his earned subtest scores on the Weschler Intelligence Scale for Children–Revised show a wide scatter and during the WJ-R testing Bobby frequently had difficulty finding words to express his thoughts. She recommends the team consider a language evaluation to assess the perceived difficulty he had in finding words to express his thought and to determine if his demonstrated lack of knowledge of written and oral expression techniques is due to a language processing problem.

What is interesting in this summary is the weight given to the results of the WISC-R. In examining the two sets of test results it is difficult to establish any validity for the connection that was made between the two sets of data. However, a connection was made that eventually led to the special educator and the psychologist ascribing a learning disability to Bobby.

The student support team chose to look more closely at the ways Bobby was participating in the learning activities taking place in his fifth-grade classroom. Again the questions that framed their analysis of the information centered around the ways in which Bobby created order out of the complexities of his everyday life, constructed and used language, and participated in problem-solving situations. The discovery process began with an analysis of Bobby's portfolio. The portfolio contained summer book reports, his dialogue reading journal, assigned writing, and letters. One letter, written October 7, 1991, caught the attention of Bobby's student support team:

Dear Kelly,

You have been very nice to me. I wish I wish I could pay you back. I wish I could get to know you better. Do you like hunting? How many animals do you have? I got som I have chickens, a goose, And many more.

Sincerely,
[Bobby's signature]
Bobby [printed]

P. S. You may think I am dum but I am really smart.

The support team was impressed by the fact that Bobby had written this letter to Kelly, but what really made them stop and think was the postscript. His statement seemed to encapsulate what was happening to him in school. They recognized that Bobby was aware of the evaluation process and that he was probably painfully aware that he had not done too well on some of the tests that he had taken. This realization increased their resolve to focus on what Bobby could do instead of what he couldn't do. It also increased their resolve to gain a better understanding of what was happening from Bobby's point of view.

The student support team began by considering the social contexts in which he was learning. Bobby participated in several meetings with individual members of his support team, and on one occasion he was asked if he thought he was experiencing difficulties with any of his classroom assignments. Bobby answered that he was having difficulty writing. He said he had a spoon in his desk on which he was making a pattern. He said that he worked on the pattern when he was supposed to be writing. The conversation then focused on the ways in which people often try to avoid tasks that are difficult for them. When he was asked why he thought that he was experiencing difficulties writing, Bobby said that he had been to eight different schools. "Eight schools," he said. "That ain't helpful at all. That's dreadful because I didn't learn much." Bobby named the states in which he had attended school, and at a later meeting his mother, who worked closely with the team, confirmed that he had indeed been to eight schools in five different states. Looking back in Bobby's school folder, there was a note from his kindergarten teacher in which she writes, "Frequent absences make it difficult for him to keep up with his classmates." So Bobby had attended eight schools and was also often absent. Bobby explained that his father was a truck driver and he would come and take him out of school and he would travel for weeks, sleeping in his father's truck. Bobby said, "One time I remember he took me out of school because he had to go away for a real long time so I missed all these lessons and I didn't have extra homework and they didn't help me make it up." Bobby's mother also talked about his many absences from school, including a six-month period in third grade when Bobby was abducted by his father and did not attend any school at all.

From the conversation with Bobby, it appeared to the support team that he felt that his difficulties were due to these frequent relocations and his numerous absences from school. Debbie, Bobby's teacher, was already seriously concerned about the number of times he was being removed from the classroom to be tested. Bobby's comments on being absent and on missing work increased her concern, and she advocated that the number of times that Bobby was removed from the classroom be kept to a minimum.

Bobby's student support team accepted his interpretation of why he was having difficulties with his academic assignments. The support team felt that the many changes in school location and frequent absences had had a significant impact on his reading and writing. They also talked about the differences in philosophies of local schools, and of the social and academic consequences of moving back and forth between synthetic approaches to reading and more holistic/process approaches to instruction. The consensus was that Bobby's reading and writing had been affected by not only his moving from one school to another and his repeated absences, but also by the different approaches to instruction that he would have encountered on his never-ending journey. The student support team talked about the way in which first-, second-, and third-grade activity provided a

Assessing the Complexity of Students' Learning

foundation for fourth- and fifth-grade tasks. It is assumed that students have been enculturated into the academic life of the school. It was decided that if Bobby were to experience any difficulty with an academic task, it was important that the member of the support team who might be working with him did not assume that he had received instruction that would prepare him for the task. In Bobby's case such assumptions would lead to in-the-head explanations of socially constructed difficulties.

The student support team realized that they needed more information about Bobby's literacy development. The decontextualized information about "processing speed," "auditory processing," and "visual processing" that had resulted from the special educators' tests did not provide them with any information that they could use when they worked with Bobby in his regular classroom. The decision was made that Mary B., the school's literacy educator, would develop a running record, which would include a miscue analysis of Bobby reading.[6]

In Mary B.'s report of Bobby's reading of *The Man Who Kept House,* she begins with the directions that she gave to Bobby prior to reading. The next section of her report reads as follows:

> *Information gathered during the oral reading.* As Bobby read the text he used his finger and pencil interchangeably to point to the words. During the beginning of the reading, Bobby appeared to be focused on the words, intent on and reading each one correctly; but as he progressed through the story his fluency, expression and interjections about the events in the story increased. During the second half of the story, he punctuated his story with little asides such as:
>
> > "It would have just been easier for him to get some grass," when the woodman put the cow on the roof,
> >
> > "How can he do that with a fire on?" when the woodman pulled the end of the rope out of the fireplace,
> >
> > "Man that must be hot," when he read the description of the wife coming in to see the husband with his head in the porridge pot and his feet in the chimney.
>
> As he was reading one of the sentences Bobby said, "There's a word missing here." After he called my attention to it I realized several articles (the, a, the) had been inadvertently left out of the text when it was typed. I explained to him what had happened. Then, he immediately picked up a pencil and began to insert the missing words as he continued to read. Bobby looked to me for confirmation about the correctness of a few words and in doing so lost his place on two occasions. Bobby used

repetition as a self-correcting strategy and occasionally for the purpose of processing a problem in the text. His retelling included an accurate summary of the story and its characters. Many of the events were named and sequenced. He included statements which indicated his understanding of character development and inferential thinking.

Information gathered from the analysis. Bobby's uncorrected miscues have a high degree of syntactic and semantic acceptability with the original words. They were of the same grammatical function as the original word. Over fifty percent of his miscues kept the meaning unchanged. Many of his miscues had some degree of graphic similarity; but most of them have very little similarity in sound with the original word.

Bobby's reading of this story consisted of:

Running Words—777 (no illustrations)
Miscues—19
Omissions—4
Insertions—1
Self-corrections—17

This data can be looked at in the following ways (the uncorrected miscues, omissions and insertions were all included in computing each rate):

Error rate—1:34
Accuracy rate—97%
Self-correction rate—1:2

The majority of his self-corrections appeared to be made without having to orally read the text to the right of the word he was self-correcting (usually proficient readers are visually scanning ahead). Three of his self-corrections appeared to be made by reading one or two words beyond the self-correction. Two were made by rereading two or three words to the left of the self-correction.

Reflection. Bobby read this text with a great deal of proficiency. It appeared that he was reading for meaning and self-corrected his miscues to achieve this purpose. Billy's oral reading indicates that he relies on context and meaning to help him analyze unfamiliar words. From this sample it appears the majority of his miscues and self-corrections are tries at words that will fit. In a few cases he appeared to be attempting to sound out a word. Bobby would probably benefit from the continuation of instructional activities designed to help him internalize the use of a range of strategies and cueing systems.

Mary B. recommended the development of a biographic literacy profile that would incorporate the information derived from his portfolio with a spelling profile and both dictated and independent writing samples.

Bobby's student support team continued the discovery process, gathering as much information as they could about Bobby so that they could best fit the ways in which they were working with him to support his academic needs. Debbie and Bobby watched a segment of "Nova," the Public Television program, called "The Making of a Junk Food," and then Debbie asked Bobby to tell her about the show. She then transcribed sections of the audio recording that she made of his description, and the transcript and audio tape became a part of the corpus of information that they were developing on the ways in which Bobby was learning in school. (Interestingly, after listening to the audio tapes of Bobby's miscue analysis and his response to the "Nova" program, the speech and language pathologist could find no reasons for testing.) For Debbie, Mary B., and Mary C. the process continues, and the insights that they are gaining into the ways in which Bobby uses language and participates in problem-solving situations are being utilized directly on an ongoing basis, as they both support his learning and provide him with opportunities to develop a better understanding of his own learning. In Phase Three of this student advocacy model of instructional assessment, a detailed account is presented of the ways in which this support is being provided for Bobby.

Summary and Conclusions

The student advocacy model of instructional assessment maximizes the opportunities that teachers have to work as student advocates, collecting information that is directly related to instruction. No leaps of faith are required. Teachers can provide documentation as evidence of the ways in which students are learning in classroom settings. No labels are necessary. Teachers can use their informed opinion (the basis of the Supreme Court's decision-making process) to develop narrative descriptions of the ways in which students use their academic abilities. When Sharron presents a systematic account of the ways in which Nicola is learning both the functions and forms of written language, her description makes it unnecessary for comparisons to be made between Nicola's academic development and the academic development of other five-year-olds. Nicola's life cannot be standardized. Sharron makes it plain that for teachers who are working within a student advocacy model of instructional assessment, student diversity is *not* a problem.

Honoring diversity is central to the student advocacy process. To honor diversity, teachers need both the time and the opportunity to meet together to discuss the lives and the work of students for whom they are especially concerned. The student advocacy model of instructional assessment is based on the underlying assumption that it is the shared knowledge and expertise of teachers that create windows of opportunity for students who are experiencing difficulties. *Teacher assessments directly inform practice.* Classroom teachers and teachers providing specialized instructional services have the opportunity to collect information *over time.* They can look for patterns in the ways individual students learn. They can describe the complexities of students' personal and shared literacy configurations. They can develop common goals for instruction, and their assessments can be used directly to inform practice. The ways in which Debbie, Mary B., and Mary C. are working together provide a blueprint for this approach to instructional assessment. Their work has made a difference. They have made noticeable changes in Bobby's life. He talks about the ways in which he is learning. He is eager to show his work to those who are interested in what he is doing. And there are clearly definable improvements in his reading and writing.

PHASE THREE: ANALYZING INFORMATION AND MAKING DECISIONS ABOUT THE TYPES OF SUPPORT THAT WILL BEST FIT THE STUDENT'S NEEDS

The student advocacy model of instructional assessment assumes that classroom teachers and teachers providing special support services will be provided with the opportunity to gather information about their students, and that their theoretical understanding and practical experience will guide the assessment process. There are no elaborate interventions that separate students from their peers. This is *not* a deficit-driven model. In "The Special Education Paradox," an article published in the *Harvard Educational Review,* Skrtic (1991) adds his own words to those of Reich (1990, p. 202) to come up with the following statement:

> The system of education needed for the post-industrial economy is one that prepares young people "to take responsibility for their continuing education, and to collaborate with one another so that their combined skills and insights add up to something more than the sum of their individual contributions." (p. 181)

In a system that is both excellent and equitable, students need the opportunity to learn in environments that encourage collaboration in problem-solving situations. They need to participate with other students in ways that create communities of learners who work together, and communities of learners who share their abilities to support one another's learning. In such classroom environments, teachers work closely with their students. Together, they work in an atmosphere which fosters public (group) trust and private (individual) cooperation. To remove students from their communities interferes with this educational process, separates students who are often the most vulnerable from their peers, and interferes with their academic *and social* development.

In the student advocacy model of instructional assessment, students receive the extra support that they need from the members of their student support team *within* the regular classroom setting. To illustrate the ways in which student support teams work with students in regular classroom settings, two examples will be given. The first describes the ways in which Andrew and his student support team work together, and the second describes the ways in which Bobby works with his student support team. These examples will be juxtaposed to emphasize that there are many ways in which support can be provided. Each example serves to illustrate the close links between the analysis of the information that has been collected, the instructional decisions that are made, and the interventions that are carried out in regular classroom settings.

Learning How to Support Andrew's Academic and Social Needs in a Regular Classroom Setting

Maria has been Andrew's teacher and student advocate for two years. When Andrew was a second-grade student in her classroom, Maria kept a running record of his learning. In her notes for October, November, and December she wrote:

> Andrew uses print in many ways. He has submitted weekend news about something he has done, written notes to me, made signs "Do Not toch! AndreW"), recorded information in his computer log, and he continues to write in his journal. Andrew involves himself in many of the writing assignments for the class. He made a mobile for a book project for *In the Night Kitchen.*
>
> Andrew remains very quiet about his work. He will give limited information when questioned and often uses a shake or nod of the head to answer. When he has finished a piece, Andrew will locate himself close to me and may remain standing there without comment with his work in hand. Usually the interchange follows this pattern:

T: Looks like you have some work with you.
A: Um-hum. (Stays near)
T: (Pausing, then) would you like to read it to me?
A: (begins to read)

In February Maria noted:

Andrew continues to bring his work to me when he has finished. I now wait and look to him to begin the conversation. He now starts with "I made a book" or "Want me to read it to you?"

Later in Andrew's second-grade year, Maria chose to focus on him when she met with an extended student advocacy group of teachers that meets on a regular basis in the school in which she teaches. Maria chose to focus on Andrew because of his shyness and because of his early history in school, when he was regarded (according to the special education records) as "slow." Maria talked with the extended student advocacy group about Andrew's participation in the classroom, about his disposition, and about his relationships with children and adults. She described his activities and interests, his formal learning, and his strengths and vulnerabilities. In her notes on his activities and interests she wrote:

Andrew speaks often of Nintendo games and is familiar with a variety of current movies—Dick Tracy, the Turtles, Home Alone, etc. . . .

Information in his work—books with the Mario characters, Dick Tracy, Air Wolf. There is action in his work particularly the illustrations. The text provides the sounds that support the actions.

Andrew also likes jokes and riddles. His work often includes humorous bits directed to his audience and sometimes between characters. He wrote his own riddle book early in the year. . . .

Andrew uses scrap pieces of paper, oaktag, cardboard and tubes for construction. He assembles them with staples. His interest seems to last only a short while after the construction.

For a project during our Cinderella study in November, he chose to design a board game. He is presently working on a second game with no direction from me. This is his own idea.

He also enjoys books with tapes. He will sit through a second playing of the book.

Based upon their consideration of the information that Maria had collected, the extended student advocacy group helped her formulate instructional strategies that she could use to support Andrew's academic and social development. These included the following:

- Within socially accepted parameters, give Andrew an environment in which he can show his strengths.
- Try using audio and video recordings with Andrew so that he can create images of himself that will be an outlet for his creativity and documentation of who he is.
- Try to tap the social aspects of Nintendo. Perhaps Andrew could become an "expert" among the Nintendo buffs in his class. Perhaps he could connect with older children through his interest.
- Search out books such as *Crow Boy* to make visible the value of people who are different, people who make meaning out of life in ways that are not common.

Maria's instructional strategies during Andrew's second-grade year were achieved through small interventions that she made on a day-to-day basis. Much of Maria's attention focused on enabling Andrew to participate with other students in the activities that were taking place in the classroom and on enabling Andrew to feel more comfortable talking with her about his work. Maria became the "significant other" in Andrew's academic life. She worked to open up opportunities for him to use his abilities in ways that demonstrated his considerable talents.

This year Maria and Mary B. have worked together as Andrew's student support team. Both Maria and Mary have become increasingly aware of the importance of literacy technologies (computers, Nintendo) in Andrew's life. They have spent time considering the impact that his interest in such technologies has on both the ways in which he approaches academic tasks in the classroom and the ways in which he tries to make friends with other students in the room. In the stories that he writes and in the games that he constructs, many of his graphic representations are computer- and Nintendo-inspired. For example, one of the games that he recently invented is called "Knights and Dragons." It is Andrew's version of the old game "Hangman," (see Figure 5–5). In Andrew's game there are boxes for each letter of the chosen word, and beneath each box a Nintendo control box. Andrew provides the category ("I put the category up here"), which in this game is "food." If the player provides a letter that is not in the word Andrew draws a knight in a box. If the player guesses the word before there are a certain number of knights, a dragon (drawn at the bottom of the page) is killed. If the player does not guess the word then the dragon goes free.

FIGURE 5–5   Andrew's "Knights and Dragons" game

Maria and Mary discuss the way in which Andrew uses his games as an invitation for other students to play with him. Maria said, "The games brought people in." It is the first time that they have observed him trying to engage others in his activities, and it is working. Students enjoy the games that he makes, and he is not short of participants when he has the opportunity to play.

In more formal learning situations, literacy technologies also play an important role, and Maria and Mary continue to explore the ways in which Andrew uses different symbol systems. In their analysis of his work, they have been using a literacy analysis grid, which helps them focus on the ways in which Andrew is developing problem-solving strategies, constructing oral descriptions, using graphic representations, using different symbolic systems, developing understanding of story structure, writing narrative descriptions, and developing conventional spelling patterns. The notes that they write are essentially analytical memos to themselves, scratch notes that enable them to focus their attention on the ways in which Andrew is learning. (See Figure 5–6.)

Maria remains the principal student advocate for Andrew. Mary B. sometimes works with him, but for the most part it is Maria who provides him with the extra support that he needs to enable him to function successfully within his third-grade classroom. Mary explains that her daily visits to work with other children in Andrew's classroom provide Maria with the opportunity to work with Andrew. Thus, while Mary B. and Meg (a Chapter One teacher) are in the room, Maria takes a few extra minutes to talk with Andrew about his work. Maria's student support plan consists of small instructional interventions that take place on a daily basis. The interventions are based upon her in-depth understanding of the ways in which Andrew is learning. She makes the most of her opportunities to provide moment-to-moment assistance. For example, she focuses on creating comfortable opportunities for Andrew to talk about his work and to share what he is doing with the other students in the class. In addition, knowing that he will be expected to produce more handwritten texts when he moves, she is working with him to strike a balance between his graphic representations and his accompanying writings. This is not an easy task for Maria, who knows that Andrew's graphic representations are at the center of his intellectual development. Maria's task is to expand upon the ways in which he uses his creation of visual abstractions so that he is successful within the academic community of his classroom, and within other academic communities that he might encounter when he moves and attends a different school.

Learning How to Support Bobby's Academic and Social Needs in a Regular Classroom Setting

This is the first year that Debbie has worked with Bobby. At the beginning of the fall semester, Bobby injured his hand and his arm was in a cast. After that he contracted pneumonia, and was unable to attend school for several weeks. When he was in school, he was out of the classroom for a considerable amount of time because he was being evaluated to discover whether or not he "qualified" for special education services. Although Debbie tried to keep his absences from the classroom to a minimum, she was concerned that she was not spending enough time with Bobby to allow her to gain some understanding of the ways in which he was learning in her classroom. There were very few opportunities for her to observe him as he

FIGURE 5–6   Andrew's literacy analysis

BLiPP LITERACY PROFILES ANALYSIS GRID - 1   Name: Andrew Feb

Problem Solving	Oral Descriptions	Graphics	Symbol Weaving
10/91 - uses clay to make dice for his games. - uses paper of different sizes for books. - uses post-its for "hidden work" - look behind door A, B or C. - Flag game - uses a variety of different materials to construct flags and prizes. - Remembers books by author. - Locates books by exact title - e.g. Rand McNally Picture Atlas of the World. - Mazes, Logo, Where in the World is Carmen Sandiego.	Remarks: "This is a game." "I put a category up here." "I finished my book." Science lab: Sand "There's a treasure in there."	Characters have "active" "thought balloons." 9/91 Jr. News - illustrations accurate - working at computer. - having a meeting Detailed graphics - Support story.	9/91 Duck Tales - uses cut out parts of pages as "windows" e.g. "we found! [money] flap flap (with pictures) - Illustrations have text within - "The Scariest Ride" (hat on man) e.g. [leaving Dracs] [volcano] [come back soon] [brouttes voitantes]

Story Structure	Narrative Descriptions	Developmental Spelling	Other
10/91 Non Fiction - the Jr. News - tells the initial activities & classmates - includes about the author on his own. - "What do they do next?" - "look at #4" - "to be continued." - Writes series "The Alien 1, 2, 3.	Adding text to Logo	Mid - trasitional Phonetic elements Blends Digraphs Vowel combinations. Extensive sight words.	Chooses to use markers, crayons. Prefers not to use pencil, presently Pentech Firecracker pens.

Assessing the Complexity of Students' Learning

wrote, and very few opportunities for her to observe his reading. However, as the semester progressed, Debbie was able to spend more time with Bobby, and gradually, over a period of several months, she was able to gain a better understanding of his learning so that instructional decisions could be made and appropriate interventions developed.

Given Bobby's social history, Debbie, Mary B., and Mary C., his student support team, agreed that there should be no major interventions that would either remove him from his classroom or separate him from the other students working in the room. They agreed that it was important that Bobby see himself as a fully participatory member of his classroom community. Both Mary B. and Mary C. worked with several students in Debbie's room, so it appeared to be socially acceptable for them also to work with Bobby. Thus, for Bobby, there are times when he receives concentrated help from his classroom teacher, from the school's literacy educator, and from the Chapter One teacher. Each teacher focuses on different areas of Bobby's academic development although, since they often worked as a team, there is considerable overlap in the academic support that they provide.

The instructional decisions and intervention strategies that Debbie, Mary B., and Mary C. are using have emerged from their observations of Bobby, from their conversations with him, and from their analysis of the information that they have collected, including the running record and miscue analysis. Debbie and Mary B. work together using a literacy profiles grid to help them focus on Bobby's academic development. They use the grid as a prompt for their analysis as they look across the curriculum at the ways in which Bobby develops problem-solving strategies, constructs oral descriptions, and so forth (Figure 5–7). Then they look more specifically at reading, writing, and math strategies, and similarly at mechanics (Figure 5–8).

The following example is included to show how one such analysis was made. In the "Problem Solving" category of Bobby's literacy analysis grid (Figure 5–7) Debbie had written, "uses environmental situations (i.e. listening to other students' instructions to build his own understandings." Debbie explained the cryptic comment. She said that she had given the calculation to the whole class "as a method of assessment." Debbie went on, "What startled us is that we were not instructing him in the model that he used. He had received some instruction at home but again not in the model that he used." Without specific instruction in school Bobby had multiplied 46 by 53. Debbie continued, "Mary [C.] had been working with Bobby

FIGURE 5–7   Bobby's literacy analysis grid I

BLiPP LITERACY PROFILES ANALYSIS GRID - I

Name: Bobby

Problem Solving	Oral Descriptions	Graphics	Symbol Weaving
D & D · map · flexible strategies. Recombined names of towns to change orig. into a larger list. Writing orig. w. collaborator. Theorizes about his own learning. B. uses environmental situations (i.e. listening to other students' instructions to build his own understandings.	Detailed retelling — Nova video — Class read aloud. Underground Room · His own writings · His own readings — Articulate about his learning processes etc · Eager to share detailed factual info. as well as opinions on various class issues.	Bobby uses generalized sketching to demonstrate his ideas & explore the plot line. example: demonstrating making a law. B. recognizes his own ability to draw and offers to take materials home to work with markers.	— Dungeons & Dragons — Choose your own Adventure

Story Structure	Narrative Descriptions	Developmental Spelling	Other
Uses a variety of story structures/genre — Constellation story — Owl story "Did you know" "To take care of that." — Choose your own Adv./Dungeons & Dragons — 51 ways to —		— Early transitional — blends — initial & final consonants — vowel markers. Uses environmental print.	

FIGURE 5–8   Bobby's literacy analysis grid II

Name: Bobby

BLiPP LITERACY PROFILES ANALYSIS GRID - II

READING	WRITING	MATHEMATICS
Strategies	**Strategies**	**Strategies**
- Rereads. - Reads on. - Substitutes unfamiliar words (words syntactically & semantically appropriate) - Reads for meaning - Visualization of story - Uses pictures & diagrams	- Appears to use prewriting time as an opportunity to think through the story which he then appears to write from beginning to end. example: Constellation Story ½ thinking time followed by verbalization then ½ hour of writing - When B. follows this process Minimal revision for content needed. - Uses others for spelling support especially for some letters within words	- relies on doubling and partial sums to arrive at multiplication sums. example: 4 ⟩ 8 ⟩ 12 indicating with lines 4 ⟩ 8 ⟩ 20 associations 4 ⟩ 8 ⟩ 4 - uses hash marks - uses Calculator computation in isolation and problem solving situations
Mechanics	**Mechanics**	**Mechanics**
	- uses end punctuation - Capitalizes proper nouns, book titles, greetings and closing of letters, pronoun I, sometimes at beginnings of sentences. - edits spelling as he rereads.	"getting my numbers straight" - Bobby is able to perform successfully double digit Multiplication (direct instruction was in rounding & estimating)

on rounding and estimating, while some of the other students were multiplying double-digit numbers. What surprised us was that he must have picked up the model from other members of the class." (See "Mechanics" on the literacy analysis grid II.) Debbie talked about his explanation and emphasized that he obviously understood the model that he had used. "That was his writing without support," she said. Then she continued, "The irony was that he learned how to multiply that way by picking up a model that was way beyond what we were expecting him to learn. It emphasizes how critical it is that he [be] in the room. It also emphasizes that we need to be aware of the way in which he learns. He may be busily working on some project of his own (such as learning to multiply) while we're expecting him to be working on something else (such as rounding and estimating)." The writing that Debbie referred to is as follows:

I touk 46 and I rand
    × 53
I took 46 and tim it and cum up with 128
    × 3
and touk the 5 and put it like 46 and time it
    × 50
and I cout 2300 and add 128 and I got
    2300
my antser 2428

Again Debbie spoke about the significance of the calculation. "Bobby learns from what's happening around him," she said. "That's a learning strength that many of us don't have."

Bobby's student support plan focuses on small instructional interventions that take place on a daily basis. Mary C., the Chapter One teacher, works with Bobby, helping him with specific math skills, with spelling, and with writing. Much of her time with Bobby is spent providing him with support as he works on his regular classroom assignments. Mary uses (embeds) her instructional interventions within the general assistance she provides for Bobby as he works to complete his regular class assignments. Her intent at all times is *to make the interventions relevant.*

Mary B., the literacy educator, works in a similar way. Conferences between teachers and students are a regular event in Debbie's fifth-grade classroom. There is nothing unusual about them; every student participates in them on a regular basis. So Debbie, Mary B., and Bobby went through a period of conferring every day. Given the opportunity, Bobby avoids reading. He talks about how difficult it is for him to read, and he speaks about his younger sister, who can read much better than he can. Debbie and Mary B. are trying to help Bobby "understand the process." Debbie said that the purpose of the meetings was to help Bobby get involved with some of the reading activities that were taking place in the classroom. Debbie said that he wasn't reading and that he was jumping from one book to another. To encourage him to choose a book and "stick to it," Mary suggested that they could be reading partners; but Bobby said that he didn't like the idea. On a subsequent occasion, when Debbie and Bobby were talking about reading, Debbie asked Bobby why he didn't like the idea of partner reading. Bobby said, "You just want me to finish the book." Debbie said, "He seemed upset at the thought of partner reading, so I asked him, 'What is it that bothers you about partner reading?' and he said, 'Making mistakes.' I told him that making mistakes helps, that those mistakes help us understand how you read. Then I asked him, 'Why do you think we look at your mistakes?' He said, 'To see how dumb I am.'" Debbie said that she then took a book out of his desk and opened it to the first page. With a series of "What if you" scenarios, Debbie explained what she learned from various miscues. With each "what if" she demonstrated the positive information that Bobby's mistakes provided. Debbie then told Bobby, "We listen to mistakes because they help us." She said, "He seemed visibly relieved." It was at this moment that Mary arrived and joined in the conversation. The three of them talked about different ways to partner read. Debbie said, "We got into other ways to help him. We suggested that he write difficult words on a bookmark so that he could find out what they were when he had finished reading. We looked at a page in a book he had been reading, and he picked out a word that he had trouble reading, and we told him that if he had a bookmark he could have made a note of it and asked someone what it was when he had finished reading. Bobby said he wouldn't have needed to do that as he had worked it out later on in the book." Debbie went on. "We pointed out that that probably meant that he was using context clues, and he became really interested in that. So on Monday we talked about what books he might like to read. On Tuesday we talked about miscues. On Wednesday, Jim [the school counselor] took him to McDonald's with some other kids and he missed reading. But you know that day he stopped writing ten minutes early and read and made an entry in his reading log. On Thursday he read for about forty-five minutes." Debbie said that she and Mary B. were getting worried that they were taking so much time talking about reading that there was little time left for Bobby to actually read, but when he started reading on Wednesday, they knew the investment had been worth it. If they had any doubts left they quickly faded on

Friday when Bobby came into school with the book that he had just finished reading. He had gone home and invited his grandmother to be his reading partner, and together they had read the book. Debbie said, "He was beaming, just floating on air."[7]

Debbie went on to talk about the instructional interventions that she and Mary B. had agreed to make next. She said, "Bobby is so interested in his own learning, we've decided that talking about miscues might help." Mary B. says their primary goal is to encourage Bobby to spend more time reading. She explains, "We think it will help him if he increases his awareness of the ways in which he reads. We are trying to make the process visible." She said that next week the three of them are going to look at the running record and miscue analysis that she had made of Bobby reading *The Man Who Kept House*. Mary B. said, "It is important that Bobby is aware of what he is doing and why he is doing it. Looking at his miscues helped him understand the way he reads. It's a very specific instructional intervention that is ongoing for Bobby. We are trying to help Bobby take control of his own learning. This is one of the ways that we can accomplish that."

A final comment from Debbie. When she had finished talking about Bobby's reading she went back to the lunch that he had had with Jim, the school counselor. She said that when Jim returned he told her that Bobby was visibly upset when he arrived at McDonald's and that he was "fighting back tears." Jim said that when he asked Bobby if he was okay Bobby said, "I don't get to go to places like this." Debbie said, "I keep thinking of all the situations that we put him in, situations in which he has no experience to draw upon, such as watching the film on fast food with me. He doesn't even get to eat fast food."

Summary and Conclusions

The third phase of the student advocacy model of instructional assessment provides opportunities for both classroom teachers and teachers providing specialized instructional services to work together to analyze the information that has been collected, to make instructional decisions, and to carry out instructional interventions. The student support teams are "ad-hocratic."[8] They are formed in recognition of the fact that the development of innovative instructional interventions is not a solitary endeavor. Skrtic (1991) writes that when innovation occurs "it is a social phenomenon that takes place within a reflective discourse" (p. 178). The student advocacy model creates a framework for such reflective teacher discourse. Again, the model provides teachers with the opportunity to assume the role of the novice within the framework of their own expertise. Assuming the role of the novice means that teachers acknowledge the need to understand from the perspective of individual students how learning takes place, what students know, and what they can do. Understanding learning from the perspective of the student provides teachers with opportunities to use their professional expertise in problem-solving situations that take into consideration the social, cultural, and political circumstances of their students' everyday lives.

In the two case studies used in this section to illustrate the ways in which teachers come together to analyze the information that has been collected, the ad-hocratic patterns of intervention differed in ways that enabled the teachers to provide the types of support that appeared to best fit the individual student's needs.[9] In these particular case studies the classroom teacher, the literacy educator, and the Chapter One teacher worked together. In other situations it might be, for example, the classroom teacher, the special educator, and the school counselor who form the ad-hocratic student support team. (Every attempt should be made to include a family member or significant other as a member of each student support team.)

Andrew's student support team continues to work collaboratively. Most recently they have used a video of Andrew's working on a science project as a basis for an analysis of the ways in which he participates in a complex problem-solving activity. Viewing the video created a context for the ongoing conversation that is taking place about the ways in which the team can support and enhance Andrew's learning opportunities. While the team watches the video to gain some understanding of the complexities of Andrew's intellectual activity, they also take seriously the seemingly irrelevant details[10] of his everyday[11] school life. The student support team makes a conscious effort to see what they have learned not to see. For example, the notes that students pass and the games that they play are rarely the focus of teacher attention, yet Andrew's hangman game provided clues to the ways in which he is negotiating his place as a member of the community of learners in his second- and third-grade classroom. Examining the ways in which Andrew constructed the game provided Maria, his classroom teacher, with an opportunity to see how he uses the material and technical resources at his disposal to create a social activity that he can share with the other students in his class. This is critical information that Maria shares with Andrew's student support team as they reflect upon the ways in which they can support his social and academic development.

It is impossible for Bobby's student support team to work with him without trying to understand *from his perspective* how his nomadic life and his long school absences have affected his academic development. Understanding the impact of the events that have taken place in his young life critically affects the intervention strategies that the student support team develops to help Bobby. The team's innovative intervention strategies have evolved within the framework of the reflective discourse that characterizes the conversations that occur when they meet to discuss the student support plan that they are constantly revising as they gain a better understanding of what works and what doesn't work—*from Bobby's point of view.*

It is important to emphasize that students themselves and members of their families can participate in the creation of instructional interventions. For example, Bobby began partner reading with his grandmother. In the past few weeks they have read four books together, and Bobby's grandmother often acts as the scribe for his book journal entries. These entries consist of pages of text dictated by Bobby and written in his grandmother's hand. Debbie, Bobby's classroom teacher, talks on the telephone with Bobby's grandmother at least once a week. Debbie talks enthusiastically about the changes that she sees in the type of support that Bobby is receiving at home, and it is clear that Bobby's grandmother has become a vital member of the ad-hocratic student support team.[12]

It is also clear that Bobby has become a team player. He is aware of the efforts that are being made to understand the ways in which he is learning, and he talks about the progress that he is making. On one occasion he talked about the narrative that Debbie had written about the ways in which he is learning, and then he talked about the ways in which he is reading with his grandmother. He said, "I started reading with my grandmother. We partner read. We read a chapter a person. We read every single day. At the weekends we read once. My goal is to finish a book every single week." When Bobby was asked "What's changed?" he said, "What's changed is that reading is too fun and I can't stop. I like to read."[13]

PHASE FOUR: ADJUSTING THE STUDENT SUPPORT PLAN BASED ON THE ONGOING COLLECTION OF INFORMATION

In "The Special Education Paradox," Skrtic (1991) writes:

> Student disability is neither a human pathology nor an objective distinction; it is an organizational pathology, a matter of not fitting the standard

> programs of the prevailing paradigm of a professional culture, the legiti-
> macy of which is artificially reaffirmed by the objectification of school
> failure as a human pathology through the institutional practice of special
> education. (p. 169)

The student advocacy model of instructional assessment makes visible the artificial objectification of the human pathology paradigm that currently dominates special education. Within the instructional assessment framework the triannual rituals of I.Q. and diagnostic testing are no longer used as rites of passage for students whose learning does not fit the narrowly defined definitions of school learning. Yearly "IEP's" are no longer relevant, and triannual reviews are rendered obsolete.[14] Students are not handicapped, and neither are teachers. What students know counts. What teachers know counts. It is the combined understanding of students and teachers that forms the basis of instructional assessment.

In the student advocacy model of instructional assessment, understanding how students actively participate in the construction of problem-solving situations, how they know what they know, and how they use what they have learned to generate new knowledge is part of teachers' instructional practice. Teaching becomes a problem-solving activity that brings professionals together to form dynamic student support teams that seek innovative solutions to the practical difficulties many students face as they participate in the social and academic activities of American educational institutions.

Documenting the students' participation in the social and academic life of the classroom becomes increasingly important. The portfolios of students who need the extra assistance of a student support team become more elaborate as the team works with the student to gain a more in-depth understanding of the ways in which the student learns. Scratch papers are collected as well as final products, as teachers and students try to understand *the social construction of knowledge in practice*. Reconstructing the evolution of a problem-solving situation becomes important. The finished product is only one part of the puzzle. A "right" or "wrong" answer provides very little information about the ways in which an individual student set about particular tasks. "Answers" do not necessarily reflect the complexity of intellectual activity.

Further documentary evidence of student advocacy learning is also collected and placed in the student's portfolio. Biographic learning profiles, graphic representations of problem-solving activities, and literacy analysis grids, together with accounts of miscue analysis, are all collected over time and added to the students' portfolio. At any time, the student support team can conduct an intensive analysis of the documentary evidence that has been collected to verify past interpretations and to modify, refine, and expand upon present instructional intervention strategies.

Thus the fourth phase of the student model of instructional assessment provides an opportunity for teachers to hold themselves accountable for the instructional decisions that have been made. Adjustments to the student support plan are based upon the student support team's reflection on their observations of student's learning, the notes they have collected, the portfolios they have analyzed, the analysis grids that have been constructed, and the biographic literacy profiles they have written. Team members are given the opportunity to step back and look at the descriptions of the student's learning that they have created. Invariably this time is well spent as new insights are gained and new instructional interventions are developed.

COMMENTARY

The student advocacy model of instructional assessment will require a cooperative effort if educational institutions are to overcome the discriminatory practices that have resulted from traditional reductionist assessment procedures. In *Voices of the Mind: A Sociocultural Approach to Mediated Action,* James Wertsch (1991) writes:

> We have many isolated, often arcane pieces to a larger puzzle, but we have no coherent, integrative picture of the whole. We can answer detailed questions about neuronal activity or neonatal reflexes, but we have very little to say about what it means to be human in the modern world (or any other world for that matter). (p. 1)

Referencing the work of Rogoff (1990) and Rommetveit (1979), Wertsch writes of the individualistic orientation of psychologists and of the decades of research that have been carried out that explored mental processes in vacuo, including such decontextualized phenomena as "IQ, memory strategies and grammatical skills" (p. 3).

As an antidote, Wertsch argues that "an approach to mental action" be taken "that emphasizes diversity rather than conformity in the processes involved and a concern with the cultural, institutional, and historical situatedness of mediated action" (p. 8). Wertsch explains this approach as follows:

> Human beings are viewed as coming into contact with, and creating, their surroundings as well as themselves through the actions in which

they engage. Thus action, rather than human beings or the environment considered in isolation, provides the point of entry into the analysis. (p. 8)

In the student advocacy model of instructional assessment, student support teams focus on what students can do, and how they use the social, symbolic, technical, and material resources at their disposal in the accomplishment of everyday academic tasks. As stated at the beginning of this chapter, it is the teachers' expertise that creates significant ways of knowing the local complexities of students' lives, the ways in which students construct and use language, the ways in which students participate in problem-solving situations, and how students' learning can be supported in school. The student advocacy model of instructional assessment is action-oriented, problem-solving assessment that is dynamic, vital, and in tune with diversity *from the student's point of view.*

To work within the framework outlined above will require a paradigmatic shift, a reformation in thinking, which recognizes that "student disability is neither a human pathology nor an objective distinction; it is an organizational pathology, a matter of not fitting the standard programs of the prevailing paradigm of a professional culture" (Skrtic, 1991, p. 169). While many professionals within the field of education have already made this shift, many have not. For some entrenched policy makers and administrators, the paradigmatic shift that the model necessitates will be viewed with suspicion and even hostility. Sharing power with teachers will be too threatening. For others, especially test producers and test administrators, the prospect of diminishing profits will be viewed with alarm. At the present time the State of California spends $2.4 billion a year on special education, and as in other American states it is assumed that a significant percentage of this money is spent on "diagnostic" testing. For example, in Colorado, Shepard and Smith (1981) found that the amount of money spent on assessment was almost equal to the personnel costs for direct special education instruction and support services for the average special education student (see also Rueda, 1989). In addition, in California an estimated $600 million are spent every three years on triannual reviews of students receiving special education services. None of this money goes directly to teachers to support instructional interventions for students receiving special education services. In every American state, scientifically indefensible assessment practices continue to be used for power and for profit in what could legitimately be described as the biggest waste of money in the history of American education.

The argument that some test makers and test givers have voiced in reaction to the student advocacy model of instructional assessment is that "teachers won't [or can't] do it." The immediate response to this statement is that not only are teachers doing it, but it is teachers who *volunteered* to participate in the research that has resulted in the development of the model, and it is teachers who are *pioneering* the student advocacy model of instructional assessment in schools.[15] The following table briefly outlines some of the reasons for teachers' voluntary participation.

Traditional Reductionist Assessment	**Holistic Constructivist Assessment**
Developed by researchers in studies that isolated mental processes (in vacuo) for separate analysis.	Developed by researchers in studies that acknowledge that "mental events are never directly available for analysis; they can only be modeled by inference from people's behavior in extremely well-defined environments" (McDermott and Roth, 1978; see also Wertsch, 1991).
Developed by researchers working for commercial test development companies.	Developed by researchers working with classroom and special education teacher-researchers.
Imposed on teachers. Many teachers resent the imposition.	Voluntarily developed by teachers. Many teachers embrace the opportunity.
Teachers treated as technocrats administering achievement tests.	Teachers recognized as professionals who can develop instructional assessment procedures.
Teachers regarded as lacking the specialized training necessary to administer psychological tests (e.g., WISC).	Teachers recognized for their specialized skills, which enable them to develop in-depth analyses of students' observable learning behaviors.
Teachers' knowledge often disregarded (see Mehan et al., 1986). Test results (often referred to as "objective measures") prioritized.	Teachers' knowledge (systematic subjectivity) recognized as a rich source of information about student learning.

Assessing the Complexity of Students' Learning

Assessment unrelated to teaching.	Assessment part of teaching.
Assessment side-tracks teachers. Time is taken away from instructional practices.	Assessment informs, assists, and supports teachers as they work with individual students.
De-skills teachers. Imposes limits on the opportunities that teachers have to assess students in authentic problem-solving situations.	Re-skills teachers. Expands on the opportunities that teachers have to assess and learn more about students' observable learning behaviors.
Financial resources allocated to test packages and test administrators.	Financial resources directly allocated to teachers and students for instructional support.
Separates classroom teachers and teachers who provide specialized support services.	Creates a collaborative framework for classroom teachers and teachers who provide specialized instructional services to work together.
Students removed from regular classrooms to receive specialized instructional services. Resources go with them.	Students participate and belong to a community of learners in their regular classrooms. Teachers providing specialized services enrich the classroom. All students benefit.
Standardization creates the potential for discrimination.	Diversity honored. Understanding learning from the student's point of view creates a framework for nondiscriminatory educational practices.
Interventions preplanned in September (yearly individual educational plans) do not take into consideration, nor are they relevant to, ongoing changes in learning behaviors that take place on a daily basis throughout the year.	Interventions relevant at the moment of instruction. Close link between the analysis of the information that has been collected, the instructional decisions that are made, and the interventions that are carried out.

Students removed from regular classroom activities for the assessment procedures to take place. Assessment for a student thought to be learning disabled could result in twenty-one hours of assessment or the equivalent of two weeks of school (see Shepard and Smith, 1981; Rueda, 1989).	Students assessed as they participate in regular classroom activities.
Limits learning. Focuses on what students *cannot* do, then remediates.	Enhances learning. Focuses on what students can do.
Students excluded from the information-gathering process.	Students participate in the collection of information, which they gather in their portfolios.
Students do not usually see the assessment reports, which contain detailed accounts of what individual students cannot do. Negative statements have no instructional value.	Students can read the assessment reports. The reports become a vehicle for students to think about their own learning. The information can be used by students to develop their own instructional interventions.
Language of assessment reports is foreign to both students and their parents.	Language of assessment reports descriptive of students' learning. Parents can use the biographic assessment reports to gain a more in-depth understanding of the ways in which their children learn in everyday academic settings.

Teachers involved in the research and development of the student advocacy model of instructional assessment have moved beyond the constrictions of reductionistic psychometric assessment, and they are fully articulate in holistic constructivist ways of thinking and ways of working with students. However, they remain caught between two paradigms because of federal and state regulations that require the ascription of pathological conditions to students whose learning does not fit the artificially defined grade-level expectations of the dominant bureaucratic educational establishment. On a daily basis, teachers advocate for students whose complex learning configurations reflect and are part of their everyday experiences, but whose learning does not register on the narrowly defined scales that are acceptable as indicators of intellectual ability currently used in American schools. When teachers work within a holistic constructivist paradigm, diversity is expected. Teachers know that, as Wertsch (1991) states, it is "difficult if not meaningless to isolate various aspects of mental processes for separate analysis" (p. 14), and yet they are expected to ascribe to such procedures when they request extra support for students whom they are teaching.

As teachers become more articulate in presenting their interpretations of students' learning, they also become more effective as student advocates. Their pioneering struggle to develop alternative ways of thinking about students' learning has made a difference at both the local and national level. However, other teachers should not have to repeat their pioneering work. In the implementation of the student advocacy model of instructional assessment, teachers should not be expected to ascribe to obsolete paradigms while developing new ways of thinking about instruction and assessment. Successful implementation of the student advocacy model will depend upon the commitment of policy makers, educational researchers, administrators, classroom teachers, and special educators to work closely together, to construct new organizational frameworks, to reallocate resources, and to provide opportunities for parents to participate in the process. Teachers will require intensive retraining and on-site support as they learn new ways of thinking about students whose lives they have been taught to medicalize (Mehan, Hertweck, and Meihls, 1986). If this happens, students who learn in ways that do not meet traditional school expectations will not be labeled. Students who are poor will not be penalized. Students of color will have the chance to succeed. Students for whom English is a second language will be heard. Students whose young lives have been damaged by life's circumstances will have the opportunity to recover. Discriminatory practices will be harder to conceal. Understanding learning from the student's point of view forces educators to examine their own ethnocentricities. Other ways of thinking and doing are made visible. Diversity is no longer regarded as a liability; instead, it becomes the driving force of innovation as the learning of *all* students forms the basis of instruction.

IMPLEMENTATION OF THE STUDENT ADVOCACY MODEL OF INSTRUCTIONAL ASSESSMENT

The student advocacy model of instructional assessment provides teachers with the opportunity to use their professional expertise. For most of the teachers presently working as student advocates using an instructional assessment model, the training has come in the form of personally defined apprenticeships served in classrooms with on-site support. Each apprenticeship has begun with participation in an alternative assessment institute, followed by a series of workshops that explore specific aspects of student advocacy through instructional assessment.

Training of Teacher-Leaders

Based upon the research and development completed to the present time, the following are considered likely candidates as teacher-leaders to participate in the implementation of the student advocacy model of instructional development:

1. Teachers who volunteer to participate, who are interested in the reformation.
2. Teachers who have a theoretical and practical background in holistic/constructivist educational practices.
3. Teachers who have experience of leading teachers through processes of change.
4. Teachers who are teaching at schools in which the student advocacy model of instructional assessment would be a natural extension of current innovative practices.

Training institutes for teacher-leaders would take place over approximately one year. During this time teacher-leaders would:

1. Attend student advocacy instructional assessment institutes, which would include an initial two-week institute held during the summer and three follow-up three-day institutes held during the school year.
2. Teach in holistic/process classrooms learning to observe, to take notes and develop portfolios, and to use instructional assessment procedures in working with students for whom they are concerned.

3. Participate in a second two-week summer institute, which would focus on preparing teacher-leaders to mentor other teachers who will be using the student advocacy model of instructional assessment.

On-site support for teacher-leaders in training would be essential. Visits would be made to their classrooms on a monthly basis. These visits would include demonstrations of note taking, critical analyses of students' work, and discussions that focus on the questions of teacher-leaders.

Training of Teachers

The training of classroom teachers and teachers providing specialized instructional services would also take approximately one year. During this time these teachers would:

1. Attend student advocacy instructional assessment institutes with a teacher-leader who would act as the mentor for six teachers in training. The institutes would include an initial one-week institute held during the summer and three follow-up three-day institutes held during the school year.
2. Work closely with teacher-leaders throughout the school year. Teacher-leaders would visit on a regular basis and would spend time working collaboratively with teachers in their classrooms, observing, note taking, analyzing students' work, and constructing biographic descriptions of students' learning.
3. Participate in on-site meetings with the teacher-leader's team of six teachers in training. At these meetings the teacher-leaders and teachers in training will form student support teams for students for whom they are concerned.

The implementation of the student advocacy model of instructional assessment would provide opportunities for intensive collaboration to take place between teacher-leaders and teachers in training. Teachers will need time in their classrooms to develop their own observational and note-taking procedures. They will need time to analyze students' work and to participate in student support teams made up of other teachers in training and the teacher-leaders who are mentoring them. The following organizational changes will be necessary:

1. A reallocation of resources will be essential at both the state and local levels. Money presently spent on external psychological

evaluations would be redirected for internal use by classroom teachers and teachers providing specialized instructional services.

2. New organizational frameworks that would allow student support teams to meet and work with students on a regular basis will need to be established.

3. Classroom support will need to be made available to teachers on a regular basis. Some of this support could be provided by classroom aides who have some understanding of holistic/constructivist education.

Finally, all the sites chosen during the first year of the implementation should have the potential of becoming demonstration sites. These critical sites should be chosen in schools in which:

1. There is a cohesive holistic/constructivist philosophy, or in which teachers are developing a holistic philosophy.

2. Holistic/constructivist research projects are being conducted, such as Project OLE in California or the Philadelphia Writing Project.

3. Mainstreaming has already taken place or is in the process of taking place.

A final caveat: It has been the tradition in American schools to exclude teachers from the decision-making process. In implementing the student advocacy model of instructional assessment, it is essential that teachers' voices be heard. One teacher from an East Los Angeles school talked about the assessment programs that had been tried in the high school in which she taught. She said that the eighty teachers who taught in the school would be summoned to the gym for a meeting, and that at the meeting they would be handed a package and told that it contained the new assessment materials that they were to use. She said there was no explanation of the materials and no training provided. The student advocacy model of instructional assessment is different. It will require time and effort. It is theoretically grounded, practically situated in the everyday classroom practices of teachers. The reformation that this model advocates *will* take place if teachers are treated as professionals who have the expertise to make critical decisions about students' learning. However, if the financial resources are not reallocated, or if the organizational structure of schools stays the same, all that will be handed to teachers is just another assessment package that they will be unable to implement.

Assessing the Complexity of Students' Learning

APPENDIX: THE PRESUPPOSITION OF HUMAN PATHOLOGY

In a letter from the California Association of School Psychologists to the Policy and Planning Committee of the California State Board of Education (October 21, 1991), Loeb Aronin, chair of the Special Education Committee, states:

> CASP believes that a psychological report offers a wealth of information leading to interventions to help a child benefit from education. A sample psychological evaluation is attached.

In fact the sample psychological report attached to the letter provides *no* specific information about the student J.R.'s observable learning behaviors. The reader learns that, during the extensive period of testing by the school psychologist, J.R. "exhibits poor concentration" and "poor ability to maintain physical calm when transitioning from one task to another." The reader is informed of his "learning weaknesses," "learning deficits," and "attentional difficulties." The reader is also made aware of his "articulation errors" and his "grammatical and syntactical errors," although there is no description of the specific "errors" that J.R. is making. "Psychological processing disorders" are mentioned in "short term visual memory for abstract symbols," but again there is no hard data of symbolic systems in use to back up the statement, and no examples of processing disorders are described. The recommendations that are made provide no specific information that can be used to support J.R.'s learning. Recommendations such as "(s)chool personnel to consider a structured learning environment with much positive reinforcement" serves only to emphasize the asininity of this type of report. *All* students need to be in a structured learning environment, and *all* students need to be supported by their teachers. By reporting on what J.R. supposedly *can't* do and by focusing on the in-the-head deficits ascribed to him, CASP misses the opportunity to provide detailed systematic documentation on J.R.'s observable learning behaviors that teachers could use as they work with J.R. The report is of interest historically as an example of largely abandoned isolationist (in vacuo) psychological theories; however, such potentially discriminatory unscientific reporting is of little interest, relevance, or value to classroom teachers.

NOTES

1. The appendix illustrates the presupposition of human pathology by presenting excerpts from a report sent to the Policy and Planning Committee of

the California State Board of Education by Loeb Aronin, chair of the Special Education Committee of the California Association of School Psychologists.
2.   In *The Paradigm Dialogue*, Egon Guba (1990) writes: "The press to predict and control places great emphasis on the statement of formal theories— and preferably, broad based, reductionist ("grand") theories. The development and testing of these theories characterize much of scientific activity. But such grand theories, while abetting generalizability, often are not found to 'fit' or 'work' (Glaser and Strauss, 1967) in local contexts" (p. 22).
3.   In developing the student advocacy model I have built upon the between-heads view of learning, which is presented in the first chapter of this book. Consistent with an ethnographic perspective, within the student advocacy framework, learning is defined as a social process. Teachers focus on students' *observable learning behaviors.*
4.   In the fall of 1992 Andrew changed schools. On the first day of school Maria received a telephone call asking about Andrew's status. Andrew had been in his new school for approximately three hours when the call was received. Maria was asked if he was coded. She said that he was not. Maria went on to explain that among the concerns that were expressed was that he wasn't participating in the basal reading activities and that his writing was a mixture of upper- and lower-case letters.
5.   The latter statement is confusing because the psychologist wrote in his report that Bobby's "strengths lie mainly in the visual manual area."
6.   Miscue analysis provides teachers with opportunities to examine and learn from the types of miscues that a student makes. It also provides them with the opportunity to describe the observable reading behaviors of a student. For Mary, the approach provided her with an opportunity to focus on what Bobby actually does when he reads a text. Paraphrasing Goodman, Watson, and Burke (1987) she writes in a footnote to her report: "Unlike other diagnostic instruments, miscue analysis can be both a qualitative and a quantitative analysis of reading proficiency. It allows a teacher to go beyond the surface behavior to examine strategies such as self-correction and repetition, which are in fact necessary for proficient reading."
7.   Another example of Bobby's sensitivity to and interest in the ways in which he learns was provided during one recent conversation. When Bobby was asked how he could be helped to overcome the difficulties he is experiencing in writing, he talked about the problems he has spelling. He said, "If somebody would tell me [how to spell a word] I'd be writing it. If I need help they would help me. I'd probably be able to spell because I'd be writing so much more."
8.   In *The Structuring of Organizations*, Henry Mintzberg (1979) describes various organizational structures. In his introduction to "adhocracies" he writes: "None of the structural configurations so far discussed is capable of sophisticated innovation. . . . The Simple Structure can certainly innovate, but only in a relatively simple way. Both the Machine and Professional Bureaucracies are performance, not problem-solving structures. They are designed to perfect standard programs, not to invent new ones. . . . A focus on

control by standardizing outputs does not encourage innovation. *Sophisticated innovation requires a . . . very different structural configuration, one that is able to fuse experts drawn from different disciplines into smoothly functioning ad hoc project teams"* (p. 432; emphasis in original).

9.   Teachers providing specialized instructional services work as adjuncts to classroom teachers (see Pugach, 1992). Mary B., the literacy educator, states, "I could be in Debbie's classroom for an hour every day, but I'd still only see an *n*th of what she can see."

10.   In *Voices of the Mind: A Sociocultural Approach to Mediated Action,* James Wertsch (1991) explains how conversations based on children's life histories or on personality characteristics are viewed in traditional instructional settings as "irrelevant digressions." The student's perspective is replaced. Thus the teacher loses the opportunity to understand from the student's point of view what is happening (mediated action) as a particular learning activity takes place.

11.   In *Cognition in Practice,* Jean Lave (1988) defines "everyday" as follows: " 'Everyday' is not a time of day, a social role, nor a set of activities, particular social occasions, or settings for activity. Instead, the everyday world is just that: what people do in daily, weekly, monthly, ordinary cycles of activity. A schoolteacher and pupils in the classroom are engaged in 'everyday activity' in the same sense as a person shopping for groceries in the supermarket after work and a scientist in the laboratory. It is the routine character of activity, rich expectations generated over time about its shape, and settings designed for those activities and organized by them, that form the class of events which constitutes an object of analysis in theories of practice" (p. 15).

12.   Debbie often talked on the telephone with Bobby's grandmother. However, some conversations took place on paper. In one conversation in Bobby's homework log his grandmother writes: "Bobby tells me you haven't given him his next book to read. He seems to be confused about the group reading and his book for home reading. Tonight I'll have him read a short story and do a summary on it." Debbie wrote back: "Bobby gave me this at 2:00 so my response is short. He is starting a reading book with a group of students tomorrow. If you have a book for him to read tonight that would be fine." Bobby's grandmother wrote back with reference to a telephone conversation that took place that day: 'It was good talking to you—I will come to the conference Monday, March 23 at 5:15."

13.   Even as this chapter is being edited, Bobby's life circumstances are changing. His student support team is meeting on a regular basis as they try to support his learning. Mary B. says that the team is building upon the shared reading and writing strategies developed by Bobby and his grandmother, who is no longer able to work with him.

14.   Writing of alternative paradigms for practice, Elliot Eisner (1990) states: "Behavioral prescriptions might work for bank tellers and airline attendants but they cannot work for teachers in schools concerned with education" (p. 98).

15. In one school district in New York State, teachers are conducting literacy review meetings that are described as "a vehicle for bringing teachers together." These meetings are initiated by the classroom teacher, and the ad hoc discussion focuses upon "concrete observations of a child" to gain a better understanding of the child's strengths. The goal of the meeting is to "brainstorm suggestions to support the child's growth."

REFERENCES

Cobb, Vicki. 1983. *The Monsters Who Died: A Mystery About Dinosaurs.* New York: Coward-McCaun.
Doll, William E., Jr. 1989. "Complexity in the Classroom." *Educational Leadership* (September): 65–70.
Eisner, Elliot. 1990. "The Meaning of Alternative Paradigms for Practice." In Egon G. Guba, ed., *The Paradigm Dialogue.* Newbury Park, CA: Sage Publications.
Figueroa, Richard A. 1989. "Psychological Testing of Linguistic-Minority Students: Knowledge Gaps and Regulations." *Exceptional Children* 56: 145–52.
Glaser, B. G. and A. L. Strauss. 1973. *The Discovery of Grounded Theory: Strategies for Qualitative Research.* Chicago: Aldine.
Goodman, Yetta M., Dorothy J. Watson, and Carolyn L. Burke. 1987. *Reading Miscue Inventory: Alternative Procedures.* New York: Richard C. Owen Publishers.
Guba, Egon. 1990. "The Alternative Paradigm Dialogue." In Egon G. Guba, ed., *The Paradigm Dialogue.* Newbury Park, CA: Sage Publications.
Lave, Jean. 1988. *Cognition in Practice: Mind, Mathematics, and Culture in Everyday Life.* Cambridge: Cambridge University Press.
Lytle, Susan and Marilyn Cochran-Smith. 1992. "Teacher Research as a Way of Knowing." *Harvard Educational Review.* 52(4): 447–74.
McDermott, R. P. and D. R. Roth. 1978. "The Social Organization of Behavior: Interactional Approaches." *Annual Review of Anthropology* 7: 321–45.
Mehan, Hugh, Alma Hertweck, and J. Lee Meihls. 1986. *Handicapping the Handicapped: Decision Making in Students' Educational Careers.* Stanford, CA: Stanford University Press.
Mintzberg, Henry. 1979. *The Structuring of Organizations: A Synthesis of the Research.* Englewood Cliffs, NJ: Prentice-Hall.
Moll, Luis, ed. 1990. *Vygotsky and Education: Instructional Implications and Applications of Sociohistorical Psychology.* Cambridge: Cambridge University Press.
Poplin, Mary. 1988a. "The Reductionist Fallacy in Learning Disabilities:

Replicating the Past and Reducing the Present." *Journal of Learning Disabilities* 21(7): 389–400.

———. 1988b. "Holistic/Constructivist Principles of the Teaching/Learning Process: Implications for the Field of Learning Disabilities." *Journal of Learning Disabilities* 21(7): 401–16.

Pugach, Marleen C. 1992. "Unifying the Preservice Preparation of Teachers." In W. Stainback and S. Stainback, eds., *Controversial Issues Confronting Special Education*. Boston: Allyn and Bacon.

Reich, R. B. 1990. "Education and the Next Economy." In S. B. Bacharach, ed., *Education Reform: Making Sense of It All*. Boston: Allyn and Bacon.

Rogoff, Barbara. 1990. *Apprenticeship in Thinking: Cognitive Development in Social Context*. New York: Oxford University Press.

Rommetveit, R. 1979. "Deep Structure of Sentence Versus Message Structure: Some Critical Remarks on Current Paradigms, and Suggestions for an Alternative Approach." In R. Rommetveit and R. Blakar, eds., *Studies of Language, Thought, and Verbal Communication*. London: Academic Press.

Rueda, R. 1989. "Defining Mild Disabilities with Language-Minority Children." *Exceptional Children* 56: 121–28.

Ruiz, Nadeen T. 1989. "An Optimal Learning Environment for Rosemary." *Exceptional Children* 56: 130–44.

Shepard, L. and M. L. Smith. 1981. *Evaluation of the Identification of Perceptual-Communicative Disorders in Colorado*. Final report. Boulder: University of Colorado, Laboratory of Educational Research.

Skrtic, Thomas M. 1991. "The Special Education Paradox." *Harvard Educational Review* 61(2): 148–206.

Taylor, Denny. 1988. "Ethnographic Educational Evaluation for Children, Families, and Schools." *Theory into Practice* 27(1): 67–76.

———. 1989. "Toward a Unified Theory of Literacy Learning and Instructional Practices." *Phi Delta Kappan* (November): 184–93.

———. 1990. "Teaching Without Testing." *English Education* 22(1): 4–74.

———. 1991. *Learning Denied*. Portsmouth, NH: Heinemann.

———. 1993. "Early Literacy and the Mental Health of Young Children." In *From the Child's Point of View*. Portsmouth, NH: Heinemann.

Wertsch, James. 1991. *Voices of the Mind: A Sociocultural Approach to Mediated Action*. Cambridge, MA: Harvard University Press.

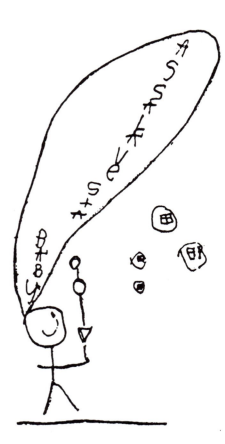

INDEX

Aberrant theory and practice, 34, 123.
  See also Assessment; Testing;
  Theories
Abused child and print, 6, 143–175
Academic: ability, narrative of, 202;
  endorsement of testing, 90;
  information,invisibility of, 17
Accomplishments, situated and
  practical, 12, 14, 16, 65
Across the curriculum, 56
Adams, M.J., 6, 144–145, 167–173
"Adhocracies," 130, 215–217, 229n
Adult-controlled learning process, 26,
  144
Advocacy Model of Instructional
  Assessment, 176–234. *See also*
  Assessment; Biographic Profiles;
  Special Education; Testing
Affluence, bearing on child's cognitive
  experiences, 168
Alphabet book, 161
Alternative evaluation, uncertainty of,
  in face of budget reduction, 24. *See
  also* Budget Cuts; Funding; Special
  Education; Statistical Analysis
Analytic: evaluation, 26; memos, 75,
  208
Ancient Greek Mythology, study of,
  100–106
Anecdotal information, teacher's
  traditional province, 178
Anthropology Newsletter, 57
Apgar, Terri, 119–120
Aphasia Screen, 11
Applebee, A.N., 48
Aronin, Loeb, 228, 229n
Artifacts, collecting of, 111
Artificial: boundaries, 111; classroom
  environments, 92–93; concepts, 47–
  48; training sessions, 171
Artwork: integrated with print. *See also*
  Drawing; Graphics; Illustration;
  Print; integration of, with print, 35–
  37, 39, 101
Assessing complexity of children's
  Literacy Learning, 3, 6, 7, 52–142
Assessment
  alternative, 54, 55–57, 117–118, 135
  authentic, 8, 118, 134, 184, 192

of complexity of student's learning:
  Student Advocacy Model, 4, 7–8,
  176–234
decontextualized, 117
informing practice, 203
negative, 198–199
in New Zealand, 126
practices, 220–221
procedures, 7
tests, as merely validating the
  numbers, 119. *See also* Advocacy
  Model; Biographic Literacy
  Profiles; Special Education; Testing
and fourth-grade reading test, 125–126
and third-grade testing, 133–134
Association: for Childhood Education
  International, 27n; for Supervision
  and Curriculum Development, 27
Assumptions, underlying reductionist
  educational argument, 49. *See also*
  Reductionist; Special Education;
  Statistical Analysis; Testing
At-risk students, and advocacy model,
  172, 178, 192–203
Atkinson study, 91
Attention Deficit Disorder, 11, 26, 119
Atwell, N., 78
Audience: reaction, arousal of, 85–86,
  136
Audio: recording, 111, 135, 206
Auditory processing, 200
Ausubel, D.P., 170
Authentic assessment. *See* Assessment
Authenticity, opportunity for, 26, 71,
  107, 191–192
Authorship, spontaneous, 53
Autobiographical writing, 63, 193
Awareness, meta, 66

Barnwell, Ed, 120–123
Basals, 38, 46, 102, 117, 134, 229n
Bateson, G., 12, 14
Beery VMI, 11
Beginning, with child, 145
Beginning to Read, debate with, 6, 144–
  145, 167–173
Behavior patterns, nonlinear nature of,
  32
Bender-Gestalt, 119

Benton, Mary, 56, 69–70, 84–85, 88–89, 118–120, 131–132
Best Friend Book, 83
"Between-heads" view, 2, 10–12, 23–24, 229n
Big Books, 158
Bill and Ted's Excellent Adventure, child's version of, 100
Biographic Literacy Profiles: "across the curriculum," 54–56; constructed by teacher and student, 178; evolution and change of construction, 87–88, 113–115; intensive analysis of, 115, 191–197; kindergarten through grade four, 53–57, 79–142; making process manageable, 89, 114–115; note-taking procedures for, 42, 78–79, 106, 111, 184, 191; reflecting development and support of each child, 106
Biographic Literacy Profiles Project (BLIPP): beginnings of, 123; documenting process of change in, 59; kindergartener's year, 145–175; major question of, 57; multiple layers of interpretation in, 88; participants in, 137–138; Summer Institutes, 143–175; and teachers literacy configurations, 118; "Teaching without testing," 3–6, 52–142
Biographic Portfolio. *See* Advocacy model; Assessment; Biographic Literacy Profiles Project
Blake, W., 69
Blame, 19
Bloome, D., 49
Bond, G.L., 167
Bony Legs, 84
Book of the Week, 83–84
Books: from found objects, 52; with tape, 205
Bresnahan, Lori, 84, 120
Brown, R., 32
Browne, M., 128–129
Budget cuts, 24, 131. *See also* Assessment; Funding; Special Education; Testing
Bureaucracy and democracy, mutual exclusivity of, 136

Burke, C.L., 20, 229n
Bush, President, 56

Cadieux, Sharron, 80–83, 113–115, 117–118
California: Achievement Tests, 131–132, 134; alternative assessment for, 7–8, 136; Association of School Psychologists (CASP), 228, 229n; Research Institute on Special Education and Cultural Diversity, 7; State Board of Education, 228, 229n; State Department of Education, 7–8
Canterbury Tales, child's version of, 100
"Captain N The Game Master," 99–100
Carbo, M., 3, 31–51
Carraher, D.W., 43, 64, 90
Carraher, T.N., 43, 64, 90
Caswell, Sue, 78
Cat on the Mat, 108–109
Categories for classroom observation, 88–89
Categorized conditions, of educational researchers, 145
CELF Screen, 11
Center for the Study of Reading, 173
Chall, J.S., 3, 31–51, 32, 33, 34 46–48, 90, 167
Chaos: Making a New Science, 31–32
Chaos theorists, 112
Chaotic discovery in language learning, dialectics of, immersion in, 33, 46–50, 60, 62, 65
Chapple, E.D., 14
Chapter books, 39, 85, 87, 185
Chapter headings, use of, 39
Chapter One teacher, 197, 213
Charlotte's Web, 40
Charts, kindergarten, interest in, 158
Chester Cricket's Pigeon Ride, 40
Child abuse, rising incidence of, 5–6
Child-structured writing, 92–94. *See also* Writing
Child-study team, 135, 194. *See also* Student Support Team
Children: everyday lives, description of, 13–14, 20, 26–27, 57–60; and perspective on own reading and writing development, 34; potential of, 26, 134

"Children Unlimited, Inc.," 57
"Choose-Your-Own-Adventure" books,
    39
"Chronic fear-of-failure" syndrome, 26.
    See also Labeling
Cinderella board game, 205
Class meetings, 110
Classroom: academic life in, 24;
    artificial construction of, 90, 92–93;
    change, 58; from child's
    perspective, 18–19; as critical sites
    of inquiry, 10, 130, 178, 179–192;
    environment, 12–13, 91–96; life,
    complexity of, 16–17, 21–27;
    noncorrective environment in, 24;
    as safe haven, 6; teachers. *See*
    Teachers
Clay, M., 20
Clinical psychologist, testing by, 10–11.
    See also Assessment; Psychologist;
    Special Education; Testing
Co-informants, teachers and students,
    42
Cobb, V., 182–183
Cochran-Smith, M., 129–130, 177–178
Coding, 27, 56, 135, 229n
Coe, R.N., 13
Cognition in Practice, 230n
Cognitive tasks, social construction of,
    58
Coles, G., 33
Collaboration, 66, 177
Community: of learners, 58; support for
    schools, 122
Complete, OT, 119
Complexity: of children's symbolic
    activity, 52–142, 69, 100, 112;
    creating order out of, 58, 192; in
    learning behaviors of young
    children, 3, 33–34, 46, 49–50, 65,
    68, 100; of students learning,
    assessing the, 96, 110–11, 176–234;
    theory and restructuring of
    educational and political practice,
    125–129
Computer: club, membership in, 13–14,
    23–24; games, 13–14, 18, 185–186;
    writing and editing stories on, 19,
    186–189
"Computer metaphor" of mind, limits
    of, 90

Conferring, student-teacher, 76, 86, 107,
    213
Confidence, in ability to write, 76
Confirmational reading, 62
Congressional mandate, 144
Consonants, use of, 53, 82, 86, 145
Constructivist perspective, as what
    students can do, 177–180
Constructor of own environment,
    student as, 13–14
Content-variety (sources/inspiration),
    113
Context-specific analysis of language
    structure and skills, 38
Contextual worlds of childhood, the,
    13–14
Conversation: with family members, 15;
    recording of, 74
Cook-Gumperz, J., 17
Coping mechanism, writing as, 6, 143–
    175, 169–170
Copying words, 36–37
Counseling services, lack of, 150
Crow Boy, 206
Crowell, S., 115–116
Cuban, Larry, 117
Cuing systems, 114
Cuisenaire rods, 19
Cullinan, B., 173
Cunningham, J.W., 172
Cunningham, P.M., 172
Curriculum generated learning, 102
Cursive writing, scribble lines to
    represent, 81

Dahl, Martha, 71–76, 113–115
Daily life, language of, 17
Damaged students, opportunity to
    recover, 176–177
Data: collection and organization of, 40,
    89, 102, 176–192. *See also* Note-
    taking; Observation
Day book: as forum for experimenting
    with language and thought, 38–41,
    85, 101–111
Day-to-day intervention, 206
de la Rocha, O., 43, 64, 90
Dead tasks (workbooks), 106
Debate, emotional, in creating
    assessment objectives for 1992
    fourth-grade reading test, 125–126

Debunking reductionist research, 31–33
Decision-making process, traditional
    exclusion of teachers from, 227
Decontextualized phenomena, skills,
    tasks, 23, 48, 219
Defensive strategies of teachers, 117–
    118
Deficit-driven model, 203
Defining and describing student
    competence, who's role, 4
Democratic: ideal for learning, 130, 137
Democratic Society, active participation
    in, 50
Demonstration sites, for training
    institutes, 227
Developmental: Dyslexia, 11, 26;
    language disorder, 11
Dewey, J., 5, 14, 27
Diagnostic testing. See Assessment;
    Special Education; Testing
Dialectics of activity and setting, 64–70
Dialogue, use of in story writing, 85
Dick Tracy (movie), 205
Dictionaries, personal, 77
Difficult tasks, avoidance of, 198–199
Dillon, D., 11–12
Dinosaur books, 43–46, 181–184
Disablement of children, through
    severing link between life and
    learning, 7
Discarded paper bits, as writing tableau,
    148, 154
Disciplined research approach; Student
    Advocacy model, 176–227
Discriminatory: practices, 219;
    reporting, 229n
Disenfranchisement, 42, 173
Disruptive classroom behavior, 146
Distar, 19, 24
Distortion of language learning, 34
Diversity: as driving force of
    innovation, 176, 202–203, 224
Documenting process of change, 57–59
"Doing", child's own theory of, 58
Doll, W., 60, 92–93
Donovan, Kathy, 76–78
Dorsey-Gaines, C., 20, 60
Doubt, parental, 16
Dracula, 37
Draw Your Family, 10
Drawing: golden age of (second-third
    grade), 68–69; gross motor, 147; in

journal, 80; labeling of, 168; large,
    101; people, 147; single color, 83.
    See also Artwork; Graphics;
    Illustration
Drug addicted mothers, children of,
    143–144
Durkheim, E., 12
Dykstra, R., 167
Dyson, A., 68

Early Childhood Research Quarterly, 88
"Early Literacy Development and the
    Mental Health of Young Children,"
    6–7, 143–175
East Los Angeles, pre-packaged
    curriculum in, 227
Eaves, Brenda, 55–56, 83–84
Editing, 86
Education: based on child assumptions,
    107; localization of, 90;
    medicalizing of, 57
Education Week, 125–126
Educational: establishment, 224;
    evaluation, 10–30; influences, 14;
    institutions, 16; practices, 115–122;
    publishing, 26, 173; reading, 62;
    theory, 47–48; writing, 63
Educators, task of, 49–50. See also
    Principals; Teachers
Eliot, T.S., 47
Emotional well-being, training sessions
    effect upon, 172
Empiricism, unquestioning dedication
    to, 172
Empowerment, pessimism regarding, 5
English Education, 3–5
Enjoyment of learning, 20
Enoki, Dr. Donald, 136
Entertainment writing, 53
Environmental print, 106, 156–157, 193–
    197
Environmental writing and reading, 62–
    63
Environments: classroom, 91–96;
    educational, 12–13
Erickson, F., 15, 17
Errors, specialists seeking out, 1
Ethnicity, 176, 224
Ethnocentricities, educators examining
    own, 224
Ethnographic accounts: from
    perspective of learner, 79

Ethnographic evaluation: as superior
educational tool, 1–3, 10–30, 15, 18,
79; theoretical constructs of, 10–30,
12–13
Ethnographic studies: in family,
community and school, 60
Ethnography: as antidote to "in-the-
head" analysis, 10, 12
Evaluation: alternatives, 11–12, 22–30,
27; of practical accomplishments
only, 12; procedures, duration of,
10; synthesis of, 176. See also
Ethnographic evaluation
Everyday: definition of, 230; lives of
children, 13–14; nature of literacy
behavior, 49; record, 77; writing,
106–107
Experience, actual and its relation to
education, 27
Expert: learner as, 66; relinquishing role
of, 14–16
Expertise, in teacher, 177–178
EXP.O-WPT, 119
Expressive One Word Picture
Vocabulary Test, 11
Expressive reading, 84

Facilitating children's language
development, 20–21
Failure: as institutional inability to
respond to child's need, 121;
measurement of, 47; as result
of large-scale manufactured
evaluation methods, 26; of
system as historically located
in social organization of
classrooms, 23. See also
Assessment; Special Education;
Testing
Families: as educators, 14–16; in
jeopardy, 26; kindergartener's
drawing of, 159; as participants in
creation of instructional
intervention, 178, 217, 230n
Family literacy: characteristics of, 60–
62, 69–70; notes and stories written
at home, 111
Featherstone, H., 132
Federal and State regulations based
on pathological model, 223–
224
Federal umbrella, 120

Feelings, writing about, 40–41
Fenton, J., 49
Ferreiro, E., 144
Figueroa, R.A., 7–8, 179
Financial resources, reallocation of,
227. See also Assessment; Budget;
Funding; Special education
Financial writing, 63
First experience in school, should
not be in testing situation,
125
Form, observational, 72. See also
Grids; Learning logs; Literacy
analysis; Note-taking
Forms and functions of written
language, 3, 6, 31–51, 89–90, 162,
169
Formula language, to begin and end
stories, 87
Four-day work week for teachers, 131–
132
Fractal Nature of Geometry, the, 69
Fragility of some young children's lives,
143
Frake, C.O., 15
"Frames of reference", academic,
social, instructional, material, 17–
19, 23, 26–27
Frog and Toad stories, 85
Functions, uses and forms of written
language. See Forms and functions
of written language
Funding, 125, 137, 144. See also
Assessment; Budget Cuts; Special
education; Testing

Gates-McGinitie Reading test, 131
Geertz, C., 16
Generic learning patterns, teaching,
fallacy of, 38, 90
Gesell, 11, 16
Glaser, B.G., 229n
Gleick, J., 32, 34, 112, 128
Global patterns: observation of, 46–51,
74
Golden, J.M., 17
Good-enough Draw-a-Person Test, 11
Goodman, Y.M., 20, 144, 229n
Gospodarek, F., 56–57
Gould, S., 116, 123
Graham, K., 17
Grandmother's Trunk, 161, 166

Graphic: images, on computer, 186–187,
207–208; representation of problem-
solving activities, 218
Graphics, 112–113. *See also* Artwork;
Drawing; Illustration
Graphophonemic concepts, 32, 45, 49,
70, 172
Grass, G., 69
Graves, D.H., 2, 20, 27, 91
Green, J., 1–2, 16–17
Grids as analytic tool, 8, 113–114, 135,
207, 210, 218–219; examples of,
209, 211, 212
Grouping of students, 26, 93
Guba, E., 229n
Guidance, direct and indirect, 49–50
Gumperz, J.J., 17

Hall, N., 20
Hamblett, Cathy, 122, 133
Hard data, as "safer" than alternative
assessment, 135
Harker, J.O., 17
Harry and the Terrible Whatzit, 37
Harste, J.C., 20
Harvard Educational Review, 203–203
Hawaii, teacher change in, 136
Heath, S., 60
Hertweck, A., 178, 221, 224
Hierarchical, models of human behavior
and skills, imposition of, 32, 46, 50
High-frequency words, 42
Historical reading, 62–63
Holistic constructivist assessment
versus traditional: outline of, 221–
224
Holistic constructivist perspective, 58,
112–114, 118, 177, 179–181. *See
also* Advocacy model; Assessment;
Biographic Literacy Profiles
Holistic reading, commercialization of,
113–114. *See also,* Pre-packaged
teaching programs
"Hollow Men, the," 47
Home Alone, 205
Home and role of print, 147, 150. *See
also* Families
Homeless shelters, children from, 143
Hop, Skip, and Jump Book, 84
Horizontal placement, 53
Human behavior, as socially ordered, 12

Human pathology paradigm,
presupposition of, 177, 218, 229–
231n
Humor, students choice of, 85–87, 205
Hymes, D., 17

"IEP's," 218
Ignoring of children in research, 171
Illustration: integration of, with print,
35–37, 39, 55, 68–70, 76; as
mirroring or supporting text, 55, 84.
See also Artwork; Drawing;
Graphics; Symbol weaving
Images, graphic: as different way of
knowing, essential to describe, 69
Imaginative: evaluation, 26;
interpretation and analytic
resources, combining of, 19
Imagining world from individual and
shared perspective of child, 4, 52–
142
In-service institutes, participation in,
180–181
"In-the-head": analysis of human
behavior, 2–3; educational system,
26
In the Middle, description of note-
taking procedure, "Status of the
Class," 78. *See also* Note-taking
Individual activity, preventing its
demise, 123–124
Influences in children's lives, visible and
invisible, 57
Informants, students as, 12–13
Information collection, systematic. *See*
Data-collection; Observation
Information writing, 53
Informed opinion, and teachers, 75, 202
Ingenuity, 71
Innovation: diversity as driving force
of, 176; as social phenomenon
within reflective discourse, 215; and
talk without action, 136–137
Insignificance, guarding against, 124
Institutional: change, teacher's lack of
power to affect, 122; inability to
respond to child's needs, 123;
structure of schools, change in, 117
Instructional: approaches, different,
social and academic impact of, 199;
intervention strategies of student

support team, 219; practices and
literacy learning, toward a unified
theory of, 31–51. *See also* Literacy;
Student Support Team
Instrumental reading and writing, 63
Intellectual: ability, narrowly defined,
224; activity, complexity of, 218;
harm, through testing programs,
127; use of environment, 91
Intensive resource room, 194
Interactional reading and writing, 63,
186
International Reading Association, 20,
27–28n, 29, 173
Interpreters, families as, 14–15
Intuitive evaluation, 26, 115
Invented forms of written language. *See*
written language
Invented reading, 72
Invented spelling, 37, 46, 53, 55, 72,
106, 113; and at-risk readers and
writers, 172; encouragement of, 20;
in stories following writing process
model, 106; unable to use on own,
81
I.Q. tests, 218
Irreducible plurality of functions and
forms of language of children, 124,
128
Isolated learning activity, symbols
manipulated apart from experience,
48
Isolated tasks, performance of, 171

Jack, Betty, 43–46
Jaggar, A., 27n
Jagged edges, in children's work, 115
Jervis, K., 32
Johnston, P., 32, 128
Jottings, quick, 149
Journal, 101, 106, 111; conversational
tone of, 85; drawings, 185; home
and school, 87; illustrating of, 84;
kindergartener's, 147–148; reading,
38–41, 87. *See also* Learning logs
Judgments, nuanced, 65

Kaleidoscopic patterns: as image for
use of written language in
classroom, 46, 65
Kappan, 48

Kaufman ABC, 119
Key words, 77; use of in kindergarten
student, 35, 37
Kindergarten: screening, 184;
traditional, predetermined literacy
program in, 165–166
Kindergartener's Literacy configuration
profile, 34–42, 52–57, 145–175
"Knights and Dragons" Game,
illustration of, 207

Labeling: absence of, in advocacy
model, 145, 176; art work with
beginning sounds, 36–37; of
children, 26, 145, 202
Laboratory. *See* Research
Langer, J.A., 48
Language: as constructed and used by
children, 34, 58, 145; how child
utilizes when not being tested, 1;
learning and usage, connection
between, 48; problem, diagnosis of,
185, 197; skills, pre-school, as base
for literacy activities, 20. *See also*
Advocacy model; Assessment;
Biographic Literacy Profiles; as
topic of study and means of
communication, blurring
boundaries between, 42–46, 48
Language Arts Curriculum, hampering
of, 11–12
Large print, representing sound effects,
39
Lateral Dominance Examination, 11
Lave, J., 43, 64, 90, 230n
Learner, perspective of, 20, 57, 90–91,
106, 216
Learning: based on who students are,
"not" who they are not, 177;
commercialization of, 113–114;
conditions, initial literacy behaviors
dependent upon, 20, 34; disorders
currently in fashion, 26;
environments, construction of own,
26, 31, 102; lost, children's, 47;
opportunities, enhancement of, 17,
20, 49–50, 177. *See also* pre-
packaged teaching programs
"Learning Denied," 2, 7, 34, 172
Learning disability: diagnosis of, 184,
198; label, 26, 145; as prerequisite

Learning disability (*cont.*)
  for Special Services, 24. *See also*
    Assessment; Biographic Literacy
    Profiles; Special Education; Testing
Learning logs, 40, 77, 92, 101, 107, 111
Learning to Read: The Great Debate,
  33–34
Least-effort strategies, 43, 45, 64, 183
Left-right progression, 80, 81, 156
Lehman College, 3
Leichter, H.J., 14
Leontief, W., 31–32
Lesson construction, elements of, 17
Letter: combinations, recurring, 83;
    forms use of, 20, 35, 148–149, 160,
    168, 198; knowledge, as predictor of
    reading achievement, 167; writing,
    40
Linear models of behavior and learning,
  32, 34, 46, 70
Lists, 107–108; as literacy event, 148
Literacy
  archaeological reconstruction, 52–53
  behavior: children's observable, 33–
    38, 56, 88; profile of second grader,
    27
  complexity and transformation of
    through dialectical relationship
    between activity and setting, 38, 89
  configurations: developing,
    kindergarten through grade four,
    79–142; teachers exploring their
    own, 52, 124
  multiple interpretations of, 60, 88
  personal understanding of, 33, 49
  in problem-solving activities, 58, 64–
    68
  profiles of third-graders, 38–42
  types and uses of, 36–38, 69–70. *See
    also* Biographic Literacy Profiles
    Project
Literacy biographies. *See* Biographic
  Literacy Profiles Project
Literacy development
  early: and mental health. *See* Early
    Literacy development; reductionist
    methodological approach, 31–34;
    what kindergartners can teach us,
    167–173
  of individual children, 106
  infinite variety in patterns of, 47

methods of capturing complexity,
  111–112
in pre-first grade, 20
Literacy educator, 197, 213, 230n
Literacy learning and instructional
  practices, toward a unified theory
  of, 31–51
Literacy portfolios. *See* Biographic
  Literacy profiles Project
Literacy profiles. *See* Biographic
  Literacy Profiles Project
Literal formats, departure from, 43, 45,
  64
"Literary" activity, dictating of, 109–
  110
Literate, becoming: as dynamic
  process, 20; particularity of each
  child, 76
Local: knowledge, importance of in
  advocacy model, 8, 31–32, 74, 115,
  177–178, 000n; school districts,
  participation in BLIPP, 125
"Local knowledge" (Geertz, C.), 16
Localization of education, 90
Logo log, 87
"Low income pre-readers", artificially
  defined group, 145. *See also*
  Labeling
Luis, 181
"Lunch Count and Attendance", form,
  78
Lytle, S., 129–130, 177–178, 178

Mager, Marcy, 53–54
Magher, Bob, 78–79, 99–100
Malnourishment, and school
  performance, 144
Man Who Kept House, the, 200
Mandelbrot, B., 69
Map-making, 101
Marginalization, of students, 42
Marston, Betty, 116
Marston, C.H., 133
Material resources, children's use of,
  111
Math biographic profiles, 56
Matthews, Kathy, 38–42, 85–86, 88–89,
  100–106, 114–115, 117, 131–132,
  134, 136
McDermott, R.P., 12, 17, 27n, 221
Mead, M., 14

Meanings, significance of shifts in, multiplicity of, 14
Medical care, inadequate, 144
"Medical model" of observation, 57, 88
Medicalizing of students, educational system, 57, 128
Mehan, H., 17, 178, 221, 224
Meihls, J.L., 178, 221, 224
Meisels, S.J., 32
Memory aid, 63
Mental activity disembodied, 90
Mental health: and early literacy development, 135, 143–175
Mental processes, explored in vacuo, 219–224. See also Assessment; Psychological Testing; Research; Statistical Analysis
Merit pay, linked to achievement test results, 116
Message writing: on classroom notice board, 93–94, 106–108; as instrumental and substitutional print, 154–155, 169, 194
Metaphor, mentalistic, 12
Methodologies, dominant, debate over reductionist disagreements, 3, 31–51
Mickey Mouse, 35
Mintzberg, H., 229n
Miscue analysis: collected in portfolio, 218, 229n; and speech and language pathologist, 202; and student involvement in utilizing, 214–215
Mixed classroom, fifth grader's visiting kindergarten for literary activity, 160–161
Model-making, 108–109
Modified classrooms, 56
Moll, 181
Monsters, 80–81
Monsters Who Died, the, 44–46, 182–183
Mother, as problem, 15
Mrs. Wishy Washy, 158
Mullis, I.V.S., 48
Multimedia centers, classrooms as, 69
Multiple perspectives of practical complexity of children's symbolic activity, 112
Multiple solutions, 65
Murphy Durrell Reading Readiness Test, 11

Murtaugh, M., 43, 64, 90
Myopic research, 173. See also Research

Naming letters, things, 150, 168
Narrative descriptions, writing of, 207. See also, Biographic Literacy Profiles Project; Literacy
National Academy of Sciences, criteria for assessment reform rating scale established by, 8
National Assessment of Educational Progress (NAEP), 48, 122, 125–126. See also Assessment; Statistical Analysis; Testing
National Association for the Education of Young Children (NAEYC), 28n, 126–127
National Association of Elementary School Principals, 28n
National Conference on Research in English, 27n
National Council of Research in English (NCRE), Ethnographic research for, 2
National Council of Teachers of English(NCTE), 1–2, 27, 28n
National Reading Council, 1–2
National testing, as public fetish, 134. See also Assessment; Statistical Analysis; Testing
Negotiating place as member of community of learners, 216
Neophyte. See Novice
"Neoprogressive," 117
New Hampshire: deconstruction of state school system, 3, 5; project schools, 132–134, 137; State Department of Education, 58, 133–134, 137
New Zealand Department of Education, assessment report, 126
Newkirk, T., 49, 68–69
News related reading, 63
Nintendo. See Video
Non-mainstream label, 145. See also Labeling
Norm-referenced material, 120
Normal label, 145. See also Labeling
"Normed" tests, 91
"Normed tests." See also Testing

Note-taking, 70–79, 89, 105–106, 113,
135, 151, 176–192
Note-writing, students, 40, 151, 216
"Nova" public TV program, audio
recording of students description,
202
Novice
student learner, 66
teacher-researcher: expertise in
assuming role of, 14–16, 177, 183,
216
Numerical assessment model, 179

Objectivity, 128
Observable literacy behaviors, 57, 60,
191. See also Biographic Literacy
Profiles Project; Literacy
Observation: as basis for instruction,
57; of children, in families and
classrooms, 48–49; disciplined, of
children's reading and writing, 34;
focusing of, 135; learning how, 112;
of student' learning, 180; tentative
nature of, 13
Observational form, 72. See also Grids;
Learning logs
Observational notes. See Data-
collecting; Note-taking
"Oddity tasks," 171
Oral description, 113, 207
Oral language, 20
Oral reading, information gathered
during, 200
Oral Sentence Completion Test, 10
Order out of Chaos, 102
Organizational pathology, 220
"Overall contextual perspective"
(Erickson, F.), 15
"Overlearning," 170

Packaged programs. See Pre-packaged
teaching programs
Pagination, use of, 39
Paradigm, prevailing, of professional
culture, 217–218
Paradigm Dialogue, the, 229n
Paradigmatic shift, in
teachers,administrators, students,
parents, 60, 65, 70, 115–129, 179,
192, 220

Paradigms: alternative, 12, 25; physical
sciences, plagiarism of, for social
phenomena, 127–128
Parent: of abused child, lack of
psychological support for, 150;
communication, through biographic
profiles, 56, 74, 125; conferences,
42; volunteers, 183
Participant-observer, 18, 52–142
Past and present, interplay between, 56
Patterning, of early literacy behaviors,
52–53
Patterns: in child's work, 115;
emergent, from disorderly data
collection, 42; teaching with eye
toward, 112
Peabody Picture Vocabulary, 11
Pearson, P.D., 173
Pedagogical: gadgets, 144; practices, 34;
strategies, 23
Peers, separation from, 203
Peetoom, A., 26
Perceptual motor difficulties, 197
Personal Knowledge, 25–26. See also
Social construction of knowledge
Personal record writing, 53
Personal-writing, 53, 80. See also Note-
writing,students
Personality Inventory for Children, 11
Perspective of the learner, 57
Peter Pan computer composition, by
"at-risk" student, 186–187
Phi Delta Kappan, 3
Phoneme task completion, training in,
172
Photographs of children collaborating in
literacy life of classroom, 112
Physically abused kindergartener's
literacy profile, 143–175, 192–197
Pictures accompanying text, 68–69, 88.
See also, Artwork, Drawing,
Graphics,Illustration
Piers Harris Children's Self Concept
Test, 10
Pigeonholed, students as, 34. See also
Labeling
Playing with print, in kindergarten, 36
Pluto, 35
Policy makers: redefining public
schools, control through tests and

restriction of local level innovation,
136; and statistical proof of
learning, 121–122
Political: activity, testing as, academic
endorsement of, 90, 125–129, 132–
137; framework of educational
system, 121
Poor school districts, funding cuts in,
137, 176, 224. *See also* Assessment;
Budget cuts; Funding; Special
Education; Statistics
Poplin, M., 177
Portfolios. *See* Biographic Literacy
Profiles
Portrait, student. *See* Advocacy model;
Assessment; Biographic Literacy
Profiles
Post-it notes, 72
Potential, children's, underestimation
of, 3
Power and profit in testing bureaucracy,
220–221. *See also* Special
Education; Testing
PPTVT-R, 119
Practical intelligence studies, 90. *See
also* Research
Pradl, Gordon, 3–5
Pre-packaged teaching programs, 34, 48,
71, 113, 120–121
Pre-reading programs, rigidity of,
pressure in, 20
Prigogine, I., 101, 123, 127–128
Principal, the, 132
Principal's perspective, and
participation in literacy approach,
120–122, 124–125
Print: activities, purposeful engagement
in, in kindergarten classroom, 36–
38, 193–195; autobiographical use of,
193; awareness of in environment,
37; in classroom, across the
curriculum, 42; educational use of,
193–194; environmental use of,
194; instrumental use of, 169;
knowledge, entering school
without, 144–145; social uses
of in symbolic play, 88; specific
skills, 172; using for everyday
purposes, 82–83; as vehicle
to communicate in world, 166

Problem-solution relationships,
reconstituting, 64, 66, 104
Problem-solving: with classification
skills, 108; documenting complexity
of, 101, 113, 135, 177–178, 183, 192;
as focus in advocacy model, 177,
179, 182, 192, 218; in Greek
mythology study, 101–102;
impeding children's innate
capability for, 48; practical
complexity of, visual representation
of, 66, 102–103; routine and non-
routine, 65–66; strategies,
development of, 207
Problems: complex, becoming visible in
child's use of print, 143; generation
of, 43, 45, 58, 64; as school defined,
16
Procedural possibilities, examine
variations in, invent new, 43, 45,
58, 64, 183
Process writing, commercialization of,
113–114. *See also* pre-packaged
teaching programs
"Processing speed," 200
Proctor, Lee, 78, 108–110, 114–115
Professional: bureaucracies, as
performance structures, 229n;
culture, prevailing paradigm of, 220;
expertise, 124
Professionals, teachers as, 71, 124, 132
Proofreading, 86
Pseudoscientific experiments, 172
Psychological: counseling, 10;
evaluation, 10–11, 16, 197;
reporting on what student "cannot"
do, 228, 229n; theories, isolationist
(in vacuo), and irrelevance to
classroom teachers, 229n
Psychological testing. *See* Special
education; Testing
Psychologist, reading: misleading
pronouncements of, 146
Psychologists: individualistic
orientation of, 219
Psychologist, school: and dismissal of
alternative assessment, 135
Psychometric assessment, reductionist,
moving beyond, 136, 179, 223
Public imagination, inhibition of, 134

Public law 94.142, Special services requires that student be tested to continue funding, 119–120
Pugach, M.C., 230n
Punctuation: awareness and use of, 39, 41, 81, 87
Puppetry, 101
Puzzles, 85, 86, 156
Pyramids, drawing of, 2

Questionnaire, preset, restriction of, 15
Quick-fix solutions, 144

"Rainbow park," 56
Raloff, J., 116
Read-aloud time, 40
Reader, seeing self as, 25
Reading: behavior, social construction of, 20; being in the mood for!, 85; development, theoretical explanations as deficient in profiling one child, 146; questioning invariant, linear, cognitive models, 146; research and analysis, 171; storybook, in family, 27; theoretically grounded explanations of, 31–51; types and uses of, 62–63, 196
Reading and writing: artificial separation between, 47; behaviors of young children, 20–22; from child's point of view, 3; as problem-solving activities, 43, 45
Reading Coordinator, 56
"Reading group conference record sheet," 77
Reading logs, 111. See also Learning logs
Reading own writing, 35
Recall, 119
"Recess literacy", notes written on playground, 111
Reconstitute relationship between problems and solutions, 43, 45, 183, 218. See also Problem-solving
Reconstructing functions and forms of written language, 60, 75–76, 124. See also Forms and functions of written language

Recording of student activity, legitimization of, 181. See also Advocacy model; Assessment; Biographic Literacy; Learning logs,Literacy; Note-taking
Recreational writing and reading, 63, 194
Recurring themes, in child's work, 115
Reductionist arguments, 3, 47–49, 127, 173, 179. See also Research
Reductionist learning theory, paradigmatic shift away from, 6–7, 177
Regression, as result of abuse, 166
Reinventing written language, 52
Remediating by reteaching, 179
Removal of student from community, 204
Repetition, as self-correcting strategy, 201
Representations, irreducible multiplicity of, 101
Representative examples of child's work for illustrating Biographic Profile, 115. See also Biographic Literacy Profile
Research: current, on young children's literacy behaviors, 20, 46–51; in laboratory or artificial settings, 12, 46–51, 90; and marginalization of teachers, 130; methods, sensitivity to children; teaching (in BLIPP), 49, 71; reductionist, debunking of, 31–33, 46–51, 97. See also Reductionist arguments
Resnick, L., 48
Resource rooms, 56
Respect, for child's pre-school language skills, 20
"Response/Comments", record of oral discussion between teacher student, 77
Responsibility for failure of student, institutional not individual, 121
Retarded range," 197
Retention: as result of testing, 27; of students, 26
Revision, 42, 85–86
Rhetoric: of the head, 12; of warmth, openness and great promise, 34

Rhyming patterns, use of, 84
Riddles, jokes, 40, 205
Right answers provide little
    information, 218
Risk-taking: with and for the child, 24;
    in story-writing, 86
Ritalin, in treatment of "Attention
    Deficit Disorder," 26
Road Warrior, the, 99
Rogoff, B., 219
Role-playing, in story composition, 40
Rommetveit, R., 219
Roth, D.R., 12, 221
Rothman, S., 125–126, 128
Rueda, R., 179, 223
Ruiz, N.T., 179

Sacks, O., 123–124
Saturday morning TV show, 99–100
Scavenging objects to write on, 148,
    154
Schickedanz, J.A., 20
Schliemann, A.D., 43, 64, 90
Scholarship, essence of, 33
School: as academic and social
    institution, 16–20; definition of as,
    "teaching and learning," 115;
    failure, objectification of as "human
    pathology," 218; models of
    learning, as intrusive, 15;
    organizational structure, 228;
    as performance organizations,
    176
School psychologist, 197
Schotanus, Helen, 59, 70, 125
Schrader, C., 88
Science News, 116
Scientific paradigms, and their influence
    on prevailing thought, 123, 127
Scientific writing and reading, 63–64
"Scope and sequence chart," 60
Scratch notes, 208
Scribbles into letters, 152
Scribner, S., 43, 64, 90
Seeing: child's learning process,
    excitement of, 109; from multiple
    perspectives, 112; "what we have
    learned not to see," 216
Seeing Voices, 123–124
Segregation, of students, 56

Self: correction, 84–85, 201–202;
    evaluation, 114; initiated print
    exploration without risk,
    166, 171; organization, as
    constitutive of classroom life,
    92–94, 101–110; portrait, of
    kindergartener, 163; selections,
    85
Sensory and perceptual exam, 11
Setting. *See* Environments
Sexually abused kindergartener's:
    Literacy profile, 143–175, 192–197;
    use of print as coping mechanism,
    135
Shannon, Pat, 137
Shared-book time, 40
Shepard, L.A., 32, 117, 220, 223
Shickedanz, J., 34
Shifting focus. *See* Assessment,
    Authenticity; Paradigmatic shift
Show Your Tongues, 69
Shultz, J., 57
"Side by side" next to children, 4, 57–
    59
Sight words, 37, 113
Skill and drill exercises, reification of,
    173
Skills, decontextualized, 20, 60, 113,
    169
Skrtic, T.M., 203, 215, 217–218, 220
Slow-learning label, 145. *See also*
    Labeling
Small group activity, 76
Smith, M.L., 220, 223
Social: construction of knowledge in
    practice, 218; construction of
    literacy, 10–27, 49; problems of
    children, disconnection from
    reading-writing instruction, 144;
    resources, children's use of, 111;
    text, 17
Social scientists, definition of, in
    educational field, 49
Sociocognitive organization of functions
    and uses of literacy, 47
Socioeconomic discrimination, 171. *See
    also* Labeling; "Low-Income
    Prereader"
Sociohistorical context, examining
    student's learning in, 192

Soft arts as record of student's work, 112
Solutions: cuddly, none, 34; embedded, acceptable, 66; generated and arrived at, 43, 45, 58, 64, 183; simple, to complex problems, 144. *See also* Problem-solving
Sorting, of students, 26
Sound/symbol relationships, 33, 37–38, 69–70, 72, 89, 105, 109; in early literacy development, 144–145, 165
Sounds: hearing and labeling of, 80–81; and letters, making connection between, 85, 162
Southern California Sensory Integration Tests, 11
Special Education: in California and Colorado, 220; evaluation and qualification for, 178, 197; folder in first grader, already "thick," 1; global testing for, 56; institutional practice of, 218; instructional services and changes in educators, 24, 118–120, 197; for kindergarten child, 167, 194; "loop," non-participatory status of student in, 24, 135; and over-representation of ethnic population, 7, 178; and pathology as disciplinary grounding, 2, 177; teachers, lack of sustained contact with student's served, 178. *See also* Assessment; Statistical analysis; Testing
"Special Education Paradox, the," 176, 203–204
Speech and language pathologist: brief availability of, 149–150, 185
Spelling developmental patterns, 37, 39, 41, 86, 182, 201, 207
Spiegel, D.L., 172–173
Stage theories, security of pre-packaged programs, 34, 47. *See also* Pre-packaged teaching programs
Standardized measure of alphabet knowledge, 168
Standardized testing. *See* Assessment; Testing
Stanford Achievement tests, 11, 134
State Board of Education, lack of support from, 122, 125. *See also* Assessment; Budget cuts; Funding; Statistical information
Statistical: information, collection of as drive for funding, 4, 122; procedures and research, reductionist nature of, 31–33, 46, 121
Stengers, I., 101, 123, 127–128
Stereotypes and myths, embedded in popular culture of reading instruction, 173
Sternberg, R., 90
Stimuli, "correct" order for presenting symbol-sound relations, 144
Stone Fox, 87
Story composition: role playing and conferring with fellow students in, 39
Story language, awareness of, 81–84, 157
Story structure, 113, 207
Storytelling in pictures, 151–152. *See also* Artwork; Drawing; Graphics; Illustration
Strategies: flexible, 66; no step-by-step or classroom-tested, 124–125
Straus, A.L., 229n
Strickland,D., 20, 60, 102, 173
Structuring of Organizations, the, 229–230n
Struggle: assessment, divisive questions, 4; continuing the, 137
Student advocacy: documentary evidence of, in Biographic Literacy Profiles, 218–219
Student advocacy model of instructional assessment: arguments against, 221; four phases of, 178–219; implementation of, 225–228. *See also* Advocacy model; Assessment; Biographic Literacy Profiles.
Student disability as organizational pathology, 217–218, 220
Student needs: analysis of information regarding, 203–217
Student Self-Assessment, 42
Student sensitivity to and interest in learning, 229n
Student support plan: development and implementation of, 179, 203–

217; ongoing adjustment of, 217–227. *See also* Student support team

Student support team, 178–179, 197, 202, 216, 218–219

Studies. *See* Research

Sub vocalizing, in composition, 39

Substitutional writing, 64

Subversive activity, teaching as, 4, 129–137

Success: dedication to helping all children achieve, 121; ensuring children's feeling of, 20; measurement of, 47; shifting burden of, from child to school, 121

Sudden leaps, in children's work, 115

Sullivan, Susan, 95–96

Sulzby, E., 20

Super Mario Brothers, 96–98, 110–111, 205

"Superior range," 197

Support and intervention, within regular classroom setting, 204–219

Support team. *See* Student support team

Survival, reading and writing for, 194

Sweet, Peter, 121–122, 131–133

Sweet Valley High (series), 41

Syllables as separate words, 86

Symbol/sound relations. *See* Sound/ symbol relationships

Symbol systems,incorporated into text, 106, 207

Symbol weaving, in situationally specific literacy activities, 68–70, 97–100, 128

Symbolic activity, complexity of: making visible in children's everyday lives, 101, 112, 123–124, 204

Symbolic forms, understanding interrelationships between, 168

Symbolic inventions, transformed into functional forms, 48–49

Symbolism, multiple forms of, 68–70, 111

Syntactic structures, 69

Synthetic phonics, 46–47

Systematic data-collecting procedures, 177, 180, 191. *See also* Biographic Literacy Profiles; Note-taking; Observation

Talking with children, importance of, 135

Task simplification and reorganization of, 66, 183

Tasks at school, completion of, for survival, 25

Teacher: accountability, 26; burn-out, 121, 132; at center of problem-solving process, 8, 177; defined tasks, 102; education programs, changes in preparatory curriculum, 57; exploration, support of, 60; impact beyond classroom, 195–197; leaders, training of, in student advocacy model, 225–226; perspective, of change in classroom, 117–118; training, in advocacy model, 226–227

"Teacher Research as a Way of Knowing," 129–130

Teacher training: training, 58

Teachers: and change, 26, 58; and daily observation, importance of, in advocacy model, 178; and powerlessness; lack of control over professional life, 5, 121–122, 136; as special interest group, 5, 137; and volunteer research, pioneers in student advocacy model of assessment, 221–224

Teaching: learning, and schooling from perspective of learner, 4, 57–60, 115; as subversive activity, 129–137

Teaching from the child's perspective, 58–60

"Teaching Without Testing: Assessing the Complexity of Children's Literacy Learning," 3–6, 7, 52–142

Teale, W.H., 26

Technical: expertise of children, functional nature of, learning from, 97, 185–189, 206; reading and writing, 63–64

Technological adventure stories, transmuting archetypal fairy-tale structure into new form, 96–100, 111

Technologies, literacy, children's use of, 111, 206
Test: from emphasis upon, toward emphasis upon child, 118; teaching to, 128
Test makers diminishing profits of, 136, 220
Testing, 10–11, 16, 24, 25–26 90–91, 128; as child's first experience in school, 125; as commercial enterprise, 90; diagnostic, 218; "lightweight," 120; linked to merit pay, 116; mass, mandated through federal laws and state regulations, 123, 125–129; mushrooming of, 119, 131; standard format, how to function within, 117; Standardized diagnostic. *See also* Assessment; Special education; standardized diagnostic, 48, 55–56, 65, 116, 125–137
Testing bureaucracy, power over professional decision making of teachers, 4
Testing of Young Children: Concerns and Cautions, 126–127
Text-picture/picture-text approach to story creating, 84
Texts, inert, print without knowledge of production, 106
Thayer, Judy, 137
Thematic Apperception Test, 10
Theme, use of in early writing, 54
Theoretical framework, building of, 112, 127
Theories: becoming fact, 47–48; broad-based, 25; commercialized and politicized, 48; scientific, created from research, 32, 126–127
Theory into Practice (TIP), 1–3, 8
"Things", importance of, to abused child, 148, 165
Thinking, shifts in. *See* Assessment; Authenticity; Paradigmatic shift
3 Wishes, 10
Tightrope walking, 49
Time, necessary to observe patterns in student learning, 202–203
TOLD-P, 119

"Toward a Unified Theory of Literacy Learning and Instructional Practices," 3, 8, 31–51
Traditional expectations, advocacy for students who fail to meet, 178, 192–203
Traditional skills, more to literacy than, 69–70
Trail Test, 11
Training: educator, pushing beyond, 124; programs, for students, 32–38; sessions, and literacy development, 172; in student advocacy model, 225–227
Transition from adult understanding of literacy to child's, 118
Trauma, using print to cope with, 143–175, 194
Triannual reviews, 218
Trivial details, as important to education of child, 15
Trust, fostering of, 204
"Tuck-In Service" flyer, characteristics of, 65–70
Tuning out, 19
Turnquist, Bruce, 79, 86–88, 131–132

Underachievement Syndrome, 10
Underestimation, of children's potential to participate in construction of own learning environments, 3, 31
Underground, going, 135. *See also* Subversive, teaching as
Unique personal configurations of children. *See* Advocacy model; Assessment; Biographic Literacy Profiles; Literacy
Unknown words, strategies to determine, 85
Unmasking children, 145
Unmet needs of children, 57
U.S. Department of Education, 144

Valentine card, example of interactional print, 193
Variation, infinite, in everyday classroom life, 46
Verbalization, allowing it to occur, 93
Vertical placement, 53

Video games, use of in story-writing, 96–100, 185, 205–209
Video recordings of specific literacy events to explore some self-organized problem-solving activity, 112, 135, 216
Visual representation of problem-solving activity, 102, 200
Vocabulary, 37, 53
Voices, of children, 49
Voices of the Mind: a Sociocultural Approach to Mediated Action, 219, 230n
Vowels, use of, 53, 82, 86, 145
Vygotsky, L., 74, 181

Wagner, R., 90
Walls, Leigh, 34–38, 79–80, 86, 88–89, 113–115
Watson, D.J., 229n
Weade, R., 17
Well-trained evaluation, 26
Wertsch, J., 219, 221, 224, 230n
Weschler Intelligence Scale for Children-Revised, 197
"Who Stole the Cookies from the Cookie Jar?," 158
Wide Range Achievement Test, 11
Wildsmith, B., 108
Williams, Sharon, 94–95, 107–108
Windows of opportunity for students experiencing difficulty, 203
WISC-R, 10–11, 119, 135, 197, 198, 221
Witcracks, 87
WJ-R, 197
Wolcott, H.F., 15
Woodcock-Johnson Standard Achievement Battery-Revised (WJA- R), 197
Woodward, V.A., 20
Word: centered school culture, 69; recognition skills, testing of, 126–127. *See also* Assessment; Testing; splitting, 145
Words: to express thoughts, difficulty with, 197; letters to represent, 168
Workbooks: as dead tasks, 106, 117; phonics, restrictions of, 38, 47

Working document, *From a Child's Point of View*, 8–9
Working hypothesis, 75
Working strategies, variations of, 114–115
Working together, teachers, in constructing Biographic Literacy Profiles, 124. *See also* Biographic Literacy Profiles
Writer, seeing self as, 25
Writing
    behavior, social construction of, 20
    conference, Super Mario Brothers story, 99–100
    conventions, use of, 182
    creative, 63
    for educational purposes, 87
    initial attempts at, 20
    as recording, 169
    samples, dictated and independent, 201
    as "saving" things for you, 83
    for social interactional purposes, 87
    strategies, 76
    students talking about, 72
    theoretically grounded explanations of, 31
    types and uses of, 53–55, 63–64, 106–108; chart, 195
Writing portfolio. *See* Assessment; Biographic Literacy Profile; Literacy
Written language: concepts, of third grade student, 39; construction and use of, 177; in everyday classroom life, 46; function, use and forms of, 33, 49–50, 53–54, 89, 184; reinvention of, 36–38, 52, 71; respect of student's understanding of, 26; social reconstruction of in everyday lives, 20, 113

Yates: Katie, 52–53; Mary, 52–53, 96–99, 111

"Zero-failure" attitude, 121

4472